MEMORIALS FOR CHILDREN OF CHANGE

In Memory of

Doctor

HERBERT MANN,

who with 119 failors with Capt.ⁿ
James Magee Mafter, went on board
the Brigg General Arnold in Bof-
ton harbour Dec.ʳ 25 ᵗʰ 1778.
hoifted fail and made for the fea,
& were immediately overtaken
by the moft tremendous fnow
ftorm with cold, that was ever
known in the memory of man,
& unhappily parted their Cable in
Plymouth harbour in a place call'd
the cow=yard & he with about 100
others were frozen to Death, 66 of
which were buried in one Grave.
He was in the 21ᵗ Year of his age
And now LORD GOD Almigh=
ty juft & true are all thy ways,
but who can ftand before thy cold?

The Doctor Herbert Mann stone, 1778, North Attleborough, Massachusetts. Slate.

Memorials for Children of Change

THE ART OF EARLY NEW ENGLAND STONECARVING

by Dickran and Ann Tashjian

WESLEYAN UNIVERSITY PRESS

Middletown, Connecticut

The publisher gratefully acknowledges the support of the Andrew W. Mellon Foundation toward the publication of this book.

Library of Congress Cataloging in Publication Data
Tashjian, Dickran, 1940–
    Memorials for children of change.
    Bibliography: p.
    1. Funeral rites and ceremonies — New England.
2. Stone carving — New England. 3. Puritans — New
England. I. Tashjian, Ann, 1942– joint author.
II. Title.
GT3203.T37   736′.5′0974   73-6006
ISBN 0-8195-4061-7

Manufactured in the United States of America
First edition

Contents

Illustrations

Photographs and rubbings were taken by the authors unless otherwise noted in the legends.

Preface

THIS study developed from what can only be described as a nearly maniacal passion to see all the seventeenth-century and eighteenth-century gravestones in New England — after seeing the first one. No doubt, the faults of this study can be largely traced to personal responses to particular stonecutters and their works. We have tried, however, to emphasize these carved gravestones as works of art within their cultural context. An understanding of the relationship between art and culture — despite the complexities involved — can illuminate both the individual work of art and the culture in which it was created. In working through the gravestone to early New England culture, we hope to dispel some prevailing misconceptions about Puritan attitudes toward art. But we began our exploration with an appreciation of the gravestone, and it is to the gravestone that we return in an effort to apprehend the nature of this early American art.

Others have taken a different approach. Allan I. Ludwig's iconographical study *Graven Images: New England Stonecarving and its Symbols, 1650–1815*, first published in 1966, confirmed our sense that many gravestones are visually exciting and possess an aesthetic dimension hitherto ignored. Several years later, after our manuscript was written, Mr. Ludwig generously clarified some of our ideas on iconography. We are indebted not simply for his criticism, but also for his willingness to share scholarly insights.

We also wish to acknowledge the early work of Harriette M. Forbes. Her enthusiasm must have been great indeed to permit her to travel the back roads of New England during the 1920s, looking for graveyards and toting a large view-camera. The terrain may have changed, and roads and cars may have been improved somewhat, but the logistics of gathering data remain formidable. Her work *Gravestones of Early New England and the Men Who Made Them* and the Forbes Collection of photographs at the American Antiquarian Society provided the first basic indication of the scope of material in graveyards. Most importantly, at a time when antiquarians were engaged primarily in the task of collecting data, Mrs. Forbes began to perceive the cultural implications of gravestone carving.

The study of material culture in America has perhaps advanced to the point that it is no longer enough to collect, identify, and catalog artifacts. We must begin to make sense out of the objects as they were significant to those who made and used them. To do so requires a recognition of the artifact first as a concrete manifestation of culture in its own right, then as part of the intangible network of ideas, attitudes, and values that brought it into being. The presence of an object encourages an examination of its own formal logic, which reveals an otherwise invisible context. To move back and forth from the visible to the invisible is the process that recreates the artifact most completely.

The illustrations of gravestones in our study are mostly rubbings. Photographs were taken when the carving was in such relief that rubbing was impossible. The rubbings were done with a vellum tissue stretched tightly across the face of the stone. An oil-based pastel applied with a piece of felt captures the surfaces of the carving in relief. A rubbing records the actual size of the marker and transcribes the texture of the stone. Moreover, the abstraction of line made by the rubbing permits the carving to be read with greater ease in many instances. But neither rubbing nor photograph can provide a literal rendering of the artifact. Such limitations of illustration, inherent in any medium, will perhaps send the reader to local graveyards to see the works of art standing there.

These works of art may not be available for many more generations. Since the summer of 1971, two important stones have simply disappeared from the graveyard in Franklin, Connecticut. These are the Pember children stone of 1773 *(Fig. 100)* and the Daniel Squier stone of 1783. Also, we have been told that the Daniel House stone of 1762 has been removed from the graveyard in East Glastonbury, Connecticut, for no apparent reason. Vandalism, of course, is not limited to rural graveyards, and rare is the city like Boston that has taken steps to preserve its graveyards. It is true that graveyards are difficult to maintain and that conservation is costly, but since local historical societies and other interested groups can do only so much to prevent vandalism and erosion, municipal action is needed. Graveyards are indeed New England's "museums without walls," and responsibility for their preservation ultimately rests with the community that recognizes its heritage. If our study accomplish nothing else, we should be gratified to have sparked such recognition.

There are many institutions that offered us support and hospitality. We should particularly like to thank Rosemary Pierrel, who as Dean of Pembroke College kindly facilitated our residency at the Otis Smith Farm and at Miller Hall. We are also grateful to the staffs of the Rhode Island Historical Society, the Newport Historical Society, the Rockefeller Library and the John Carter Brown Library of Brown University, and the Instructional Media Services and the

Program in Comparative Culture at the University of California at Irvine.

To the many persons who fostered the growth of our ideas and offered encouragement in singular ways, we extend our appreciation and gratitude. We should like to note particularly the following: Harold Snedcof, for his patience, understanding, and friendship; Susan Bliss and Carol Bratley, who share our mania; James Deetz, whose approach to the subject broadened our own perspective; John T. Kirk, who as director of the Rhode Island Historical Society helped us to mount an exhibit of Rhode Island rubbings; Esther Fisher Benson, who allowed us to examine the account books of the John Stevens Shop; Ronald Kotrc, for his translations of Latin inscriptions; Philip B. Johnson and Richard Slotkin, for reading the manuscript; James J. Flink, whose generous criticism and encouragement sustained our efforts during crucial periods of writing. And finally, a very special measure of gratitude is offered to George Monteiro.

Dickran and Ann Tashjian

September, 1973

MEMORIALS FOR CHILDREN OF CHANGE

Introduction:
Puritan Attitudes toward Art

THE curious conception of a colonial New England barren of art—as though any culture could be so bereft—can be traced to the demonstrable anti-art attitudes of the Puritans in England. Beginning in the reign of Elizabeth I these dissidents sought to reform the Anglican Church by purifying its outward or "visible" forms. While their most crucial reform centered around the limitation of church membership to a congregation of God's Elect, they also attacked the liturgy and administration of the sacraments as corrupt and contrary to scriptural teaching. With like feeling, they stripped from their churches the "idolatrous" arts of painting, free-standing sculpture, and stained-glass windows as signs of pernicious Roman Catholic influence.[1]

Needless to say, these Englishmen met resistance from civil and religious authorities. Although the Puritans were at first a scorned minority, they gradually gained power in Parliament until civil war became inevitable. During the two decades prior to 1640, however, groups of dissenters migrated to New England, where they presumably continued their religious aversion to images. The harshness of the environment fostered a practical concern for survival which, combined with their iconoclasm, would have allowed scarcely any art to exist.

This, at least, has been the prevailing view. In *A History of American Literature* Moses Coit Tyler states the case in perhaps its most extreme form:

> In proportion to his devotion to the ideas that won for him the derisive honor of his name, was he [the Puritan] at war with nearly every form of the beautiful. He himself believed that there was an inappeasable feud between religion and art; and hence, the duty of suppressing art was bound up in his soul with the master-purpose of promoting religion. He cultivated the grim and the ugly.... In the logic and fury of his tremen-

dous faith, he turned away utterly from music, from sculpture and painting, from architecture, from the adornments of costume, from the pleasures and embellishments of society.[2]

Writing with biases pervasive throughout the nineteenth century, Tyler is betrayed by an excessive rhetoric which distorts the historical Puritan beyond recognition. But while other historians and critics have been less prejudiced and more sophisticated than Tyler in their portrayal, they continue to share his sense of the matter.

In *The Colonial Craftsman*, for example, Carl Bridenbaugh advances the functionalist position: "In the seventeenth century, craftsmen and husbandmen who came to America faced the compelling problem of hewing a living out of the forest; they had little time and less energy for fashioning artifacts beyond absolute necessities." Likewise, in his Introduction to *Colonial American Writing*, Roy Harvey Pearce claims, "There is little of what we may, properly speaking, call 'literature' in this collection, as there was little of the sustained aesthetic attitude in colonial America. Colonial Americans were determined to make a new way of life in a new world. . . . They had little or no time for that disinterested contemplation which is essential in making works of art."[3] In a social history of technology Bridenbaugh's view is at least understandable if not entirely valid, whereas Pearce's assertion suggests a fundamental myopia which reduces our early literature to historical curiosity.

Against these notions stands the gravestone in silent but dramatic profusion throughout the burial grounds of New England. These markers bear witness to New England culture during the seventeenth and eighteenth centuries. Their designs carved in slate and sandstone, marble and schist, the memorials also bear witness to themselves. In pointing to those who came before, their eloquence is drawn out of visual repose. Their silence has been misconstrued, however, to indicate an anomalous existence in a pragmatic if not an iconoclastic culture. As a result, a comprehensive study of the art of gravestone-carving has not been realized.

Appreciation, let alone understanding, of this early New England art is hardly possible without a proper sense of its cultural context. Allan I. Ludwig has pursued one aspect of this dimension in *Graven Images: New England Stone-carving and its Symbols, 1650–1815*. Rejecting a twentieth-century diminution of the carved images as merely "quaint," he proposed to ascertain what they meant to the people who cut the markers, purchased and erected them.[4] By assuming, therefore, the traditional role of the iconographer, Ludwig established the visual meaning of the carved images in terms of their contemporaneous literary sources.

Ludwig, however, accepts the basic premise of Puritan iconoclasm. Thus the title of his work puns on the biblical sense of "graven images" as against the literal sense of images carved upon stone. To account for the proliferation of gravestones throughout New England, he is forced to assert: "Religious art is born only when there is a burning need for imagery. It is a need so ingrained that even when the mind dreads imagery for fear of idolatry, religious art endures. The New England Puritans found their need for imagery so great that not even their storied fear of idolatry could come between them and the thousands of stone images they carved and rooted in the hilly New England landscape for a period of some 165 years." Ludwig's presentation of Puritan iconoclasm is far more sophisticated than Tyler's, but in the final analysis there is little difference. Tyler also claims that "the Puritan did not succeed in eradicating poetry from his nature. Of course, poetry was planted there too deep even for his theological grub hooks to root it out. Though denied expression in one way, the poetry that was in him forced itself into utterance in another."[5]

Both writers, then, have conceived of the Puritan as one who, because of his religious dictates, attempted to repress his artistic impulses, but without success. In this view artistic creativity is an inevitable process, bound to occur despite stringent censure. This will to art becomes rooted in human nature rather than culture. Such location is subject, of course, to controversy, a twentieth-century dispute not unlike metaphysical speculation of previous times. While we may prefer to avoid such thickets, we are nonetheless asked, most crucially, to accept Ludwig's hypothesis that the Puritans changed their minds about art, at least on gravestones, after they came to New England.[6] Yet all the other cultural continuities between old and New England render the possibility of a radical switch extremely suspect. Consequently, a reappraisal of both Puritan functionalism and iconoclasm is in order. Long-standing misconceptions must be resolved and set aside before the gravestone can be seriously considered as a work of art.

Although no longer so widespread, a functionalist view of early New England settlement remains nonetheless pernicious in its distortion of Puritan creativity. Historians and critics have often pointed to an anonymously written economic tract published in Boston as an early eighteenth-century summation of practical attitudes derived from the Puritan work ethic, and hence a demonstration of New England hostility toward art. The pertinent passages require, however, another consideration: "The *Plow-Man* that raiseth Grain, is more serviceable to Mankind, than the *Painter* who draws only to please the Eye. The *hungry* Man would count fine Pictures but a mean Entertainment. . . . The *Carpenter* who builds a good *House* to defend us from Wind and Weather, is more serviceable than the curious *Carver*, who employs his Art to please the Fancy. This condemns not Painting or Carving, but only shows, that what's more substantially serviceable to Mankind, is much preferrable to what is less necessary."[7]

A careful reading suggests that this polemic does not altogether proscribe art, which is considered a luxury only under certain economic circumstances. Indeed, with material surplus, an undertaking of the decorative arts is preferable to idleness. Most important, the functionalist criterion of worthy endeavor was not limited to physical labor. The tract recognized that "the studying of *Languages, Arts, Sciences, Divinity, Physick, &c.* and the employing the skill or knowledge obtained by such Study, may greatly promote the *Glory of God*, the *Persons own benefit*, and the good of those he is concerned with."[8]

The functionalist explanation for the supposed lack of New England art lies rooted in the exaggerated image of the Puritan in a hostile wilderness, exclusively engaged in fighting off the Indians, famine, and disease, and thus lacking the time or the inclination to write poetry or paint a canvas. Such a view fails to take into consideration the fact that the Puritans possessed a strong and vital European heritage which, to the best of their means and ability, they brought with them across the Atlantic. They consciously chose to expend time and energy on writing sermons without reducing their attention to matters of physical survival. It has become increasingly apparent, moreover, that the Puritans probably composed as many poems as they did sermons. The substantial body of poetry written during the seventeenth century, combined with the sermons, further challenges any simplistic notion of functionalism. If this concept is to have any meaning at all, it should be broadly defined to include cultural as well as physical necessities for survival.

A theory of iconoclasm would appear to bear closer scrutiny than the functionalist explanation. The fact that the Puritans rarely mentioned the gravestone would suggest that it could exist only at the price of being verbally taboo. Silence on the matter of gravestones had its sources in causes other than iconoclasm, however. It must first be realized that the gravestone carver was an entrepreneur whose shop undertook a variety of stonecutting commissions. Cutting markers was thus only a part of his employ by the community. Consequently, an apprentice-master relationship was never rigorously institutionalized and enforced, as was the case in other crafts such as cabinet-making, printing, and smithing. Because of the informality of craft tradition, a coherent gravestone aesthetic may never have been recorded. Certainly the few documents pertinent to carving, such as diaries and account books, do not mention gravestones in any artistic sense.[9] And yet, though carving was thus not subject to extensive discussion in Puritan literature, the process should not be considered primarily one of unconscious creation emerging from a folk tradition. There were, to be sure, many conventional images and forms, but there were also infinite variations within the limits of convention, not to mention unconventional designs, which suggest, rather than residual embellishment, an artistic consciousness at play in the carving process itself. The greater part of our study attempts to convince the reader of this view.

The artistic consciousness of the stonecarver in the seventeenth and eighteenth centuries hardly could have coexisted with iconoclasm, nor could the other arts and crafts of early New England. In addition to hymns and limner portraiture, there were the necessary domestic crafts: weaving and needlework; furniture-making (virtually works of sculpture at the hands of the Townsends and Goddards in Newport) and the allied arts of stencilling and painting furniture, particularly in Connecticut; not to mention the wide variety of metalwork from crude smithing to the wroughting of elegant silver. To restore his art to the Puritan does not imply that he lived in a Boston somehow akin to the Florence of Renaissance Italy, nor, on the other hand, does it imply that the Babbitts of our Main Street have a direct and simple lineage to the New England Puritan. Such exaggerations obscure the significance and vitality of Puritan art, created as it was to meet the needs of a culture in revolutionary transition.

From this perspective of Puritan culture, iconoclasm persists as a crucial question for consideration. After all, the Puritans *did* strip their churches of art; they even destroyed gravestones and monumental sculpture in old England not only during the early reign of Elizabeth but again during the Civil War. Why, then, did the gravestone, not to mention the other arts, become established and eventually flourish in New England? The question assumes an even more perplexing guise in an examination of the relationship of the gravestone to the dominant religious concerns of the Puritan community.

The cultural historian would be forced to treat this issue as a paradox were it not that gravestone carving was considered a civil craft, practiced with the tacit consent of the religious authorities. This approval was predicated upon carefully drawn distinctions between civil and ecclesiastical jurisdictions over the functioning of the community as a whole. Iconoclasm was unequivocally reserved as an ecclesiastical concern. The gravestone with its images and designs was thus exempt from charges of idolatry since it was erected as an integral part of the funeral ritual, explicitly defined as a civil event, while retaining a dual cultural function, both religious and social. As a result, the graveyards which harbored these monuments were public grounds legally distinct from meetinghouse property.

In *A Testimony from the Scripture against Idolatry & Superstition*, first published in 1672 and reprinted in 1725, Samuel Mather, a member of the powerful Mather family which had removed itself to New England, offered his interpretation of the Second Commandment, so crucial for the approval or prohibition of graven images:

> 1. *That it is not meant of Images for Civil use, but for worship; thou shalt not bow down to them, nor serve them.* For the Civil use of Images is lawful for the representation & remembrance of a person absent, for honour and Civil worship to any worthy person, as also for ornament, but the scope of the Command is against Images in State and use religious.   2. Neither yet is it meant of all Images for religious use, but *Images of their own devising,* for God doth not forbid his own institutions, but only our inventions.[10]

The instances of legitimate civil use that Mather cited could have served as implicit references to gravestones, not only as markers but also as bearers of images. According to the first argument, gravestones would have fallen under civil rather than ecclesiastical jurisdiction. The second argument would indicate that even if the gravestone fell under religious authority, the use of images would have been approved if they were derived from the Scriptures—God's "own Institutions," certainly not man's "inventions." Similar views concerning idolatry were upheld by another influential Puritan divine, Samuel Willard, in his *Compleat Body of Divinity*, a collection of his sermons published posthumously in 1726 upon the request of the Boston clergy.[11]

Mather's publication of 1672 was a compilation of two sermons he had delivered in England a decade earlier against Roman Catholic and Anglican ceremonies, and so approximates the time when gravestones were beginning to proliferate throughout New England.[12] No direct cause and effect relationship should be inferred, however. At best, Mather summarized the Puritan position with regard to idolatry and thus indirectly sanctioned the erection of markers, which began as early as 1650. In all likelihood he was simply articulating that which the New England divines took for granted about gravestones. Consequently, there is no reason to postulate, as Ludwig does, a conspicuous reversal of attitudes once the Puritans had left England. The iconoclasm under Elizabeth had been directed against "Papist" images within the Church of England, which was the object of purification. The renewed destruction of churches and churchyard monuments during the Civil War was more likely a zealous eruption of submerged animosities exacerbated by the reign of Archbishop Laud than a reasoned military action based upon religious ideology. At the same time, however, the latter cannot be completely discounted. Since graveyards belonged on the grounds of the Anglican Church, Puritan vandalism of gravestones in England could have been justified by religious doctrine.

In contrast, the Massachusetts Bay settlers extended their destruction outward, against the wilderness and against the culture of the native Indians. Even their departure from England was not considered a violent rupture. Intent upon establishing a Bible commonwealth as a model for corrupt Europeans to follow, these migrating Puritans had the opportunity to start anew, at least to the degree that their societal group held common religious assumptions upon which to build their outpost of piety. As a result, their leaders exercised extensive control over social behavior, including, if they so desired, the erection of gravestones. The dangers of individual interpretation leading to heresy with respect to the carved images were circumscribed by tacit communal agreement on their meaning, with the Bible as the final authoritative source.

Originally an artifact marking the presence of the deceased beneath the earth, the gravestone would have been approved by the Puritans for its didacticism. Thus the innumerable stones that bear the legend, "As I am now, so you shall be," warned the passerby of death's inevitability. More than this function, however, generated the gravestone in early New England. The ironies of history, redounding upon this New England settlement, played a determining role in the practice of funerary art. While enduring great hardships to establish and maintain a Bible commonwealth, these Puritans were left isolated by their English brethren who, in the midst of Civil War, embraced the heresy of toleration and valuable political allies in the process, thereby rejecting what the colonists desperately came to defend as the New England Way.

To cap matters, by the advent of the second generation in New England, the original leaders were gradually dying; the ministers felt a slackening of communal piety, further discouraged by an increasing commercial prosperity, and counterpointed by a series of natural disasters and Indian battles which lent the appearance of God's disapproval of New England gone astray. Communal anxiety was not assuaged by warnings from the pulpit, as the ministers cast jeremiad after jeremiad upon their flock.[13] Deserted by history and apparently corrupt from within, this transplanted culture needed a reassertion of the religious values which had motivated the founding scarcely a generation before. Nathaniel Morton's *New Englands Memoriall* in 1669 was but one attempt to establish a provincial history of cultural ideals from which the community could derive a spiritual and historical identity. The gravestone was another—a tangible and enduring memorial which, as Mather implied, served "for the representation and remembrance of a person absent, for honour and Civil worship of any worthy person." The gravestone, then, not only commemorated the deceased individual but also confirmed the broad cultural goals and ideals of the early New England settlement. In this respect, the gravestone was one mode of artistic expression which, along with literary forms, served to create a memorial of the past for this transplanted culture.

Once having located the gravestone within the cultural contours of early New England, as we shall do in the first two chapters, we can then more fully seek out its artistic dimensions in subsequent discussion. The following instance, however, may provide a preliminary sense of our approach and the directions in which the material will lead us.

At the North Church of Boston, Cotton Mather delivered a funeral sermon for the Reverend Grindal Rawson of Mendon, who died on February 6, 1715. Funerals were a common occurrence, so perhaps it was the death of an energetic spiritual leader which charged the sermon with elements of particular significance for our understanding of Puritan art. With a crucial phrase, Mather described the congregation to itself as "Children of Change." By thus using an explicit metaphor of transformation, he had seized upon the essential nature of the Puritan funeral ritual. These rites expressed the hopes of eternal life for the deceased. They further served to sustain the surviving members of the community in their own belief in a collective posterity, if not an ultimate conversion—the "great Change" which, as Mather envisioned, would result at death. The sources of these celebrations lay in the cultural perception of vital metamorphic processes throughout human experience. The very transience of life itself held forth the promise of spiritual rebirth. The "Children of Change" were perhaps the "Children of God" after all.[14]

As a ministerial spokesman for the dominant religious tradition of New England, Mather embodied these beliefs in transformational symbols, the widespread currency of which assumed particular form and intensity upon the occasion of death. In this context the metamorphoses of flesh and spirit which qualified these settlers as "Children of Change" found visual articulation upon their gravestones, commemorating the dead for the living. The carved designs in their totality, as well as individual images and elements within, are animated by metamorphic values which formally dramatize the spiritual changes wrought through death. The designs, moreover, are not simply of peripheral concern, creating an "atmosphere" in support of iconographic meaning, as Ludwig supposes, but rather they are central to the comprehensive meaning of these artifacts.[15] In addition, neither the designs nor their constituent elements should be considered apart from their plastic embodiment as stonecarving.

Meaning evolves out of a fusion of religious and aesthetic values manifested through the marker's total presence as sculpture.

The funeral ritual, as it was practiced and developed during the course of the seventeenth and eighteenth centuries, serves as our fundamental model of cultural behavior by which to understand the meaning and significance of the gravestone as an art form. Since the ritual did not exist in isolation, we first discuss Puritan orthodoxy from the perspective of death by recasting the theology in terms of its response to the crucial human event which visited Puritan and non-Puritan alike. Balancing multiple ambiguities and tensions within its structure, Puritan theology most strikingly, albeit temporarily, resolved the Christian paradoxes manifested in baptism, conversion, and death through the continuum of metamorphosis, which, as Sister M. Bernetta Quinn has observed elsewhere "begins and ends the history of man." Central to the Christian experience, metamorphosis in its "finite forms"[16] became a particular concern of the Puritans, preoccupied as they were by the problem of establishing a visible church which might more closely approximate the invisible order of Christ than the institutions thought to be afforded by Anglicanism. Although the broad outline of funeral celebration was most certainly brought from England, it was this intensification of metamorphic values by the Puritan orthodoxy that informed the funeral practices of early New England communities.

Out of the perceived psychological pressures of existence emerged a visible complex of cultural values reflected in commensurate human behavior dramatizing them. Thus death ritual was a dynamic and critical pattern of social response. Insofar as the practices can be reconstructed, three elements gain importance.[17] The elegy, funeral sermon, and gravestone have endured as primary documents which now serve to illuminate the societal behavior surrounding death. Their relationships are examined in the second chapter. Intrinsic differences, of course, should not be ignored. The poem remains distinct from the prose sermon, and both—as literary documents—differ from the gravestone, ultimately a visual form. But while poems and even sermons often possess a visual dimension, and gravestones bear verbal and literary characteristics, the significant area of commonality was the cultural function served within the funeral ritual. As a result, all three shared and mutually reinforced commonly held values through the intrinsic qualities of their respective media.

Metamorphosis thus emerges as the most significant process informing these three artifacts, and suggests that the transformational values evidenced by the gravestones belong within a larger expressive pattern, at once religious and aesthetic, out of which a coherent visual aesthetic for the carving of gravestones can be inferred. That the style of carving varied regionally and changed over the years goes without saying. But their essentially conservative memorializing function within the culture, combined with transformational values, established a funerary art in the graveyards which remained vital until the nineteenth century.

CHAPTER 1

Rituals for God and History

Historical Observations

IMMEDIATELY after the creation, when the world was to be peopled by one man and woman, the ordinary age was 900 years and upwards. Immediately after the flood, when there were three persons to stock the world, their age was cut shorter, and none of the Patriarchs but *Shem* arrived at 500. In the second century, we find none that reached 240. In the third, none but *Terah* that came to 200 years; the world, at least a part of it, by that time, being so well peopled, that they had built cities, and were cantoned out in distant nations. By degrees, as the number of people increased, their longevity dwindled, till it came down at length to 70 or 80 years; and there it stood, and has continued to stand, ever since the time of *Moses*. This is found a good medium, and by means hereof, the world is neither overstocked, nor kept too thin, but life and death keep a pretty equal pace.

> *The New-England Almanack, or Lady's and Gentleman's Diary, For the Year of Our LORD CHRIST 1800* by Isaac Bickerstaff, Esq. Printed at Providence (R. I.) by John Carter, opposite the Market.

Writing out of his eighteenth-century optimism in an established New England community, the chronicler of this almanac might well have been sanguine about death, whereas in contrast, his Puritan forebears had settled in a land where life and death did not yet "keep a pretty equal pace." The initial struggle for survival in the wilderness of New England was so harsh that the small group of religious exiles had constant fears of extermination. Adversities of an alien culture, a severe climate, disease, and hunger informed their experience. Only in the discourse of their religious imagination did life and death maintain equilibrium, spiritual rebirth in rhythm with mortality. Thus the Puritans would have scarcely approved "Isaac Bickerstaff"'s reduction of biblical myth to mere fable, complacently tipping their dual vision of this world and the next decidedly in favor of earthly concerns.

Whatever their dreams about the material promise of the New World, the Puritans derived their courage and persistence from their religious premises. Before disembarking from the *Arbella* as the first of the Great Migration in 1630, John Winthrop advised his constituents that "Wee shall be as a Citty upon a Hill, the eies of all people are upon us."[1] Conscious of his role in the unfolding of God's eternal plan in history, he envisioned a Bible commonwealth that would serve as a model for his corrupt churchmen back in England. These Puritans who landed at Massachusetts Bay had removed themselves only geographically from the Anglican Church. While asserting their continued membership, they nonetheless shared with the Plymouth Separatists a vital impulse for church reform. In England their insistence would help to bring on civil war by the end of the decade. The exodus to New England was but one offshoot of the social and cultural conflicts generated. In the establishment of this wilderness outpost the workings of cultural purification were to be revealed for the homeland to follow.

This quest for purification in the New World was not a dream so unrealistic that the migrating Puritans could dismiss the practical exigencies of death. As Nathaniel Hawthorne astutely noted two hundred years later in *The Scarlet Letter*, "The founders of a new colony, whatever Utopia of human virtue and happiness they might originally project, have invariably recognized it among their earliest practical necessities to allot a portion of the virgin soil as a cemetery."[2] The pattern of the novel indicates that Hawthorne's symbolic appropriation of the cemetery not only acknowledged the stark fact of death but also served as a permanent index of fundamental human limitations, not merely physical but moral, spiritual, and intellectual as well. Such finitude would preclude the possibility of a perfect society. In this respect, Hawthorne might have assented to the Calvinistic belief in human corruption, so central to Puritan theology.

More than time, however, separated Hawthorne from his seventeenth-century ancestors. They lacked the skepticism necessary for his ironic ambivalence, which would subvert religious absolutism. From their perspective the graveyard was a ground of discourse between this world and the next rather than a final resting place.[3] They acknowledged death as the termination of physical being and the start of spiritual afterlife. The fact of death was subsumed by a belief in Christian metamorphosis, where earthly change, both of a spiritual and worldly nature, culminated in the final transition to the invisible world of heavenly salvation. Crucially, however, despite such firmly ingrained expectations, the Puritans perceived ambiguities of human existence, the very same so keenly felt by Hawthorne, but they were nevertheless constrained from self-irony by the holistic structure of their theology.

The Puritans of Massachusetts Bay attempted to construct a theological system that would establish a spiritual and moral order, civil and ecclesiastical in scope, out of the fundamental relationship between man and God. Tensions ensuing from the central Calvinist concept of an infinite God and a finite man extended in due course throughout the system. It was inevitable, then, that Puritanism could not remain a static religious phenomenon with an embalmed set of eternal truths.[4] The contradictions and ambiguities of human existence were to be reconciled within a comprehensive and seamless structure. Yet the desire for a total structure was in itself contradictory, since at the same time that the Puritans tried to explain God to man, they realized that God, in the final analysis, was beyond human comprehension. Such a realization, however, did not prevent the Puritans from attempting to formulate a system. Covenant Theology, as it came to be known, thus bore a semblance of logic but also a symbolic dimension which was ultimately suprarational.[5] As an essential component of the theology, death was both a logical certainty and a disruptive force which could be discharged through symbolic modes of expression. Indeed, only on a symbolic level could these paradoxes gain full play; otherwise they assumed but a tenuous balance within the theological structure.

The logic of Puritan theology was derived from the sixteenth-century French academician Peter Ramus. He had revised Aristotelian methods commonly accepted within the universities upon the Continent, and developed a logic of pedagogy which appeared to have infinite possibility and application. He replaced the syllogism with discrete "arguments" about a subject to be elaborated upon or an assertion to be tested for its truth. The "arguments" were disposed dichotomously as subcategories of the subject or assertion at hand in a dialectic of supposedly self-evident relationships. Ramism was not accepted without extensive and bitter controversy, but it eventually found limited appeal in English universities, particularly with some important Puritan leaders like William Ames and Richard Mather.[6]

Through their enthusiasm for what was originally intended as pedagogical reform, this system of logic was generally adopted by seventeenth-century Puritans in New England as a complete mode of knowledge. Ramist logic became indispensable for explicating the mysteries of the Scriptures and thus became a rhetorical tool as well, cast into a sermonic form known among Puritans as the plain style. Their epistemology transcended mere method to assume metaphysical stature, so that the patterns of meaning afforded by the logic could ostensibly be discovered in experience itself. Fraught with difficulties in that respect, Ramism wrought further strains upon the entire theological structure. Even as this pervasive dialectic characterized the language and logic of New England Puritanism, its analytic energies were at odds with the synthesizing qualities of Christian metamorphosis.[7] The ensuing tensions would be most profoundly felt in the graveyard, where death, viewed as a process both destructive and regenerative, was recapitulated through the visual aesthetic which informed the creation of their grave markers.

The consequence of all these internal stresses was change. Puritanism could never remain or, for that matter, ever be a monolithic religious movement, not even in New England, where the opportunity for social control seemed most feasible. Because the relationship between man and God stood at the heart of the matter, the Puritans were caught between what they perceived to be the institutional corruptions of Anglicanism and Roman Catholicism, on the one hand, and the anarchy of individual religious inspiration, on the other. Within the ecclesiastical dimension of their piety, therefore, the Puritans of Massachusetts Bay were aware of the danger in separating from the Church of England. In their desire to reform the Anglican Church from within, however, they still courted schism. Even though they were isolated in a small wilderness community, the members of their own group recapitulated the entire problem. Despite the range of strictures which rendered dissent invalid, religious debate prevailed. What from a later perspective can appear tedious was quite otherwise for the Puritans, who found religious issues to be living options. Along with tracts and essays, sermons were published and circulated extensively not only among ministers but generally throughout the congregations. Not a closed circle, the ministry exerted a powerful influence in the community. Indeed, the preeminent centrality of religious values to the culture at large was such that church and state in Massachusetts and Connecticut were not completely separated until well into the nineteenth century.[8]

This gradual change developed through a series of crucial controversies over the course of the seventeenth and eighteenth centuries, and led to the creation and proliferation of dissident congregations that refused to tolerate state support of the established churches. By 1800 the Covenant Theology of seventeenth-century orthodoxy had been abrogated. Nevertheless, the subsequent dissenters from the established churches held in common with the original Puritans a desire to erect a pure church of true believers—a religious preoccupation which persisted throughout the latter half of the eighteenth century.[9]

Contrary to Oliver Wendell Holmes' popular depiction of a rickety "one-horse shay," these transformations of seventeenth-century Puritan orthodoxy attest to its original strength and vitality. The intensity of their controversies suggests the force with which their religious tenets and concept of mission struck the sensibilities of these men. Their innumerable polemics arose from the implicit tensions of the theological structure. Changes in the nature of the visible church during the seventeenth and eighteenth centuries were predicated upon evolving conceptions of the Christian experience. What was the nature of the true believer? What distinguished him from the Christian who was baptized but incapable of professing saving faith in Jesus? These essential questions revolved around the concept of metamorphosis, by which a professing Christian was somehow a new man, different not only from his own previous state but from his fellows as well. The predominant and traditional metaphor for this spiritual redemption was rooted in the natural cycle of birth and death, a cycle that Christ had transcended through His own Resurrection. Thus an eternal realm and an ephemeral earth became reconciled through certain kinds of change, declared in conversion to Christ and promised in death as part of God's immutable order.

Covenant Theology offered the primary vehicle of reconciliation. In applying the tenets of John Calvin, the Puritans on the Continent and thence to Massachusetts Bay had developed a contractual metaphor to lend form and comprehension to the disproportionate relationship between weak man and omnipotent God. By the first covenant, one of works, God had given eternal life to Adam in Paradise in return for his obedience. Death entered the world upon Adam's failure in the Garden, and his progeny were deemed guilty of his Original Sin until the end of time.

The Puritans thus considered death in its spiritual as well as physical dimensions. Expostulating such attitudes in a tract of 1680 entitled *The Sting of Death and Death Unstung*, Leonard Hoar, for a time president of Harvard College, offered this definition:

> 1. There is a general and meer natural consideration of Death, and so it happens not only to man, but to all Creatures living. 2. A Theological consideration of it, as it is inflicted by the just punishing hand of God, and is a part of the curse, and so it is a miserable privation of Life, and so it is to be considered here, as a judicial penal evil, and so armed with its sting it is the greatest evil in the world.[10]

In discounting the physical aspects of death, Hoar emphasized its spiritual function as God's legal punishment upon Adam and his progeny for Adam's disobedience in the Garden.

The constant presence of physical death reinforced and empirically confirmed the spiritual concerns of New Englanders. In a funeral sermon of 1721 Benjamin Colman noted, "IT is a *dying time* too, and the Lesson is seasonable, 'That by a holy and righteous life we be daily so preparing, as that GOD helping us we may not at last fear to die. God grant us this Inestimable Mercy, the *Hope of the Righteous* in our End." The occasion of death offered the preacher the opportunity to teach a spiritual lesson. His recognition that the leverage of the sermon rested upon the fulcrum of death in the sensibilities of the congregation is indicated by a footnote appended upon publication: "The *Week* after the preaching of this *Sermon, two* of the Communion *died;* and *five* more Adult persons of the Congregation, and *six* Children: and the next week but one we had above a *hundred Funerals* in the *Town.*"[11]

In the face of man's essential mortality, made even more evident by daily life in New England, the Puritans were not without their spiritual affirmations. They acknowledged the significance of Paul's assertion in his First Epistle to the Corinthians: "For as in Adam all die, even so in Christ shall all be made alive." If the Puritan divines were to have drawn upon the first clause alone, surely their theology would be open to the stale charges of morbidity. But by equal emphasis upon the concluding line the mercy of God as well as His justice was made evident through the mediation of His son Jesus Christ. Christ's triumph over death was the basis for the second covenant, the Covenant of Grace. Under the new obligation God would give eternal salvation to those human beings who responded with a faith in Christ. God would provide, moreover, the spiritual grace, the means of Christian faith to man.

Despite the apparent ease of the Covenant of Grace, the Puritans faced enormous difficulties in its application. There were, of course, the institutional modes of determining the Elect so as to accept them within the innermost circle of true believers in the church structure. The baptized Christian had first to pass through specific conventionalized psychological stages in order to establish for his own satisfaction, if not for the satisfaction of others, that he possessed the saving faith to participate in the Lord's Supper with the inner congregation. Once the arduous phases of self-doubt, guilt, humility, illumination, and so forth had been experienced, the Puritan initiate was recognized a Christian believer, a visible saint and certified member of the religious community. As one contemporaneous writer of the complexities of conversion decreed, "But you must be transformed (or metamorphosed) by the renewing of your heart and life; the old frame must be dissolved, and a new one acquired."[12] Only then would the conversion process be completed.

Or so one would think. Despite the appeal of the Covenant of Grace, in which God's free self-limitation indicated a sign of His mercy and benevolence, despite the communal guidelines provided by the elders of the congregation, and despite the spiritual roadmaps of the theologians, a Puritan catch-twenty-two was incorporated in a seemingly rational contract. Such were the mysterious ways of God, as the omnipotent and ultimate Being, that He might grant grace as He wished, without regard for human effort. Good works, then, would not lead to salvation, although such endeavor might be a visible sign of salvation. Moral behavior in itself would not bring about the resurrection of the soul, but without morality one of the vital indices of predestined redemption was lost. Partial psychological relief was provided by Calvin's tenet of perseverance, in that a visible saint could lapse into sin without loss of election; presumably the strain and pressure of maintaining perfect behavior was thus removed. But lapses, particularly serious and frequent ones, could indicate just as easily a loss of salvation and a fate that in death was more to be feared than death itself.

Psychologically and theologically hamstrung, the Puritans exercised themselves both inwardly and outwardly. Believing that they had been placed in the world by God, they were obligated to participate fully in the social order, an imperative which has come to be seen in its secular terms as the Protestant Ethic. But just as they strove to accomplish good works, which ranged from charitable acts to successful commercial transactions, they turned inward to examine their souls. Because it was difficult to maintain such an equilibrium between the inner and outer worlds, a practical Sewall or a mystical Edwards would often develop. Diaries became the incomplete vehicle for the invalidated sacrament of confession. This popular mode of introspection allowed the writers to record daily occurrences and to draw from them indices of salvation or perdition. Thus could Michael Wigglesworth, the esteemed pastor of the Malden congregation, agonize over his fitness to partake of the Lord's Supper. It was incidental to Wigglesworth that he appeared to possess all the proper credentials. He alone knew his inner life, the terrors wrought and distorted by his pride, humility, and charity, prisms of his soul so difficult if not impossible to distinguish until the advent of Judgment Day, the "Day of Doom" depicted in his widely received poem.[13]

Just as the Puritan saint had been spiritually transformed by his conversion experience, so his death would presumably lead to his resurrection, the ultimate metamorphosis. As Samuel Willard, a most venerated Puritan divine, observed, "The compleat fulfilling of many spiritual Promises is reserved till another Life. There is a near relation between things spiritual, and things heavenly: Grace differs from Glory but in degree." In this view death was no longer an event to be feared but an experience of initiation to the rewards of heaven. Leonard Hoar concurred: "Death to the Saints is the middle point between two lives, it is an harbinger and a fore-runner of their being received up. . . . No sooner are the Saints undressed here, but they are cloathed upon in heaven." A popular verse offered a portrait of the saint in relation to his impending death:

> What makes the Saints on earth desire to be
> Dissolved, and that blessed day to see?
> What makes them whilst they're here below to groan
> Against this Body of Corruption?
> Lord, they know that when they from hence do go,
> On them a glorious Kingdome thou'lt bestow.[14]

Such a portrait, however, expressed the ideal, for although it was certain that the saint would receive his heavenly reward, his earthly identification remained an uncertainty. Consequently, death was approached with both fear and exaltation, with full knowledge that it alone was the key experience out of which the Puritan saint's lifelong tensions would be resolved. As Benjamin Colman warned his congregation, "It becomes a *Saint* to meet death with fear, for he is yet a *Sinner,* and is going before the HOLY ONE, and into his ETERNAL State; and every Believer has not a full *assurance.*" Trepidations over death, psychologically real and physically palpable, were balanced by a keen interest in future rewards, ever a possibility. Thus Colman held forth the affirmations of metamorphosis: "It will be the more bright and sweet, if it be possible, to pass out of the darkness of fear into the Inheritance of the Saints in Light. O how happy to find the dark fears groundless, and pass'd away for ever! to go *trembling* out of the Body, and the Soul find itself immediately in the *imbracing Arms* of holy Angels, sent to carry it into *Abrahams* bosome."[15] Between the poles of negation and affirmation the Puritans lived, both sustained and tormented by the ambiguities of Christian metamorphosis.

It is no wonder, then, that the New England community placed such emphasis upon funeral observances. And yet there are questions about the particular nature of these ceremonies. In compliance with Puritan theology, burial of the dead was relegated to civil jurisdiction, and therefore outside of ecclesiastical authority. Funeral rituals, however, bore both religious and social implications in a duality of function; not only was the soul released to its unknown fate, but the community felt the loss all the more clearly in terms of its own uncertain existence. The infusion of religious attitudes came from the private grief of the family responsible for the burial, conditioned as the survivors were by the theological arguments from the pulpit. As the force of Puritan theology diminished or changed during the course of New England settlement, the social and increasingly secular appurtenances of funeral rituals came to the fore and made the ceremonies increasingly elaborate. Eventually the original intent of seventeenth-century Puritan divines was submerged during the eighteenth century by what would become a precursor of the hollow ritual of death as practiced in contemporary America.

In seventeenth-century New England a definite separation of authority over burial rites was never articulated, but such division was clearly a basic assumption underlying the establishment of church and town. Precedents existed with the Puritans in Europe, as evidenced in "The Points of Difference" sent by the London-Amsterdam congregation to James I in 1603. The sixth point probably set forth the general attitudes prevalent within the Puritan party in England: "That the Ministers aforesaid being lawfully called by the Church where they are to administer, ought to continew in their functions according to Gods ordinance, and carefully to feed the flock of Christ committed unto them, being not inioyed or suffered to beare Civill offices withall, neither burthened with the execution of Civill affaires, as the celebration of marriage, burying the dead &c. which things belong aswell to those without as within the Church."[16] In following Calvin, who had eliminated the seven sacraments except for baptism and the Lord's Supper, the Puritans further proscribed the church rituals through a broad interpretation of the Second Commandment. They denied, of course, the validity as well as the efficacy of extreme unction, and located related rituals concerning burial in the civil realm.

Be that as it may, this separation did not prevent the Puritan divines from commenting upon the nature of proper burial. The Westminster Convention of 1645 appended to the *Confession of Faith* a *Directory for the Public Worship of God*. Included in the *Directory* were procedures "Concerning Burial of the Dead" describing the form to be used by the Presbyterian Church of Scotland. In acquiescence to the views of Independent Puritans at the Convention, this section required that the attended body be taken to the cemetery and buried without undue ceremony. The stated reason for this procedure denied the efficacy of prayer and performance of rites with respect to the soul of the deceased, since his fate had already been determined by an omnipotent God. The theological emphasis of their position was buttressed by the liturgical: to avoid committing "superstitious" acts that had "proved many ways hurtful to the Living" in the past, all ceremonies such as kneeling, praying, reading, and singing were proscribed.[17]

In *Plain Dealing or News from New England*, printed in London on his return from Massachusetts Bay in 1642, Thomas Lechford described the funeral commonly practiced in Boston: "At Burials, nothing is read, nor any Funeral Sermon made, but all the neighbourhood, or a good company of them, come together by tolling of the bell, and carry the dead solemnly to his grave, and there stand by him while he is buried. The Ministers are most commonly present."[18] The simplicity of this account implied no negation of solemn reverence afforded the dead by the living in this civil ceremony. Even though active participation was outside their authority, the ministers' presence at burials intensified the fact of death as the final act of this life, awesome in its dimensions for what it might bring in the next.

Apparent from Lechford's description of burials, New England custom dictated a simple interment similar to that advised by the Westminster *Directory*. Although the New England divines at the Cambridge Synod of 1648 considered the work of Westminster only with respect to the *Confession of Faith*, they would have known the contents of the *Directory*. The Synod did not formally act upon the latter, however, because the autonomy of the individual local congregations would have been severely undermined by such liturgical dictation. Nevertheless, the New England ministry most likely agreed with the *Directory* on the practice of burial, a matter formulated by the Independents, Puritans in old England who were closest in sympathy to those removed to the New World. While funeral rites were never formally delineated in New England, civil customs were allowed to develop through observance which paralleled the position of the *Directory*.

As a result, there were other aspects concerning the funeral in which the *Directory* admonition matched New England practice. The *Directory* maintained a delicate balance between religious and civil aspects of burial: "Howbeit, we judge it very convenient, that the Christian Friends, which accompany the dead Body to the Place appointed for publick Burial, do apply themselves to Meditations, and Conferences suitable to the Occasion: And that the Minister, as upon other Occasions, so at this Time, if he be present, may put them in Remembrance of their Duty." By changing the emphasis of burials from mourning the dead to personal meditations, the religious consciousness of the community would be exercised. Yet the official church structure would remain independent of such involvement, thereby eliminating any remnant of supposed "Papist" interference. The somewhat casual phrasing of ministerial inclusion underscores the probability that a minister would indeed be present upon such an occasion and could not be thought overzealous should he entreat his accompanying parishioners to "apply themselves to meditations." Over a half-century later, in 1710, Cotton Mather underscored the didactic value of burial rituals in his diary. "It would be a great Service to the Kingdome of God, if the

Funerals, that are so frequent among us, were made greater Instances and Incentives of *Religion*," he declared.[19]

In quality of tone, however, Mather's diary entry differed from the *Directory*'s mild interjection of peripheral ministerial participation in burial. Mather's piety, occasionally excessive, was here a valid and understandable reaction against the social emphases that the funeral had taken on over the course of the past seventy years in New England. And yet the original sanction of what Mather came to perceive as abuses was derived from the provisions of the *Directory*. Its final clause concerning burial defined the civil sphere of authority with respect to rituals and allowed the development of an institution in tandem with both the ecclesiastical and magisterial authorities, independent of the former and virtually free by the latter. The *Directory* added the qualification that the previous proscriptions "shall not extend to deny any civil Respects or Deferences at the Burial, suitable to the Rank and Condition of the Party deceased, while he was living." This qualification appears to have been fully operative as early as 1649, when the Artillery Officers of Boston appropriated a barrel and a half of powder from the Massachusetts Bay Company to discharge at the funeral of Governor John Winthrop. The General Court, in meeting the following month, absorbed the financial loss of powder and "thankfully acknowledge[d] Bostons great worthy dew love & respects to the late honnored Governor, wch they manifested in solemnizing his funerall, whom wee accompted worthy of all honnor."[20]

During this period of one hundred fifty years, from the funeral of Governor Winthrop in 1649 to the death of President Washington in 1799, the ambivalent result of arbitrary division of authority concerning burials became fully visible. The community that initially simulated the sounds of the impending apocalypse to dramatize the violent sense of the loss of a leader had itself undergone violent upheaval. The churches' reluctance to interfere and to become, therefore, formally integrated in the rituals resulted in social excesses of the funeral observances. The magistrates, originally coordinate with the church elders in the seventeenth century, had proved ineffectual in regulating funerals which became, by contemporary accounts, excessive displays of conspicuous consumption, the bane of both clergy and General Court. Public sensibility at the time of Washington's death was so enervated by the trappings of burial that the display of mourning became in itself an indulgence of personal memorabilia.

The growth of the funeral ritual served a vital cultural purpose nonetheless. What most clearly emerged from the paraphernalia of funerals in New England was the articulated need of these dislocated people to be memorialized to the future, a need made all the more urgent by the Puritans' sense of spiritual mission to the New World. Commemoration of an individual settler by his contemporaries seemed to ensure and mark indelibly the anticipated future with the knowledge that someone *in particular* had gone before in the new land of Canaan. Through the establishment of family dynasties, made visible in the graveyards, the conscious work of a societal destiny greater than that of an individual family could emerge all the more assuredly. No accident, then, that Morton's *New Englands Memoriall* was first printed in 1669, concomitant with the popular proliferation of gravestones.

New Englands Memoriall is as much a verbal graveyard, in this sense, as the abbreviated history Morton intended it to be. In the introduction "To the Christian Reader," Morton celebrated

> *How that* God brought a vine into this Wilderness; *that* he cast out the Heathen and planted it; *that* he made room for it, and caused it to take deep root, and it filled the Land; *so that* it hath sent forth its boughs to the Sea, and its branches to the River. *And not onely so, but also that* He hath guided his people by his strength to his Holy Habitation, *and planted them in the* Mountain of his Inheritance, *in respect of precious Gospel-Enjoyments. So that we may not onely look back to former Experiences of Gods goodness to our Predecessors (though many years before) and so have our faith strengthened in the Mercies of God for our times.*[21]

Morton continued with a recording of important first documents, citing the signers of the Mayflower Compact, the names *Mayflower* and *Speedwell*, and reprinting the elegiac poems written upon the deaths of the New England leaders. His narration of the first Thanksgiving and the trials of the early settlers, particulary their interaction with the Indians, are the elements of popular history, the subjects that have lent themselves to American cultural myth.

Morton's writing was directed between individual and collective memorial. As he asserted in his prefatory note, "*So then,* gentle Reader, *thou mayest take notice, that the main Ends of publishing this small* History *is,* That God may have his due praise, His Servants the Instruments have their Names embalmed, and the present and future Ages may have the fruit and benefit of Gods great work, in the Relation of the first Planting of *New England.*" Even fifty years later, Cotton Mather pleaded, "*And Lord, lett me at my Death be found worthy of a Remembrance among the Living!*" In much the same way, Samuel Sewall, the Boston jurist and diarist, pinned a note on the door of the Old South Church: "Samuel Sewall desires Prayers, that the Death of his Eldest Daughter may be Sanctified to him, and to the Relatives."[22] Naming the dead "sanctified" them to the collective memory of the living, and perhaps perpetuated their lives to future generations, not merely for the sake of individual vanity but, more importantly, for the creation of a cultural model that the community could look back upon for guidance.

In addition to these verbal declarations, the structural elements of the funeral ritual itself reveal the communal significance of death. Sewall recorded its formal aspects in his description of the death and burial of his daughter Hannah in 1724.

> Satterday, Aug.ᵗ 15. Hambleton and my Sister Watch, I get up before 2 in the Morning of the L. Day, and hearing an earnest Expostulation of my daughter, I went, down and finding her restless, call'd up my wife. Sent for her bro.ʳ the Min.ʳ who pray'd with her. I read to her the 23.ᵈ Psalm, and pray'd with her, (Mr. Prince I think, pray'd in the evening). Mr. Cooper pray'd. I read the 34ᵗʰ Psalm, and the first and last of the 27ᵗʰ, I do not remember the exact order of these things. I put up this Note at the Old [First Church] and South, "Prayers are desired for Hanah Sewall as drawing Near her end." Her Bro.ʳ pray'd with her just before the morning Exercise. Finding that I could do her little or no Service, I went to Meeting, and join'd with Mr. Prince praying excellently for her. The Lord's Supper was Celebrated. When I came home I found my Daughter laid out. She expired half an hour past Ten. Her pleasant Countenance was very Refreshing to me. I hope God had delivered her from all her Fears! She had desired not to be embowelled. In the Afternoon I put up this Note at the Old South, "Samuel Sewall desires Prayers, that the Death of his Eldest Daughter may be Sanctified to him, and to the Relatives." After the Exercises tooke order of Mr. Fitch for a Coffin. Physicians say, Considering her Distemper, we must bury on Tuesday.
>
> Monday, Aug.ᵗ 17ᵗʰ continue in the same mind, and say that now she Canot be embowelled. Before night put her into her Coffin in a good Cere Cloth, and bestow a Convenient quantity of Lime, whereby the noxious Humour flowing from her Legg, may be suppressed and absorbed. Boston [Sewell's black servant] will not have her put into the Cellar: so she is only remov'd into the best Room. And because the Casements were opened for Coolness, Boston would watch all night.
>
> Tuesday, Aug.ᵗ 18. My daughter is Inter'd, Bearers, Maj.ʳ Habijah Savage, Mr. W.ᵐ Payn; Mr. John Boydell, Mr. John Walley; Mr. Henry Franklyn, Henry Gibbs. Had Gloves and Rings of 2pw.ᵗ and 1/2. Twelve Ministers of the Town had Rings, and two out of Town. At our Return from the Grave, her Bro.ʳ J. Sewall pray'd. *Laus Deo.*[23]

As with the death of his first wife, Hannah Hull, in 1717, Sewall concentrated on the external events surrounding the death of his daughter. In the case of his wife, no mention was made in the *Diary* with respect to a funeral sermon delivered by Cotton Mather and printed at the expense of Sewall; nor did he mention the printed elegy handed out at the time of her burial.[24] It is not known if either a sermon or an elegy were written and delivered upon the death of his daughter Hannah, but it is likely that some verbal tribute was compiled, for it was customary to pin a broadside elegy to the back of the hearse or coffin on the way to the graveyard.

Although the entry was made well into the eighteenth century, Sewall's record of death and burial can be considered representative of funeral behavior probably from the time of Governor Winthrop. The intensity of Sewall's grief cannot be hidden beneath the abstract quality of recording the events surrounding the death of his daughter. The close family involvement in the deathwatch, the prayers, and even the laying-out of her body after death brought to the immediate relatives the comfort of ritual proceedings without the public mechanisms for formalized grief so manifest in later years. The presence of a minister was certainly not a "Romish" concession, for his prayer would not bring about salvation; nevertheless, its practice was a humanized recognition of the anxieties besetting Hannah and her family before and after death, an expression of hope that affirmed their faith in the Lord's will.

The dual role of Hannah's brother as a member of the family and as a minister gives some indication of the communal ramifications of a funeral beyond the immediate privacy of the family. Sewall's posting of notes to the church doors is another indication, a public manifestation of personal grief. The external ceremony of carrying the body to the graveyard belonged entirely within the public realm and allowed the community to participate in commemorating the deceased. Thus it was standard practice to have two sets of pallbearers. The ones listed at Hannah's funeral would have been the honorary bearers: one group bore the coffin to the graveyard, while the other carried the pall over the coffin. Communal participation was further institutionalized by the common ownership of the palls held through the town governments, another indication of the ecclesiastical-civil separation of authority concerning burial.

That these practices could and did lead to excesses is well borne out. In contrast to the relative simplicity of Hannah Sewall's burial (but probably not as simple as that outlined by the *Directory*) was the entry of John Rowe's *Diary*, recording the burial of Jerimiah Gridley, a Boston lawyer, less than fifty years later in 1767:

> Sept. 12. In the afternoon I attended the Funeral of our Right Worshipful Jerry Gridley Esq, Grand Master, as Deputy Grand Master. The officers of his regiment marched in order first. then the Brethern of St. Andrew's

Lodge. then the Stewards of the Grand Lodge. then the Brethren promiscuously two by two. then the Wardens of the Second Lodges. then the Wardens of the first Lodges. then the Wardens of the Master's Lodge. then the three Masters of the three several Lodges. then the past Grand Officers & the Treasurer. then the Grand Wardens. then myself as Deputy Grand Master. then the Tyler with the Grand Master's Jewels on a Black Velvet Cushion. The Corps the Bearers were the Lieut. Governor, Jedge Trowbridge, Justice Hubbard, John Erving Senr, James Otis and Mr Saml Fitch then followed the Relations. after them the Lawyers in their Robes. then the Gentlemen of the Town & then a great many Coaches, Chariots & Chaises. Such a multitude of Spectators I never saw at anything before since I have been in New England. After his Body was Interred wee Returned in Form to the Town house (from whence his Corps was taken at the Beginning of the Procession) in the same order as wee first walked. I do not much approve of such parade & show but as it was his Relatives desire, I could not well avoid giving my Consent. I think the Number of the Brethren that attended was 161. Upon the whole it was as well Conducted & in as Good Order as the Nature of it would admit.[25]

In describing the pageantry of the Masonic funeral, Rowe reflected the general misgivings over excessive funeral displays which became subject to legislative regulation through the passage of sumptuary laws during the eighteenth century. But whereas Mather desired simplification as a reflection of religious piety, Rowe's concern centered on matters of taste and social propriety. Despite their common desire for simplification, Rowe's sentiments regarding ostentation bore little or no connection to Mather's Puritan impulses—an indication of fundamental changes in attitudes toward funeral observances in the eighteenth century.

The renewals of sumptuary laws which attempted to restrict the amount of money to be spent on gloves, rings, scarves, and rum at funerals (and other unrelated social acts as well) throughout the eighteenth century suggest that excesses occurred with frequent regularity, that the proscriptions of the magistrates failed of their purpose. Originally of religious import to the community, many of the customs increasingly took on social significance alone. For example, funeral feastings provided the community with the opportunity of participating in the loss of the deceased, as well as providing sustenance to persons who had come long distances to attend the burial. The practical and implicitly religious considerations were soon exceeded as the event became purely social. Thus a funeral dinner given to as many as one hundred ten male guests after the burial of Caleb Davis of Boston in 1797 took up most of the expenses, which amounted to 844.80 dollars at the time.[26] Nearly a century earlier, Cotton Mather noted that the social aspects of funerals were being increasingly emphasized. "We think only of *other Peoples,* never of *our Own* [death]. From the Levity at *Funerals,* it may truly be Judged so!" he exclaimed with disapproval. Likewise, he antici- pated from the pulpit laws forbidding the use of rum at funerals. He minced no words: "For them that should *Walk as Mourners about the Streets,* then to *Reel as Drunkards about the Streets,* and be fitter for the *Stocks* than for the *Streets:* Wretch, How darest thou so horribly defy the Vengeance of Heaven?"[27]

Similar developments of social excess occurred for other funeral customs. The accumulation of gloves, scarves, and rings was essential to the burial ritual. The exchange of these seemingly minor gifts was conducted in such a manner as to imply commitment to the life of the deceased by those remaining to com- memorate his death. Thus members of the community were invited to the burial by receiving a pair of gloves as a sign of their fellowship. Scarves made of lengths of white linen were given to the ministers and were intended to be sewn into shirts and worn in memory of the deceased. Gold rings were given not only to the ministers of the town who attended the funeral but also to rela- tives and special friends of the deceased. Commonly inscribed on the inside of the band with the name or initials of the deceased and his date of death, the mourning rings were engraved, molded, or enameled with death's-heads coffins, and skeletons—in short, the same kinds of images used by printers of elegy broadsides and by the carvers of gravestones. The E. H. ring, for example, given by Edward Holyoke upon the death of his wife Elizabeth in 1711, shows two skeletons flanking a central crystal and encircling the band, their feet meet- ing in a rosette upon the opposite side (*Fig. 1*).

Cotton Mather got at the heart of this exchange:

> I would never putt on the Civilities (of a Glove, or a Ring, or a Scarf) given me at a Funeral, but endeavour to do it, with a Supplication of this Impor- tance; *Lord, prepare me for my own Mortality.* And, *Lord, lett me at my Death be found worthy of a Remembrance among the Living!* And inasmuch as I have a distinguishing Share, above the most of them who ordinarily attend a Funeral, in such Civilities, I would look at it, as an Obligation on me to press after the Instances of Godliness and Usefulness, that may render me more excellent than my Neighbour; and particulary, in an holy Behaviour at a Funeral; exemplary in the Religion of the Funeral.[28]

The implicit tensions in the separation of ecclesiastical and civil authority over burial become manifest in the attitudes of Mather and Sewall (who were con- temporaries), although they missed the conflict in such terms. The giving of gloves, rings, and scarves as invitations and mementos of the deceased figured large in Sewall's diary and was present in Mather's discussions of funerals. But whereas Sewall listed with impunity the funerals at which he served as bearer

Fig. 1. The E. H. [Elizabeth Holyoke] mourning ring, gold band inlaid with black enamel, inscribed "EH / ux EH / Ob Aug. 15, 1719 / AE 28"; maker's mark "TE" [Thomas Edwards (?), Boston]. Diameter, ⅞ inch. *Courtesy of The Essex Institute, Salem, Massachusetts.*

and the gifts he received for such services, Mather exhorted himself to "purify" his acquisitions and worried about the great amounts of time spent by the citizenry at funerals.

Mather even delivered a funeral sermon on funerals, *A Christian Funeral*, with the subtitle indicating the topic: *A Brief Essay, On that Case, What Should Be the Behaviour of a Christian at a Funeral?* While affirming the observance of funeral customs, he protested against their growing social importance accompanied by a shrinking religious significance. For Mather the former was of value only insofar as the latter sustained primary import. Grasping the religious implications of death, each individual would ideally participate in the funeral service as a communal exercise, manifesting the will of God in His New Canaan. Mather's envisioned balance between the communal and the religious was not maintained, even as he delivered his sermon in 1713. Although Sewall himself was not lacking in orthodox piety, his matter-of-fact account of social exchanges in the funeral service accurately reflected what was to come. The funeral artifacts, particularly the glove and the ring, soon assumed conspicuous social dimensions. The materials used for the gloves varied from fine kid to lamb's wool, and large quantities were imported from England for such occasions. There was a direct relationship between the quality of the proffered glove and the social standing of the invited guest in relation to the family of the deceased. Likewise, mourning rings became increasingly elaborate during the eighteenth century. Common semiprecious stones as well as plaited hair were incorporated into the design of the rings. Handed out in prodigious quantity, accumulated rings could eventually create a small fortune for the recipients, as evidenced by the now legendary quart tankard of funeral rings left to the heirs of Doctor Samuel Buxton of Salem in 1758.

And yet, prevalent as these artifacts were, by their very nature they were ephemeral. It was the gravestone commissioned from the local stonecarver by the family that has endured over the centuries as memorial for the deceased.

The earliest of these memorials were simply rude markers with the name and age of the deceased painstakingly cut and etched, rather than carved, on fieldstones. At the same time, some prominent families used tombs dug into the side of a hillock. A heavy wooden door provided entrance into the crypt. Other families employed massive table slabs on which were carved their coats of arms so as to maintain their ancestral identities. The great majority of New Englanders, however, came to erect individual head- and foot-stones, generally in the shape of a doorway, suggesting the passage between this realm and the next, with the carvings on the tympanum and pilaster panels dramatizing the transition between the visible and invisible worlds.

After the funeral the length of time that the family of the deceased might take to erect a stone varied from several weeks or months to even years. The lapse depended in part upon the availability of a stonecarver in the immediate area. No doubt the head of the family occasionally had to ride several miles to another town in order to speak with a carver. Even in an urban area there were delays, since the availability of a gravestone depended upon the stock the carver had on hand. Whereas the stone was probably already cut into slabs, the design might not have been carved in advance. There was, moreover, always the delay of cutting the text and epitaph to suit the individual deceased. The task of stonecarving itself took time, as evidenced simply by the fine lettering upon many gravestones, not only those with elaborate designs but also those rough-hewn, bearing only the name of the deceased and the date of his death (*Fig. 2*).

Stonecarvers engaged in other kinds of stonework and occasionally held other occupations as well. William Young of the Worcester area was the town surveyor, a local cartographer, and justice of the peace. John Bull of Newport engaged in everything from building houses and laying foundations to privateering, and then incidentally carving some of the most masterly stones to

Fig. 2. The I. R. stone, 1688, Newman Cemetery, Rumford, Rhode Island.

be found in New England at any time before or since. Joshua Hempstead was a judge of probate, a carpenter (who made coffins), a land broker, a farmer, and a mariner. Between these occupations he cut gravestones for the New London and Norwich areas. New Englanders thus sought out the particular services of a carver through other craft and professional roles when it became necessary to mark the graves of their dead.

Neither the craft nature of stonecarving nor its memorializing function for the community should preclude its possibilities as art. Inasmuch as distinctions between craft and art are probably untenable, the stonecarver would have scarcely fulfilled salient cultural needs without an awareness of aesthetic considerations. It was not the craft as such, but rather the informality of the carver's role in the marketplace that had significant bearing on the quality of his work. Here was a factor which eludes unqualified generalization, yet it should be recognized for its possible effects.

The informality of craft operation could easily work against the quality of stonecarving. Faced with other tasks and the demands of other roles, stonecarvers oftentimes worked hastily and without aesthetic considerations in their carving. As a consequence, some stonecutters slavishly borrowed designs and patterns from fellow carvers in order to facilitate their efforts. Such copying resulted in an insidious mechanical quality of design on the finished monuments, competently cut but without any visible sensitivity or originality in the handling of material and image. On the other hand, an informal situation could allow the carver a flexibility in his selection of motifs and designs. He was free to draw upon the decorative elements of other crafts, the most popular of which was printing, which made available woodcuts and engravings in addition to the various lettering styles. The stonecarver's eclecticism was not an inevitable indication of unoriginality, and should not be so interpreted, for New England craftsmen in general shared an iconography drawn from a common cultural milieu.

By the same token, the commercial nature of stonecarving was not necessarily detrimental to creativity. Oftentimes, to be sure, there were limitations if a family were forced to accept the designs that a carver had available in his shop. But the marketplace also afforded the interaction of the carver and his customer to agree upon a gravestone appropriate to the deceased, or if not to the deceased, satisfactory to his survivors. A gravestone, then, most certainly reflected the social and emotional needs of the remaining family, but it could also reflect the person whom its erection honored. Sewall, for example, worked in close conjunction with his friend the carver William Mumford in the proper determination of the epitaph for his father, Henry Sewall of Newbury, Massachusetts.[29] In like manner, there are many stones whose carvings indicate the nature of the person deceased by virtue of the design. The markers for the ministers of a community provide perhaps the most obvious instance. A case in point is the gravestone erected in Paxton, Massachusetts, for the Reverend Silas Bigelow, portrayed addressing his congregation from the pulpit (*Fig. 58*).

In the final analysis, artistic success was dependent primarily upon the carver's aesthetic vision, a lapse of which would result in mediocrity, regardless of his sheer technical skill. His aesthetic found its source in the metamorphic process central to Christianity and particularly crucial to Puritanism, which produced a corresponding metamorphic art form on its gravestones. This aesthetic cut across regional styles and indeed accounted for their development over time. By the middle of the eighteenth century other sensibilities preferring neoclassical values became infused in the creation of the design upon the gravestone. The dynamics of metamorphosis, however, were so well established as the aesthetic tradition of the stonecarver that the designs absorbed or accommodated new sensibilities. The limits of such growth were marked by the advent of the willow-and-urn motif at the beginning of the nineteenth century. Even though Protestant Christianity in New England retained its power of belief, Puritanism had sufficiently declined so that its attitudes toward death were supplanted by a romantic sensibility that preferred euphemistic and sentimental imagery in the creation of a genteel funerary art.

CHAPTER 2

Symbolic Modes of
Christian Metamorphosis

EVEN though the Puritans eliminated elaborate liturgical forms from the church, they retained a viable sense of ritual in their death observances. However simple these were originally intended to be, the very prescription of behavioral forms signifies the presence of ritual. The funeral expressed important individual and communal memorializing needs and discharged severe anxieties about death in the process. Death and resurrection, central to Christianity, could not be constrained within the supposedly rational structure of Covenant Theology. Only ritual dramatization and other related modes of symbolic expression could adequately resolve the paradoxes and tensions of Christian metamorphosis.

Although located outside the church, the funeral ritual remained a sacred performance: "The participants in the rite are convinced that the action actualizes and effects a definite beatification, brings about an order of things higher than that in which they customarily live."[1] The funeral ritual afforded a self-conscious and formalized activity separated from ordinary life. Thus the graveyard was a circumscribed space where the main activity of burial was concentrated. Through prescribed rules which allowed repetition of behavior, the funeral ordered the profound disruption caused by death. Reassurance was limited, however, since the community of survivors could not know the spiritual fate of the deceased or, by implication, their own. It was this uncertainty of outcome, not simply each new death, which called for ritual enactment again and again, to play out the mythic possibilities of Christian metamorphosis informing the service.

The formal rules of behavior which established the funeral as ritual presuppose an aesthetic dimension. In its most general configuration the funeral service possessed a harmonious flow: events would occur as expected, offering stability and order to counteract the trauma of death. Within the ritual itself a number of elements took on an aesthetic quality as well: the fine carpentry of the pine coffin, the elegance of the mourning rings, the tolling of the meeting-house bells, and so forth. But the funeral sermon and elegy in particular were fully developed art forms. These modes of expression embodied the broad range of ambiguity surrounding death and resurrection and assumed an intensity of symbolic value as integral parts of the ritual. The elegy was often recited at the grave site; the minister delivered the funeral sermon after the burial and so drew the congregation together for meditation. In acting out these symbolic elements of ritual the Puritans were demonstrating their faith. As a result, language, recitation, and gesture coalesced in a perceived reality whereby the ritual assumed an autonomy of meaning commensurate with faith. Metamorphosis was no longer a theological abstraction but took on palpable existence through the symbolizing imaginations of the survivors.[2]

An examination of the funeral sermon and the elegy reveals the modulation between metaphor and metamorphosis on the gravestone. Notwithstanding the widespread use of death images on mourning rings and similar decorations for the funeral cortege, the sermon and the elegy were most closely related to the gravestone through the frequent interplay between their visual and verbal aspects. The published sermon occasionally carried funereal images on the title page, and broadside elegies were often decorated along the margins; likewise, the gravestone offered verbal information about the deceased, often by the convention of the elegiac epitaph, which occupied an important area of the stone surface. More important, however, these three art forms of the funeral ritual best expressed the full range of complex attitudes about death felt by the community. Consequently, although the modes were intrinsically different, their iconography as well as their formal qualities drew from the same cultural source. The minister, the elegist, the stonecarver, and the family of the deceased all shared the complex of values that their culture attached to death: Christian metamorphosis and its attendant ambiguities informed the funeral ritual to draw the community together for a sense of life in the face of death.

In the funeral sermon the preacher had an opportunity for a wide range of theological and religious discourse. But eventually he made mention of the deceased, whose spiritual course he charted from his natural, unregenerate state as a youth to his Christian conversion, which offered hopes of salvation. A similar content held true for the elegy, commemorating the deceased at the grave site. There is, for example, "A Copy of Verses Made . . . on the Sudden Death of Mr. Joseph Brisco, Who Was Translated from Earth to Heaven January 1. 1657."[3] The elegist evokes the immortal voice of Mr. Brisco himself to recall his earthly conversion, which was but a rehearsal for the final metamorphosis (indicated by the very title) as he joins the saints in heaven.

Although the pattern of spiritual conversion provided a common discursive narrative for both the elegy and the funeral sermon, figurative language was used less intensely in a funeral sermon than in an elegy. The difference in the use of language ultimately comes down to the difference between prose and poetry. And yet the demands placed upon verbal expression at certain moments during the funeral service were best met by the particular nature of poetry and prose. Although a convention, and hence vulnerable to banality, the elegy was oftentimes a personal expression of grief, written by a relative or close friend of the deceased. Poetry, therefore, was appropriate at the grave, where passion was dominant.

Samuel Sewall has poignantly recorded his feelings upon the death of his mother:

> Went ab^t 4. p.m. Nathan Bricket taking in hand to fill the Grave, I said, Forbear a little, and suffer me to say That amidst our bereaving sorrows We have the Comfort of beholding this Saint put into the rightfull possession of that Happiness of Living desir'd and dying lamented. . . . And therefore I ask and hope that none will be offended that I have now ventured to speak one word in her behalf; when shee her self is become speechless. Made a Motion with my hand for the filling of the Grave. Note, I could hardly speak for passion and Tears. Mr. Tappan pray'd with us in the evening.[4]

Prayer was one form of consolation for the survivors, but elegies at the grave were another. Whatever Sewall managed to say required great restraint in the face of such stress, lest sheer emotion prevail. Even as the passion of the grave would call forth poetry, with its concentrated, highly charged language, the elegiac form offered a verbal discipline of its own by rendering a surrogate voice for the deceased—preferable to the silence that would soon prevail.

Conversely, prose discourse requires logic and rationality, which are easier to attain after the event of death rather than during. By custom, the funeral sermon was delivered either on Sunday or as the weekday lecture immediately following burial so as to maintain the civil nature of the service. But a few days' respite after the interment was all the more imperative for the preparation of the funeral sermon, structured as it was upon Ramist logic, which was intrinsic to the rhetorical intent of explicating biblical texts. The funeral sermon, then, required and found congenial opportunity to intellectualize and elaborate on theological matters. Death became an occasion for teaching the congregation a religious lesson as well as for commemorating the dead.

THE FUNERAL SERMON AND PLAIN STYLE

Given the discursive nature of prose, the minister's use of figurative language was loose and relaxed, rather than intense and highly charged. His adherence to the plain style, moreover, may have contributed to a slackening of figurative language: the minister would shun the elaborate, the fanciful, and the esoteric in his choice of images, conceits, and literary allusions. As the Reverend Thomas Hooker noted, "The substance and solidity of the frame is that, which pleaseth the builder, its the painters work to provide varnish." According to his view, the minister should concentrate upon the logical organization of the sermon, its Ramist structure, "the substance and solidity of the frame," rather than decorative language, mere "varnish" in Hooker's eyes.[5]

Michael Wigglesworth, in his *Prayse of Eloquence* (1650) before his instructors at Harvard College, declaimed: "So that let a good Oratour put forth the utmost of his skill, and you shall hear him so lay open and unfould, so evidence and demonstrate from point to point what he hath in hand, that he will make a very block understand his discourse."[6] In Hooker's words Wigglesworth wanted to "direct the apprehension of the meanest," placing Ramist logic at the service of the plain style. Patient analysis guided by a direct outline would open a difficult biblical text to the least educated of the congregation. Plain style was thus perhaps the first popular American art form, created by a ministerial elite to convey their complex ideas to the populace at large.[7]

With this end in mind Wigglesworth affirmed the value of concrete oratory: "Let him [the orator] be to give a description of something absent or unknown; how strangely doth he realize and make it present to his hearers apprehensions, framing in their mindes as exact an idea of that which they never saw, as they can possibly have of any thing that they have bin longest and best acquainted with. Or doth he take upon him to personate some others in word or deedes why he presents his hearers not with a lifeless picture, but with the living persons of those concerning whom he speaks." Such pulpit discourse required art and skill on the part of the minister. Plain style was plain only in that it was not baroque or esoteric, and it certainly was not crude, as Wigglesworth scornfully indicated with a rhetorical question: "Why should he here discourse after the vulgar manner, and deliver his mind as a cobler would doe . . . ?"[8] Wigglesworth's insistence upon ministerial presentation of vivid language to the congregation was to reach its peak in the brilliant sermons of Jonathan Edwards less than a century later. In the meantime, a strong sermonic tradition developed in New England—a tradition of simplicity and directness, requiring all of the minister's art to conceal his rhetoric.

Puritan plain style, then, did not prohibit the use of figurative language. It only required that the figures employed have common currency and a vivid-ness made further accessible through a logical presentation. If the minister did not weave his sermon with appropriate scriptural quotations throughout—allu-sions that were to vivify as well as substantiate his argument—he might lace his sermon with metaphors that were related to the central scriptural text. As stan-dard procedure the minister began with such a text, as did, for example, Samuel Willard upon the death of John Leverett, the governor of Massachusetts: "*And I sought for a man among them, that should make up the hedge, and stand in the gap before me for the land, that I should not destroy it, but I found none: Therefore have I poured out mine indignation upon them, I have consumed them with the fire of my wrath; their own way have I compensed upon their heads, saith the Lord God.*" In explicating the text, with its apocalyptic overtones (increasing the anxiety of the congregation all the more), Willard seized, as key words, *hedge* and *gap*. He recognized their use in the text as metaphors, which he proceeded to unfold for their implications. Once he had explained the various meanings, he then made a series of "assertions" using his own metaphors consonant with those of the text. "That which God expects of a people whom he takes to be a vineyard of his own, is, that they should bring forth fruit to his glory," he declared.[9]

Within Willard's analytic presentation there was a synthetic undercurrent. His metaphors coalesced through an associational logic—a logic of metaphor, so to speak. For example, he chose an agrarian metaphor of the "vineyard" to complement the image of the hedges. Implicitly, the fruit of the vineyard would grow in the gaps of the hedges—an eminently familiar conceit, since Christ is closely associated with the grape. The predominant characteristic of this ser-mon, however, was analytic, an integral aspect of the Puritan's logical presen-tation in Ramist terms, which broke down the meaning of propositions into their constituent elements for explication and resolution.

As a result, the use of Ramist logic generally kept the figurative language of the funeral sermon in check and restrained the verbal transformations of the deceased subject as analogues for his anticipated spiritual transformation from earth to a glorified state in heaven. A poignant exception can be found in Cotton Mather's funeral sermon for his father Increase. Mather rightly took the event of his father's death as a communal loss. He framed his sermon with a biblical pas-sage concerning Elijah's chariot ascent to heaven as his son watched. "He cried, My Father, my Father, the Chariot of Israel and the Horsemen thereof! And he saw him no more."[10] Out of his anguish and grief the son could only state the essentials of his vision, the limits of verbal articulation expressing the boundary between heaven and earth. This highly charged apocalyptic ending was a ver-bal metaphor for Increase's spiritual transformation; but the metaphor was also coextensive with reality in the faith of Cotton and the congregation, as Mather, reiterating the words of the Bible, becomes the Old Testament son, articulating the same cry once again, watching his father die. If not purged by the recitation, the community was consoled by the remaining presence of the son to carry on. The figurative language of the sermon is highly successful, as actuality and biblical allusion, oral recitation and verbal text, fuse through the dramatic powers of the Puritan's symbolizing imagination.

THE FUNERAL ELEGY

The power of symbolizing, predicated upon an intensity of faith applied to common experience, gave impetus to the concentration of figurative language in the funeral elegy, in which Christian metamorphosis might be symbolically invoked for the deceased. Although Ramist logic and its restraints were never completely eliminated, basic as it was to the Puritan world-view, it was submerged in a proliferation of poetic devices that ran through the best elegies. A wide variety of metaphor, biblical allusion, telescoped imagery, rough syntax, and wit in the form of puns, anagrams, and acrostics—these were not simply decorative elements but forms essential to the poetry, dramatizing the visible saint's transformation in death, his ultimate conversion to Christ.

Being central to Puritan theology, death was a reality that could charge the survivor's imagination. Consequently, at the same time the Puritan's faith informed the rites of death with significance, the latter profoundly inspired his poetic sensibility. "In walking to a Funeral, I would be forever careful, that the Gentleman whom I walk withal shall be Entertained with some Communication, that shall be instructive to him, and assist our Praeparation for the future State."[11] Cotton Mather's diary entry of June 1713 was a self-admonition to emphasize, or possibly to restore, a custom dramatized in an elegiac poem written by either John Fiske or John Eliot as early as 1645.[12] The narrator of the poem addresses himself to Thomas Dudley, Governor of Massachusetts Bay, as they walk to a funeral. The particular situation in the poem became the occasion to write Dudley *his* funeral elegy, even though he would not die for another eight years. Thus the religious presuppositions of the Puritans permeated their poetic sensibility in such a way that everyday reality and metaphor merged in an elegy of future inevitability.

Taking his cue from Dudley's name, the narrator creates an anagram from its letters: "Thomas Dudley" came to spell "ah! old, must dye." The anagram is, of course, appropriate for the occasion as a reminder of the participant's own coming death. The narrator then elaborates upon his anagrammatic discovery:

> A deaths head on your hand you neede not weare
> a dying hand you on your shoulders beare
> you need not one to minde you, you must dye
> you in your name may spell mortalitye.
> younge men may dye, but old men these dye must
> 'twill not be long before you turne to dust.

Aside from its intrinsic delight and surprise, the wit of the first two lines serves to emphasize the meaning of the anagram: the inevitable mortality of human beings becomes the essence of Dudley, discovered in his name and correlated with his old age. The unanticipated switch of physical components in the image of Dudley (head on hand, hand on shoulder) calls attention to the funeral artifacts (funeral ring and coffin), thereby sharpening the dramatic situation of a burial procession. The second line offers a telescoped image of their roles as coffin-bearers but emphasizes primarily the hand of mortality about to select Dudley next among the living to die. The lines bear, therefore, a dual image of life and death: as the living enact the funeral rites, they are reminded of their own possible death. And yet Dudley needs no human reminder; neither funeral rings, enactment of death ritual, nor anagrams are necessary, for he carries within himself the universal inevitability of mortality.

The closing lines would be merely repetitive and irrelevant were it not for their liturgical quality:

> before you turne to dust! ah! must; old! dye!
> what shall younge doe, when old in dust doe lye?
> when old in dust lye, what N. England doe?
> when old in dust doe lye, it's best dye too.

The incantation of the anagram suggests the supernatural power of the Word, its metamorphic quality piercing the ephemeral aspects of the flesh to the eternal truths of death and mortality. The anagram conjures up "Thomas Dudley" with a new significance, the inevitability of age to succumb to the dust of death. The finality of life, lent by the exclamation marks in the anagram, establishes a break in the poem, as the narrator then turns to issues transcending the individual. What shall be the effect of death upon the community? How shall succeeding generations behave when the elders pass away? The narrator foreshadows God's controversy with New England in the latter part of the seventeenth century, when the ministers felt a decline of piety in the community.

The narrator's question is merely rhetorical, however, and completely submerges any didactic response that might be anticipated. His answer, "it's best dye too," indicates his respect for the stature of Dudley in the community. In the eyes of the narrator he is indispensable for the commonwealth. The hyperbolic affirmation of the individual leader precludes, and thus overrides, the possibility of spiritual rebirth of either the fallen man or his community thereafter. On that point ride the poem's strength and weakness. The imagined magnitude of Dudley's death raises a valid communal question which is given only a personal response. And yet the private and the public dimensions of Puritan death were coextensive. Equally important — if not more so — the iconic power of words meant that the poet was not in complete control of the direction that his poem would take. This submission to words, an assumed risk for the contemporary poet, was undertaken by the New England Puritans in overpowering moments of spiritual import.

That Dudley was also concerned about the future course of New England is indicated by his own poetic response, found in his pocket upon his death eight years later. In assent with the earlier poem, he catalogues his physical infirmities: "Dim Eyes, deaf Ears, cold stomack shew / My dissolution is in view." The physical degeneration culminates in death, with, however, spiritual resurrection. "My Soul with Christ, My Body dead," he affirms.[13]

Up to this point, Dudley appears to have approached the elegiac convention in a rather perfunctory manner, stringing out images and metaphors. His use of an analytic, almost atomistic structure is counteracted, however, in the concluding sestet, which offers some vivid advice:

> Let men of God in Courts and Churches watch
> O're such as do a Toleration hatch;
> Lest that ill Egg bring forth a Cockatrice,
> To poyson all with Heresie and Vice.
> If men be left and otherwise combine,
> My Epitaph's, I dy'd no Libertine.

Wrought in the medieval imagination, a cockatrice was a composite monster with the wings of a fowl, the tail of a dragon, and the head of a cock, hatched by a serpent from a cock's egg upon a dunghill. This horrific creature could kill by a simple glance (*Fig. 3*). The inversion of sexual imagery into multiple perversions serves as a dense metaphor for the evil consequences of religious toleration. Dudley's expression is in sharp contrast with his analytic discourse of physical degeneration and indicates the pressures on his imagination: the preservation of New England's nontoleration was of greater concern to him than his old age.

Fig. 3. Cockatrice illustration, woodcut from Ulisse Aldrovandi's *Serpentum et Dracon Historiae*, 1640. *Courtesy of General Research and Humanities Division, The New York Public Library, Astor, Lenox and Tilden Foundations, New York City.*

Even though few elegies offered communal policy in such explicit terms, New England felt constrained to engage in resolving God's controversy during the years after Dudley's death in 1653. As a result, the elegy became a public means of mourning the death of a leader whose loss would be compensated by celebrating his ideal characteristics, a model for the community to follow.[14] Affirmation of the individual, closely linked to communal renaissance, was predicated upon the Puritan's belief in salvation after death and all the envisioned transformations that would occur to the Christian soul released from a degenerate body. Christian metamorphosis found its poetic expression in the Puritan's use of metaphor.

This relationship was clearly indicated in a confessional poem written by John Danforth, who offhandedly lent the title, "A Few Lines to Fill Up a Vacant Page."[15] Revealing the fallen state of his soul, Danforth claims, "I Drave in Discontentments Sea." In the final two stanzas he develops this image of being adrift:

> Thus being Lost, wrong Course I Steerd
> While neither Sun, nor Stars appear'd
> Instead of Heav'n's Land, I made Hell,
> I knew't by its Sulphureous Smell:
>   Coming on Waters, strait my LORD spy'd I;
>   Avaunt, Foul Fiend! Avoid, fell Foe! Cry'd I;
> So vilely I mistook, and therefore spake foul Blasphemy.

By this time, the reader is aware that the image has become a psychological metaphor of purgation, describing Danforth's mind and soul as out of God's grace.

His meeting with Christ, whom he mistakes in his fallen state as the devil, quiets the turbulent waters:

> 'Tis I, quoth He, Be not Afraid.
> Which Words He had no sooner said,
> But all my Discontents resil'd;
> The Ruffling Winds, and Waves were still'd;
> By what Time, Faith and Hope my Sailes could hoise,
> I got safe and firm Anch'rage in a trice,
> Within the very inmost Bays of Blissful Paradice.

Christ, of course, saves the narrator. But what is remarkable is that Christ changes the metaphor by His actions. The transformation from troubled to calm waters signifies in metaphorical terms Danforth's conversion to saving faith. Thus the powers of Christian metamorphosis were closely associated with the dynamics of poetic metaphor.

In the elegy that Dudley wrote for himself, the intuitional and associational qualities of metamorphosis are held in tension against the atomistic structures which suggest Ramist tendencies. Otherwise, the latter fragment the poem or abstract the meaning without regard to the quality of imagery. Spiritual purpose was served to the fullest verbal dimension by a discharge of language in metamorphic play. Thus both the spiritual and playful aspects of puns and anagrams gained Puritan approval. The one aspect did not deny or preclude the other. Play as wit and verbal manipulation affirmed the Christian spirit in its metamorphic process.

The pun, so dependent upon intuitional insight and wit, oftentimes developed into a conceit that would serve as an animated structural motif for the poem. The ultimate success of the pun depended upon the elegist's recognition of the interaction between the concrete presence of words and their transcendent reality. In the elegy for Hannah Hull Sewall, John Danforth played his verbal insights to perfection.[16] After praising her father, John Hull, a leading Boston merchant, he catches the reader by surprise:

> The Hull, soon Built upon, became an Argo;
> Deep fraighted with Terrene & Heav'nly Cargo:
> Immortal Vertue gave Immortal Name;
> Long Life, Power, Honour, Added to His Fame.
> Stretching his Course, Refresh'd with Prosperous Gales,
> Quitting New-England's Coasts, to Heav'n He Sails.

Not simply the pun with its unexpected wit, not even the pun as a conceit, but rather the reader's sudden entrance into an imaginative realm where concept and concrete image coalesce, so that by the conclusion the reader sees the ship set sail and Hull himself transformed in heaven—this movement sets a dual charge, owing to the poet's skill in verbal manipulation with a view toward expressing spiritual feelings.

Like the pun, the anagram served as an integral part of the elegy and was based on fundamental religious assumptions about Christian metamorphosis. John Fiske, for example, wrote an elegy for Samuel Sharpe, "late ruling-Elder to the Church at Salem."[17] Fiske unfolded the anagram," Us! Ample-share," from Sharpe's name. The opening lines of the elegy indicate not only the communal sense of loss but also the explicit transformation of Sharpe into the "ample-share": "Us) saies, whose is the losse: The Gayner Hee / Whom changd for ample-share of Blisse you see." Put to immediate use in the poem, the anagram is a verbal correlative to the spiritual metamorphosis that Sharpe has undergone. In his discovery of the anagram the poet was simply recreating verbally that which had already occurred spiritually, demonstrating the iconic power perceived in words.

Playing variations on the anagrammatic theme—share and loss echoing life and death, death and resurrection—the narrator laments, "Oh! who shall us! us! comfort, hope, helpe, give?" The repetition of "us" suggests that Sharpe himself was the "comfort" that the narrator calls for and, by implication, recalls from his previous relationship with the deceased. Only Sharpe could provide the "ample-share" of "comfort" and other virtues. Since the anagram is of the deceased's name, the deceased himself becomes the center of the elegy, not only because he is the proper subject of the poem, but also because he constitutes the formal structure as well. In a transcendent yet concrete bisecting dimension, the deceased *becomes* the poem, chanted by the elegist, reenacting the interpenetration of word and flesh.

BROADSIDE VERSE

Images of death that appeared in the published funeral sermons were clearly of the same iconography of gravestone design. Most often, the title page bore simply a black rectangular border, enclosing the printed elements, which lent the appearance of the epitaph on a gravestone (*Fig. 4*). Occasionally, however, the design would become more complex, as the rectangle would assume an arch at the top of the title page, thereby suggesting even further the common shape of the gravestone. Within the tympanum arch, the usual skull, skull with wings, or hourglass would appear, the shapes depicted by crude woodcut (*Fig. 5*). Little, however, is revealed about the nature of gravestone design. In fact, it is

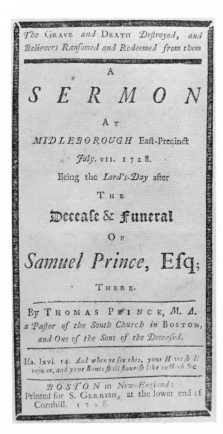

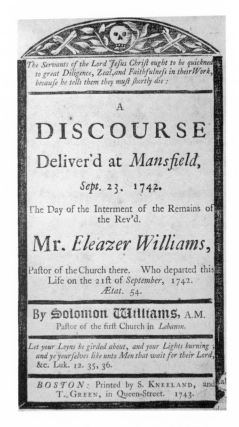

Fig. 4. Title page of *The Grave and Death Destroyed,* a funeral sermon for Samuel Prince by Thomas Prince, Boston, 1728.

Fig. 5. Title page of *The Servants of the Lord Jesus Christ,* a funeral sermon for Eleazer Williams by Solomon Williams, Boston, 1743.

the broadsides of elegiac verse, pinned to the shrouded hearse on the way to the graveyard that indicate, by their close juxtaposition of verbal and visual elements, how gravestone art was animated. Like the title page of the funeral sermon, the broadside derived its imagery from the same cultural sources as did the gravestone. But more than the funeral sermon, the broadside presented visual images alongside the verbal figures in the elegy itself, all of which were presented in a manner that paralleled the vitality of gravestone art.

One such broadside is *"Upon the DEATH of the Virtuous and Religious* Mrs. Lydia Minot . . ." (*Fig.* 6).[18] The title, which provides some biographical information, appears beneath a woodcut tableau that extends the width of the sheet. Centered between auxiliary emblems of death is the black-bordered elegy. On the lower half of the sheet three anagrammatic poems on the name Lydia Minot are printed. The poetry is far superior to the accompanying visual imagery, but as the tableau was a frequent convention for broadsides, its combination with the elegiac verse reveals much about the art of the gravestone.

The central poem poignantly confirms Puritan attitudes about death:

> Here lyes the Mother, & the Child, Interr'd in one;
> Both waiting for the same Bless'd Resurrection.
> She first to it was Life; Then to't became a Grave,
> Dead in her Womb: To fetch it thence, Death to her gave.
> The Life and Death of both, his Sov'raignty Makes known,
> Who gives and takes at will, and no Controll can own.
> The Fruit and Tree together here lyes pluck't, yet sure
> That Root whence a Saint's All doth spring, must firm endure,
> Eternal Love, in which the Sap's the same, that feeds
> Each Branch, be't Mercy or the Rod when so it needs.
> ['Cause now to God and Christ I ever live.]

The metamorphic images assume a suprarational association, as the contradictions of life and death are resolved by Christian salvation. In contrast, the surrounding motifs of an hourglass, shovel, and coffin are crude indeed, however appropriate they are for the poem. In their design they simply amount to visual analogues for death, atomistically strung out. In their presentation the three discrete images bear little or no relationship to the play of language that characterizes the poem.

The three poems, based upon variant anagrams, indicate the metamorphic progression from mortality to resurrection. "I di to Al myn'" dramatizes the sacrifice of earthly life upon death; "I di, not my Al" affirms the existence of a Christian afterlife; and, using an acrostic as well, "Dai in my Lot" reveals the glories of heavenly reward. Though each poem presents part of the metamorphic process of life, death, and rebirth, the total structure is logical and linear in sequence. Something of this mixture, the combination of linear structure with metamorphosis, can be discerned in the tableau that dominates the broadside.

At the center there is a skeleton in stride, carrying a scythe and wearing banners that extend horizontally and bear the legends *Memento Mori* and *Remember Death*. Emblems of mortality appear on either side of the figure. At the lower left, the funeral cortege is depicted moving toward the entrance of the tomb at the extreme right.

Like the anagrammatic poems, the gross structure of this design is linear and sequential. Unlike the images that surround the central poem, however, this tableau exists as a whole. Linear though the design may be, and notwithstanding

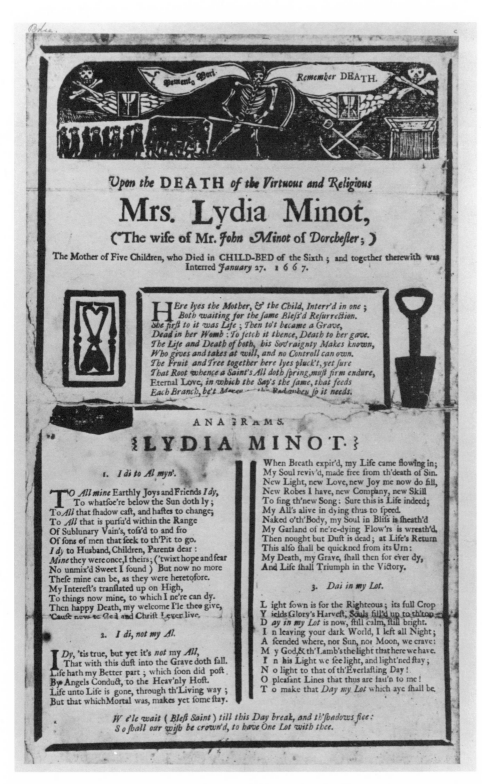

Fig. 6. "Upon the Death of the Virtuous and Religious Mrs. Lydia Minot, . . . of Dorchester . . . , " funeral broadside, 1668, Cambridge. 8¼ x 13½. *Courtesy of The Massachusetts Historical Society, Boston; photograph by George M. Cushing.*

the crudity of its woodcut technique, the rhetorical power of the tableau ensues from the metamorphic quality of the images that coalesce by visual association —directed by sequential logic, to be sure, but visually suprarational in its expression. Thus the banners of the skeleton could easily be construed as wings, thereby suggesting the possibility of resurrection. The wing motif is carried over to the hourglasses, indicating the flight of time. Flanked by the skulls, the entire sequence visually suggests the rhythm of life and death. The central figure of the skeleton, towering over the entire funeral cortege, would indicate that death is leading the procession toward the tomb. Not only does this placement of the skeleton visually unite the upper and lower horizontal segments of the tableau, but his exaggereated size places him conceptually between two worlds, a cosmic and an earthly realm. Put another way, the earthly realm becomes a cosmic vista. The human beings of the funeral are trapped by the inevitability of their mortality, marching through the dark to their own tomb as well as that of the deceased.

THE GRAVESTONE

In North Attleboro, Massachusetts, among the stones for the Maxcys, a well known family of the area, is an unexpected marker for Caesar (*Fig. 7*). Whatever "liberal" intentions the stone may, at the time, have implied in its assumption that a slave might enter heaven, it was nonetheless thoroughly racist in attitude. Nevertheless, the epitaph articulates one of the most dramatic examples of metamorphosis following death. That Caesar's unjust and inhumane lot as a slave on earth would be compensated by Christ's mercy in heaven might be expected. But the choice of color imagery as a metaphor for spiritual transformation, that Caesar's soul could literally change from black to white upon death, indicates a strong belief in the power and extent of redemption through Christ, His ability to transform that which could not possibly be changed in mortal life.

Carved at the top of the gravestone is an anthropomorphic sun with boldly delineated geometrical rays that extend their points to the outer arch. On the gravestone, the sun, ordinarily a symbol of life with its essential heat, is poised either at sunset or sunrise on a line that serves not only as a demarcation between the design and the epitaph but also as a horizon. This visual ambiguity, however, does not indicate that the carver was uncertain about death. Rather, the image embraces a dual meaning. The sun could be setting, the end of a day suggesting the end of a life. Within a Christian context, however, the sun would also be rising, the start of a new day suggesting spiritual resurrection. The sun

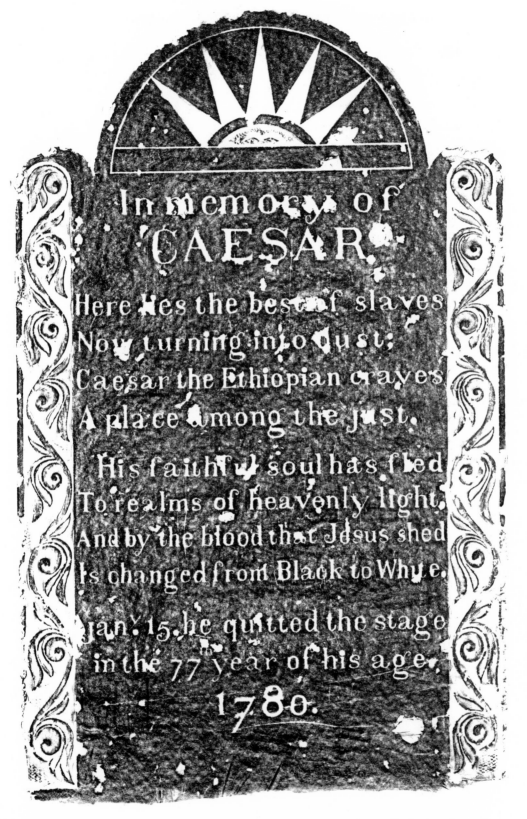

Fig. 7. The Caesar stone, dated 1780, but probably recut in facsimile during the early twentieth century, North Attleborough, Massachusetts. Slate. 25 x 16.

becomes an eternal sphere as it charts an earthly cycle of night and day, with life and death calculated not by human time alone but by God's time as well. Thus the sun visually echoes the epitaph's concept of "heavenly light." The position of the sun, neither fully set nor fully risen, also suggests that death is the moment of transition from this world to the next. Through this image the human dilemma of transitory existence takes on cosmic significance, fused with the Christian mystery of resurrection.

This dimension of metamorphosis is not unique to the Caesar stone. In Oxford, Massachusetts, there is a marker erected "In Memory of Capt Hezekiah / Stone Who Departed this Life / July ^e_y 18th 1771 in the / 61st year of his Age" (*Fig. 8*). A brief couplet indicates the stonecarver's wit: "Beneath this Stone Deaths Prissner Lies. / The Stone Shall move the Prisner Rise." The pun revolving about "stone" as the gravemarker and as the name of the deceased offers a spiritual affirmation in the face of his earthly imprisonment. Laughter is not sacrilegious but a confirmation of the sacred, a joyous acceptance of the limits and transcendence of the Christian believer. At the top of the gravestone a stylized image of a cherub, possibly a metaphor for the captain himself in his transformed state, reinforces such attitudes, as the wings arch in aerodynamic motion. The carver's skill, if not his faith, left behind a moving image of stone.

Verbal puns in epitaphs of gravestones have their counterpart in visual puns. For example, in the Copp's Hill Burial Ground of Boston there are some variant images of a death's-head with wings among the other gravestones. Like the rest, these markers bear a full-faced, rather abstract image of a skull signifying death and mortality. Its wings do not extend outward horizontally but sweep upward, meeting at their tips above the skull. Its massive weight presses

Fig. 8. The Captain Hezekiah Stone stone, 1771, Oxford, Massachusetts. Slate. 23 x 24¾.

downward toward earth, whereas the movement of its wings suggests the affirmation of heavenly ascension, a tenuous balance much in the manner of the Caesar sun, which rises and sets simultaneously. On one such design, on the Joanna Buckley stone of 1716/17 (*Fig. 9*), the interior space created by the arched wings and the skull is simply negative. On the Mary Hirst stone (1717), however, the imagination of the carver transformed the same space into a heart (*Fig. 10*) — a visual pun accentuated by the fact that this particular gravestone is

Fig. 9. The Joanna Buckley stone, 1716/17, Copp's Hill, Boston, Massachusetts. Slate. 30 x 27.

Fig. 10. The Mary Hirst stone, 1717, Copp's Hill, Boston, Massachusetts. 21 x 22½.

in proximity to those lacking hearts. Even so, the heart is not visible on first glance. Only by engaging in the intricacy of design will the viewer discern the hidden heart. Within the metamorphic logic of the design, the heart, a traditional seat of spiritual transformation, lies at the center of Christian death and resurrection. The mortal remains of the skull descend to earth, while the heart is borne up to heaven by the wings.

Both the Caesar stone and the Mary Hirst stone share common qualities in what would appear to be rather disparate images. These images display a metamorphic animus, albeit in slightly different terms. The elements of the Mary Hirst stone are transformed by visual ambiguity alone, whereas the Caesar stone achieves its metamorphic qualities through the concept of Christian death and resurrection. It is this Christian paradox that insists upon the dual significance of the sun's tenuous position on the horizon. Without the conceptual ambiguity only a single interpretation would obtain, thereby denying the design its validity.

Both symbols also bear biblical meanings that would have been well known to the colonial community. While the Mary Hirst stone is more complicated visually than the Caesar, both markers offered very direct, forthright images to those who came to the burial grounds — and not infrequently, given the death rate. The visual impact of these stones is typical of most in New England and suggests an analogy to the plain style of Puritan sermons: the most common, the least educated, could understand the carvings and profit from their didactic import.

In Wakefield, Massachusetts, a gravestone dated 1678 still stands in memory of Captain Jonathan Poole (*Fig. 11*). An early marker, erected when the Puritan orthodoxy was changing but nonetheless strong, its design presents the initial visual solutions of a carver conditioned by the aesthetic assumptions of the plain style. In the manner of the Caesar and Mary Hirst stones, this one also bears a simple, direct image — a skull with wings that is quite typical in the iconography of death's-heads in the Boston area. The image offers a concrete example which powerfully dramatizes the didactic elements of the design: *MEMENTO TE ESSE MORTALEM,* incised around the arch over the skull. Even a member of the community who was uneducated in Latin could understand the message from the image.

The message, however, was not a simplistic reminder of death, despite the unmistakable human skull, an emblem of Poole's mortal remains. As grim as contemporary sensibilities would take it — and, indeed, as grim as the Puritans themselves would have wanted the image to be interpreted — the total design is not one of despair. However dominant the skull itself may be in the design, there is also a pair of wings that suggest resurrection, a spiritual event that no

Fig. 11. The Captain Jonathan Poole stone, 1678, Wakefield, Massachusetts. Slate. 20½ x 18.

Puritan would have denied, whatever his doubts and anxieties concerning his own prospects. The symbol of the winged skull has a dual meaning, then, in which neither aspect can be assumed to have been dominant. Death was powerful, but so was Christian resurrection in the Puritans' religious imagination. This conceptual duality, moreover, was not sequential but simultaneous in its visual perception.

Just as the meaning of the image is harmoniously reconciled on a conceptual level, the design itself possesses a visual unity, derived in great measure from the structural symmetry of the stone. The space upon the planar surface is divided evenly, as the central arch of the tympanum is repeated by the two lesser arches of the pilasters. Within this gross structure the dominant image presents identical wings, each with three tiers of feathers; and the skull is symmetrical, each half of the face fully mirroring the other. Such geometric division lent itself to standardization by rule and compass for marking out patterns to be incised on stone. In addition to this functional purpose, the emphasis upon symmetrical structure conformed to the plain-style aesthetic, Thomas Hooker's insistence upon "the substance and solidity of the frame."

The unity of the design is reinforced by other visual elements, more subtle than simple geometry. For example, the full-faced skull is tightly positioned between the "shoulders" of the wings. Attention is drawn to the skull by a dentil outline which descends in a loop from the upper curve of the wings. This linear wave plays against the arc above the skull, in turn repeated by the arch of the tympanum, modulating between the pilaster capitals. Moreover, the tympanum arch implicitly intersects the inner arc, so as to carry the eye inward to focus upon the central image. The skull rests its chin upon an hourglass, thereby projecting an earthward gravity, the weight of the skull reinforced by the implicit downward movement of sand from the top to the bottom of the glass. Such a hierarchy would suggest that death ultimately dominates time. And yet the skull is balanced upon the hourglass by its wings poised for flight, the opposing movements suspended in the tension of death and resurrection. This subtle visual play, which puts forth the primary argument without calling attention to itself, complies with the plain-style view that art, although necessary, should not be flaunted in the presentation of a sermon or, in this instance, a carving on a gravestone.

The rather narrow horizontal space spanned by the upright hourglass serves as a frieze for a series of images subsidiary to the skull. To the right of the hourglass is a coffin lying on its side next to a vertical shovel that is crossed perpendicularly by a pick. On the far left of the hourglass are a pair of diagonally crossed bones, a visual variant on the pick and shovel. In syntactical sequence on either side of the hourglass is the supportive Latin phrase *Fugit Hora*. These images, of course, are additional emblems of death. On the pilasters adjoining the frieze are two vertical weapons, a saber and possibly a pike, both instruments of death, particularly appropriate for the military status of the deceased.

The articulation of such subsidiary images would suggest that they are visually ornamental in much the same way as figurative language was considered in the plain-style sermon. That is, figurative language is in part additive, a prettifying element not essential to the content of the sermon. The Ramist division of form and content had its visual counterpart in the layout of this gravestone design, in which the primary message was presented in the tympanum, while the lesser decorative elements took their places in the margins, so to speak, along the pilasters and the frieze. Thus the decorative elements of the Poole stone are subordinate to the main image, and they are laid out analytically and discretely in a line, their relationship determined less visually than conceptually by their emblematic representation of death. To be sure, there are internal relationships, as horizontal, vertical, and diagonal lines play against one another: the crossed bones are visually associated with the pick and shovel, and the vertical hourglass is further related to the horizontal coffin by virtue of their rectangular forms, which are picked up again by the outlined borders of the saber and pike. Nevertheless, these hints of metamorphic vision remain almost completely submerged by the linear, atomistic structure, a characteristic conditioned by Ramist logic. The basic skull with wings is unfolded by the subsidiary metaphors one by one.

Less than fifty years later, John Stevens of Newport, Rhode Island, carved a very different kind of gravestone for Mary Carr (*Fig. 12*). Erected in 1721, her gravestone offers a set of images and a manner of phrasing different from the Poole stone of Wakefield. The logical structure remains in the underlying symmetrical design, but it is dominated by other emphases. Stevens did not bind the total design together by a logical structure in which discrete images are related by reference to a common conceptual source. Not only had such a source changed in emphasis, but its presence was felt less as an idea behind the images than as an idea expressed by the images. Visual interest had grown, focusing upon the images themselves in relation to one another, metamorphically as well as metaphorically.

Filling the tympanum is a full-faced cherub with outspread, fluted wings. Bordering the text of the stone, simply identifying the deceased and her dates of birth and death, are two flowers the stems of which rise to the height of the pilasters. At the base of the stone are a pair of peacocks, placed in casual symmetry toward the flower stems. Between them is a balanced decorative element, its curves repeated in inverted fashion above the cherub on the tympanum. Although the text emphasizes the remains of Mary Carr beneath the earth, the images all suggest spiritual rebirth. The peacocks, for example, were traditional symbols of immortality. They face the lovely flowers that grow out of the base as if from the earth, their eternal blossoming on stone suggesting the yearly rebirth of spring. These earthly images ascend the stone, the eye led upward by the repetition of leafy pattern, to the cherub, another symbol of spiritual resurrection. Its feathered wings arched outward suggest the opening of a flower. The decorative element hanging above serves to release the cherub from downward gravitation, thereby lending an illusion of flight. Not only are these images related conceptually as metaphors of resurrection, but they are also associated visually through metamorphic forms. The birds with their wings have a parallel in the cherub and its delicately engraved feathers. The organic quality of the decorative elements is matched by the floral patterns on the pilasters. Thus the images are associated, not logically but suprarationally, by visual metamorphosis, the result being a totally articulated composition of interrelated forms.

The gravestone of Mary Carr, then, fully developed the metamorphic tendencies previously held in restraint by the structural logic as found on

Fig. 12. The Mary Carr stone, 1721, Old Common Burying-ground, Newport, Rhode Island. Slate. 19¾ x 17½.

the Poole stone in Wakefield. The tensions between metamorphic association and logical structure animated the aesthetic design of New England gravestones from 1650 to 1800. Whereas the religious counterpart to visual metamorphosis lay in the Puritan emphasis upon spiritual conversion and then resurrection upon death, the structural design of the gravestone had its source in the linear logic of Ramus allied with the aesthetic of plain style. It was the gravestone, however, that endured with these visual characteristics, derived from Puritan culture, long after Puritanism underwent its own transformations in the eighteenth century. Exhibiting the same characteristics in verbal terms, the elegy underwent a decline in popularity, signaled by Benjamin Franklin's parody of the genre in 1722.[19] Although the funeral sermon continued well into the nineteenth century, its plain-style characteristics reflected only one aspect of the gravestone design. Out of the cultural pattern that the three artifacts created, the gravestone continued to bear such characteristics well into the eighteenth century, possibly because of its essential function to the community, its conservation of cultural values upon stone—memorials for children of change.

PATTERNS OF CHANGE AND THE CRAFT OF CARVING

While the gravestone retained its metamorphic aesthetic over the years, the images themselves were not invulnerable to change. Visual metamorphosis along with shifts of religious sensibility played a central role in the development of the primary images on the stones, changing from death's-head to cherub to portraiture. Such transformations in New England fell within the three major themes of traditional Christian monuments: "The first includes everything dealing with death and the funeral, the effigy of the defunct forming the centre of interest. The second is reserved for the fate of the soul, while the third provides a retrospective summary of the life of the deceased, the latter remaining the principal figure, but now portrayed as an active participant until the moment when his mortal struggles cease on his deathbed."[20] In the concentrated period of one hundred fifty years New England gravestones recapitulated the forms and the concerns of Christian funerary art for fifteen hundred years through the Renaissance.

The general shift in imagery on New England gravestones was probably a function of change in religious attitudes. Even though the basic death's-head with wings was not an image of despair, the emergence of the cherub suggests a shift of emphasis from mortality to immortality—a change that occurred during the Great Awakening in the second quarter of the eighteenth century, when the possibility of salvation strongly gripped the religious imagination of the colonial populace. Likewise, the rising incidence of portraiture after 1750 would suggest a growth of cosmopolitan attitudes as the New England colonies along with the others stepped forth united to take their place among nations. These correlations must remain speculative, however, until statistical studies of gravestones have been completed to form patterns based on sound empirical evidence.

In the meantime, caution must be taken in interpreting the religious significance of the sequential change in iconographical emphasis. Superficially, the switch from death's-head to portrait would suggest a relinquishing of grim Puritanism for the humanistic values of the Enlightenment, or at least so a stereotypical reading would imply. However, careful examination of the gravestones would suggest otherwise. The inevitable departure from seventeenth-century Puritan orthodoxy did not entail a decline in religious belief or concomitant Christian values. Indeed, by the end of the eighteenth century, when a "new" orthodoxy became established, it in turn denounced the mild deism of Jeffersonianism as utterly atheistic and conspiratorial. The latter, of course, was neither, but the controversy suggests the strength of established religion in New England despite the transformation of seventeenth-century Puritanism.

Care must also be taken in generalizing about the change in imagery. Although the sequence from death's-head to portrait occurred as the most general development of New England iconography, change varied from locale to locale in New England, depending in large part upon the particular religious climate and visual motifs available to the local carvers. In addition, the images that the stonecarvers would eventually adopt over a period of time were all originally present in late seventeenth-century Boston. Portraits, cherubim, flowers—in short, a definite range of images—existed as minor motifs upon otherwise conventional gravestones, and on rare occasion they existed as major symbols as well. This variety would suggest that change was a function not only of religious but of visual factors as well. A change or shift in religious values might have permitted the use of such minor motifs on a large number of stones about to be cut. But working out of the transformational logic of visual metamorphosis, the stonecarver could manipulate central and subsidiary images within a design whereby decorative motifs would eventually achieve a central position.

The morphology of the central images was such that the carver could easily imagine a shift from a skull with wings to a winged cherub, or a human being with wings, essentially a portrait of the deceased before and after his death. On the Thomas Drury stone, carved in 1778 by William Young of Worcester, the shape of the head could be changed without difficulty into an urn, the same pattern serving both images (*Fig. 13*). But without even looking forward to

Fig. 13. The Thomas Drury stone, 1778, Auburn, Massachusetts. Slate. 39 x 34¾.

the urn motif, which, with the willow, would come to dominate gravestones in two decades, there is speculation as to whether this head is an incipient portrait or a cherub. Although exact identification would be desirable, it is not necessary, for the Puritans' belief in the metamorphic process would allow simultaneous interpretation. A cherub, for example, could be identified with the flight of a resurrected soul to heaven; the two images do not have to be mutually exclusive and may be aspects of a single image, since spiritual eternity would offer coextensive dimensions by definition.

The pattern of the spreading of carving styles throughout New England is as complex as are the various changes in iconography during the seventeenth and eighteenth centuries. An individual style was expressed by each carver and his occasional apprentices. Thus the work of the Stevens Shop in Newport can be distinguished from that of the Lamson family in the Boston area. Such variations generally developed and spread over some particular region where the original carver and his subsequent colleagues worked. There were, of course, exceptions to the rule. Families would occasionally import the work of a distant carver. William Mumford's commission to engrave the marker of Samuel Sewall's father brought a monument from Boston to the Newbury graveyard, where a different visual style prevailed. Carvers also moved, introducing their stones to different areas, as when Zerrubbabel Collins migrated from Columbia, Connecticut, to Bennington, Vermont, in the late eighteenth century and took with him his unique designs, which were so beautifully realized in marble.

Nevertheless, there did exist a general carving technique that determined almost any style in New England. A majority of gravestones were cut in a linear fashion rather than in high-relief or even low-relief sculpture. These shallow incisions tended toward abstraction rather than naturalistic representation for a variety of reasons. Material, technical skill, a possible desire for simplification, the copying of woodcuts and engravings, problems of production—these factors, although not necessarily in the order of their importance, and varying according to each artisan, played a part in the perpetuation of a linear mode of carving in New England.

The slate used early in eastern Massachusetts, where the custom of erecting gravestones first began, was conducive to linear incision of design. On the other hand, the red sandstone of the Connecticut River Valley allowed low-relief sculpture or at least images with planar dimensions. In either case the sandstone required images more grossly carved than the fine tracings that slate could afford. And yet when Vermont marble was used, the carvers persisted in line-engraving even though marble could be worked in sculptured relief. Clearly, then, the prevalence of linear carving was a function less of material than of other factors.

Ludwig argues that this method was related to a lack of technical skill, if not also to a lack of a visual tradition. In this view, the stonecarvers simply did not have a workbench tradition to carve in sculpted relief. They were isolated from the high baroque tradition that flourished in the urban centers of England from the end of the seventeenth century through the eighteenth. Since they came into contact with that tradition primarily through imported woodcuts and engravings, the provincial carvers of New England copied them in a manner both linear and abstract. This technique also facilitated production by means of compass and rule. Thus the process was repeated: even though the coastal carvers eventually became more adept, those inland, particularly in Vermont, continued to incise images, while their fellow-carvers in the cities began to produce naturalistic portraits based upon volumetric carving.[21]

However speculative, as it frankly is, and based upon scanty evidence available in England, Ludwig's argument remains forceful. Even so, his hypothesis tends to obscure the stonecarver's role as a craftsman and an artist. The initial lack of a workbench tradition did not necessarily mean that the carver was an inept technician with little aesthetic sense. Many carvers did develop technical skill, some to a high degree, in what became the established tradition of linear abstraction. That some of these artisans were able to carve in naturalistic detail is evident not only from the portraiture done in the latter part of the eighteenth century but also from gravestones erected almost a hundred years earlier. Carving skills, moreover, surmounted the limitations of woodcuts, engravings, and bookplates, which, from the examples extant, were generally of poor quality, especially during the seventeenth century, and of value only in presenting an idea for a design, not its realization.

In the final analysis, therefore, the aesthetic quality of a gravestone depended less upon carving technique than upon artistic sensibility. Most importantly, New England gravestones must be judged in terms of their own aesthetic, not in terms of their approximation to, or departure from, a high-baroque carving tradition that may have existed in late seventeenth-century England. The colonial stonecarver recapitulated the spiritual life of the Puritan Saint, the drama of his life, death, and hopeful resurrection. In engraving the stone, he engaged the values of Christian metamorphosis, which accounts for the eventual multiplicity of images. While some linear elements became purely decorative, the carver came to evince an interest less in sensuous material than in visual design—in images qua images, not simply for what they represented conceptually. Thus the Mary Carr stone expresses total symbolic play—a suprarational, indeed lyrical association of images superimposed upon a symmetrical structure. Linear abstraction, then, was a means of exploring fully the possibilities of metamorphic images, and their remarkable interplay constituted the art of the New England carver.

CHAPTER 3

Emblems of Mortality

THE skull was one of the earliest and most lasting figures within the variety of designs that appeared on New England gravestones, particularly in the Boston area. A brief walk through The Granary or Copp's Hill discloses the presence of this image well to the end of the eighteenth century. Although its persistence might conceivably suggest iconographic limitations or a hackneyed response to death, dismissal of the motif is not justified. A traditional medieval emblem signifying death, the skull in combination with wings became a Christian symbol of physical death and spiritual resurrection that was equally affirmative and horrific in its perceived dimension. In the middle of the twentieth century, visitors to seventeenth-century and eighteenth-century graveyards mistakenly consider these emblems morbid and the epitaphs quaint, but rarely horrific and almost never affirmative. While the Puritans were demonstrably terrified of death as fit punishment for their sins, they also retained a keen consciousness of its spiritual possibilities. Whereas death was apprehended as the final and perhaps definitive experience on earth, resurrection was taken as an article of faith in the mysteries of God. With these presuppositions the stonecarver centered the concrete emblem of the skull within a visual context which suggests spiritual rebirth. Only through a total aesthetic pattern could a full expression of the supernatural mysteries of Might Almighty be achieved.

The symbol of a winged skull conveys in didactic as well as figurative terms the concept of metamorphosis. The skull itself still remains a powerful icon of human mortality, a sign of irreversible change and decay. With its flesh stripped away, its eyes blinded within hollow sockets, and its teeth bared, the desiccated skull indicates the mortality that lies beneath the skin of every man much in the way that the elegist found mortality in Thomas Dudley's name. The *winged* skull symbolically looks forward to the Judgment Day, when, upon the Second Coming of Christ, the body bequeathed to the earth shall be reunited with its soul to ascend to heaven. Hence the exhortation engraved upon so many markers: "Arise ye dead." This eschatology, expressed primarily by the winged skull, is reinforced by other elements within the design whose animation is essentially metamorphic. During the period dating roughly from 1670 to 1700 the development of the centrally located winged skull concerned the metamorphic interplay of surrounding visual elements and their integration as a unified design.

The early work of the unknown craftsman who cut the Jonathan Poole stone of Wakefield in 1678 (*Fig. 11*) suggests an accordance with plain-style principles that gradually acceded to the lyrical associations of visual metamorphosis. As one of the first stonecutters in the Boston area, he was logically sought out to carve gravestones. The Charlestown Carver, as he has been designated, soon became a master craftsman, setting the standards for younger aspirants to the trade.[1] He established the use of the tripartite shape of the gravestone as it had been used in England and the organization of its face for generations to come, both in the Boston area and in Rhode Island after John Stevens migrated south to Newport in 1705. His work, moreover, provided the basic vocabulary of images that became the funerary conventions for stonecarving in New England. Although the Charlestown Carver has passed into historical anonymity, his monuments still stand in many graveyards north of the Charles River, and commemorate not only the lives of the second generation of New England settlers but his own carving skills and vision as well.

This achievement was derived in great part from his singular ability among New England carvers to treat stone material for its inherent qualities. As a matter of course he used a light-colored slate of good quality, roughly and thickly slabbed, dressed on only one face. The Charlestown Carver was capable of combining a sculptural treatment of stone with an artist's sense of visual communication. Even though he worked with conventional images, he was nonetheless willing to make variations within such bounds. His knowledge of Latin, attested to by many markers bearing Latin phrases that went beyond the perfunctory warnings of *Memento Mori*, would indicate perhaps a grammar-school education. Apparent, too, is a familiarity with emblem books in addition to the more widely distributed funeral broadsides. In short, his portrait limns forth as a man who belonged to the Puritan culture of Massachusetts Bay. It is possible, of course, that his clientele provided the necessary source

Fig. 14. The Cutler children stone, 1680, Phipps Street, Charlestown, Massachusetts. Slate. 24 x 32½.

material for his gravestone imagery; but in the end only he could exercise the artistic intelligence required to take and realize effectively what was available to him for his gravestone designs.

Whatever the origins of his imagery, the Charlestown Carver worked primarily in accordance with the rhetorical principles that characterized the plain style sermon, modulating a simplicity that often belied a complexity of means within a sophisticated sense of design. During the last part of the seventeenth century, however, his aesthetic sensibilities were attracted to the complex possibilities of visual metamorphosis. By 1680, with the Cutler children stone in Charlestown (*Fig. 14*), he began cutting skulls whose wings projected from behind the head rather than from the "shoulders." This departure indicated a shorthand visualization of the intended meaning by a simplification of the central image, and thus he, in one sense, still complied with the principles of plain style. At the same time, however, the Charlestown Carver placed a different emphasis upon the surrounding decoration, both on the tympanum and the pilasters. The shells on the Cutler children stone are no longer subsidiary to the winged skull, but rather each is contained within arches on either side of the central image. To be sure, the presentation remains linear, but the analytic structure is subordinated to the morphological similarities between the winged skull and the shell.

By 1700 Boston stonecarvers were able to articulate a total visual pattern upon the face of the gravestone. Their achievement required a transformation of the analytic tendencies of plain style so pervasive as an aesthetic attitude not only in the sermons of the day but in other art forms as well. Since as late as 1786 the Reverend Nathaniel Emmons could deliver a sermon on Christ as a plain preacher,[2] the year 1700 cannot be considered a turning point away from the plain style, a major force in American art that was neither easily forsaken nor entirely without its salutory effects. Thus even throughout the eighteenth

Fig. 15. The Joseph Farnum stone, 1678, Copp's Hill, Boston, Massachusetts. Slate. 29 x 22½.

century stonecarvers often worked between the polarities of Ramist analysis and the suprarational logic of visual metamorphosis. On the earliest markers an atomistic execution of visual emblems sufficed, in consonance with varying permutations of technical skill, sense of design, and didactic intent. But as more of the planar surface was included in the design statement, emblems in isolation became inadequate, and as the century came to a close, a visually integrated work became the implicit model, predicated upon the memorializing needs of anticipated spiritual resurrection. The Charlestown Carver's awareness of new aesthetic possibilities provided tentative designs that his successors were able to expand upon and develop. Predisposed by common religious assumptions in transition, Boston stonecutters during the late seventeenth century henceforth sought various visual solutions to integrate their designs on the façade of the marker.

One of the Charlestown Carver's simplest statements appears on the Joseph Farnum stone of 1678 in Cambridge, Massachusetts (*Fig. 15*). By cutting an arch into the tympanum, he created an interior depth which allowed him to work in shallow relief. The figure of a winged skull is recessed within the surface plane of the slate slab which forms the broad outer border. Flanking the death's-head on either side are a pair of crossed bones and an hourglass, shallowly incised. The presentation of these twin emblems, as on the Jonathan Poole stone of the same year, suggests the analytic characteristics of the plain style, and these discrete images reinforce the central symbol of death and resurrection. In conceptual terms the crossed bones relate to the skull, while the emptied hourglass suggests both the passage of time and hence mortality, as well as the promise of eternity borne by the outspread wings.

Unlike the Jonathan Poole stone, however, the skull on the Farnum stone is

Fig. 16. The Neal children stone, *c.* 1678, The Granary, Boston, Massachusetts. Slate. 20 x 47½.

rounder and less angular in its contours, and thus more pleasingly proportioned. The full, bisected cranium sits on a lower jaw section. The same hollow sockets, the same triangular abstraction for a nose, and the same elegant "eyebrows," actually a double-curved line to articulate the forehead, exist upon both stones. The feathers on the projecting arch of each wing are carved without tiers and then proceed downward in short, graceful curves. The asymmetricality of the feathers contributes to the particularity of the image.

Although the abstractive elements simplify the design, they do not diminish the quality of naturalism that pervades the statement. The Charlestown Carver created the lasting illusion of a skull, its image quietly conveying the horrors of death. The juxtaposition of wings and skull does not redound immediately to the concept of death and resurrection. Through a simple sculptural technique the carved image has a very real presence: this terrifying creature exists not solely as a metaphor of the theological imagination but within the aesthetic imagination as well, by virtue of its realized plastic dimensions.

Dated 1671 but probably carved six or seven years later, the Neal children stone (*Fig. 16*) appears to be as simple as the Farnum stone, erected at about the same time.[3] On this exceptional marker in The Granary is carved a winged skull; the subsidiary emblems are but three and lightly etched below the bold design. Differences, however, between the Farnum and Neal children stones are major. The latter is far more complex in design, and points to some fundamental problems ensuing from principles of the plain style.

The Neal children stone was cut as a façade of a classical temple, its pediment containing the primary symbol, a well proportioned skull, which had become characteristic of the Charlestown Carver's work. The elegant skull is set firmly within the slightly recessed triangular space of the pediment. Its wings arch and extend gracefully to the far points so as to shelter the three deceased children. Again, the carving is such that the figure has an aesthetic dimension which dramatizes the concept of Christian resurrection without sacrificing its own concrete presence. The refined directness of the pediment design embodies the rhetorical ideals of the plain-style sermon. Neither Hooker nor Wigglesworth could have required a more orthodox handling of the carved statement.

However, the Neal children stone displays precisely that conflict between structure and decoration which could ensue from the arbitrary Ramist distinctions between form and content. Beneath the frieze that accepts the weight of the winged skull are four columns which divide the epitaphs for the three children. At the top of these rectangular sections thus created are Gothic arches, each of which contains an emblem: crossed bones, an hourglass, and a pick and shovel. Close examination reveals that the columns are extended by lightly traced capitals upon the frieze. The Charlestown Carver was not simply timid in his tentative engravings, for there is an earlier stone which has the temple columns clearly cut into the surface.[4] On the other hand, the temple façade of the Neal children stone cannot support the weight of the frieze and the pediment. The lower part of the stone, then, serves primarily as an ancillary metaphor for the temple of heaven.

The structural possibilities inherent in this architectural image are unrealized on the stone. The problem lies in the necessity of cutting the capitals into the frieze, in this instance a horizontally continuous space that looks better relatively unadorned than broken up or divided. At the same time, the architectural structure would have been out of proportion if the capitals had been cut below the frieze. The Charlestown Carver's compromise of light etching retains harmonic proportion and conforms as well to Ramist dissociation of decoration from structure. Well aware of the structural inadequacies still present, he was able to devise a solid base by relegating the function of pediment support to the pilasters of the gravestone. In addition, two leaf motifs conceived geometrically within squares serve as accents that implicitly provide resting blocks for the outstretched wings of the skull above. Further support is achieved by the relationship between these motifs and the spandrels of the arches. Partly by these means, but primarily with the breadth of the gravestone base, the Charlestown Carver compensated for the lack of support that should have been provided by the columns. Although this inconsistent solution did not prevent the Neal children stone from being an eloquent work of art, it does suggest some of the visual problems facing the Charlestown Carver, predisposed as he was to the principles of plain style.

Probably during 1678 the Charlestown Carver also cut the Thomas Kendel

Fig. 17. The Thomas Kendel stone, *c.* 1678, Wakefield, Massachusetts. Slate. 24 x 22.

stone of Wakefield (*Fig. 17*), differing in conception from the marker for the Neal children but derived from the same set of values that inform the plain style. Utilizing the familiar tripartite slab once again, the Charlestown Carver lowered the tympanum space to nearly half the frontal plane of the stone, thereby making the visual statement of major importance. Beneath this large, slightly recessed area, a frieze demarcates the design from the textual statement. Its organic motif is repeated across the entire width of the stone and creates a cyclic, undulating movement that suggests the growth of the natural world.

The lack of symmetry in this organic sequence contrasts vividly with the symmetrical structure of the central design—a difference that suggests the supremacy of supernatural harmony with its cosmic stasis over the ephemeral cycles of nature. In the upper area a full-faced skull is supported by an architectural column that rests upon a plain band above the frieze. With its own metamorphic qualities, the column might well be vertebrae or a tree trunk, in either case suggesting growth culminating in death. Resting on the bottom band on either side of the column are identical cherubim, one of the earliest instances of these figures upon gravestones in New England, and cast above the skull is a winged hourglass.

The entire design might suggest a macabre balancing act were it not for the wit that successfully sustains the images and their expressions of death. Where the eye expects the convention of a winged skull, it finds instead two cherubs, which in turn become "shoulders" through a visual duplexity. Yet this surprise is not merely clever, since the cherubim function within the meaning of the design as guardian angels for the deceased. The Charlestown Carver thus placed greater emphasis than before on dramatizing the possibilities of resurrection. The hierarchical structure of the design would suggest, nevertheless, that the skull still dominates the meaning of the stone. Above the frieze of natural forms rest the cherubim, intermediaries between this world and the next, and above them stares the bleak face of death. Eternity in the form of a winged hourglass reigns over the entire tableau. The religious implications of the visual structure are supported by the verbal text: "HERE IN $\stackrel{e}{Y}$ EARTH IS LAY ON OF $\stackrel{e}{Y}$ 7 OF THIS CHURCH FOUNDATION / SO TO REMAIEN TEL $\stackrel{e}{Y}$ POWERFUL VOICE SAY RIS, INHERIT A GLOR$\stackrel{s}{I}$ HABITATION."

On the Kendel stone the Charlestown Carver succeeded in controlling the analytic tendencies inherent in the plain style. Above the cherubim and parallel with the bared teeth of the skull is a line of subsidiary emblems. Symmetrically placed are two coffins followed by paired artifacts of death: on one side, above the cherub's head, a bone crossed with a shovel; on the other side, a bone with a pick. Finally, in the outer corners of the tympanum field are squared leaf motifs like those upon the frieze of the Neal children stone. This interior phrase of death emblems upon the Kendel stone is well conceived, providing a geometric motion to match that of the organic frieze beneath. Moreover, the bones inclined toward the hourglass define an interior area of triangular structure, withstanding the analytic and fragmentary impulses of plain style.

Eleven years later, in 1689, for the commission of the Lieutenant William Hescy stone in Wakefield (*Fig. 18*), the Charlestown Carver again depicted the skull, now with wings protruding from its sides. The sculptural quality of the skull was retained by a deeply cut overhanging arch. Utilizing the same conventionalized funereal emblems, he placed the skull upon an hourglass, flanked on the extremities of the frieze by sets of crossed bones. Between these emblems were cut the recurring didactic mottoes, *Memento Mori* and *Fugit Hora*. Thus far the statement appearing upon the stone conforms to plain style, since each emblem is discrete and supportive of the central symbol.

The Charlestown Carver began to diverge from this aesthetic, however, as evidenced by the treatment of the pilasters and the frieze beneath the hourglass and crossed bones. The frieze itself is symmetrically rendered, with decorative leaves extending outward from a central geometric pivot, while the pin-

Fig. 18. The Lieutenant William Hescy stone, 1689, Wakefield, Massachusetts. Slate. 26 x 27½.

wheel suggests the cosmic motion of the heavens or the symbolic presence of angels. Visually related to this motif, although not actually connected, are the pilasters. Spiral capitals extend downward in cyclic curves on either panel. Bold clusters of grapes hang from these vines, occasionally punctuated by naturalistic detail. Simply carved, and in low relief, the pilasters achieve a lyrical quality as the vines and grapes suggest sacrifice and resurrection in the Christian tradition. This stone indicates the limits of the Charlestown Carver in his attempt to move from the principles of plain style toward a complete visual metamorphosis. The elements of the design remain discrete, even though the frieze and the pilasters are visually associated in a suprarational way which transcends the logic of plain style.

In the development of late seventeenth-century Boston stonecarving the Hescy gravestone is transitional. Preceding it in 1680 is the Rebekah Row stone (*Fig. 19*), which provided some new directions for the fellow craftsmen of the Charlestown Carver. Beneath the winged skull extends a long frieze between an hourglass and a pair of crossed bones. At the center is a star-and-petal motif alluding to Christ as well as the regeneration of nature. Balanced on each side are a series of three disks: the first two are pinwheels; the third is blank except for a circular center. As wheels, the disks would symbolize "the whole masse and body of all things under heaven, subject to continual change and mutation," according to a Christian dictionary of the time.[5] Although this constant motion of the natural order is given conceptual limitation by the emblems of mortality —the hourglass and crossed bones—the natural is transcended by the spiritual, as indicated by the presence of cherubim upon the pilasters. Wheels in biblical association with cherubim render the meaning of the frieze highly ambiguous, suggesting both spiritual and natural movement.

The statement of the Rebekah Row stone is still analytic, since tympanum, pilasters, and frieze remain distinct segments. Although, as on the Hescy stone, the frieze has discursive tendencies that threaten to fragment the structure, the Charlestown Carver achieved a cohesive design nonetheless. The skull's wings mantle the entire frieze as death and resurrection reign over the natural order. The hourglass and the crossed bones define visually as well as conceptually the limits of the frieze, as rectangular elements play against the inner series of circles. In contrast to, yet reinforcing, these simple images of mortality are the cherubim upon the pilasters. A rational structure thus dominates but allows the expression of visual metamorphosis.

Although the capitals of the pilasters are elevated to help integrate the structure, the tympanum of the Rebekah Row stone is distinct from the frieze. A late contemporary of the Charlestown Carver, William Mumford of Boston, devised a variation on the Row stone's structure by dividing the tympanum area itself horizontally into two parts. In The Granary stands a modest slate stone (*Fig. 20*) for Mary Goose, who died in 1680. Mumford continued to work from the principles of plain style, but he moved toward integration of the total façade. The tympanum is clearly divided by a thin band. The familiar winged skull completely fills the upper space, the curves of the wings and the top of the skull in neat counterpoint to the overriding arch. Beneath is a row of emblems. A floral motif within two concentric circles is flanked by leaved squares tipped on point. These, in turn, are positioned next to sets of crossed femurs, vivid reminders of mortality. With subtle form and line, the floral centerpiece relates visually to the organic gourd design on the pilasters, all of which, with their

Fig. 19. The Rebekah Row stone, 1680, Phipps Street, Charlestown, Massachusetts. Slate. 19 x 27¼.

Fig. 20. The Mary Goose and child stone, 1690, The Granary, Boston, Massachusetts. Slate. 18½ x 17½.

implications of regeneration, are in contrast with the decay of the skull and bones.

In addition to the conceptual relationships among the various images, there are also visual ties that tend to integrate the design. These exist despite the fact that the tympanum is clearly divided and, in turn, separated from the pilasters. A major step toward visual integration results from the row of emblems creating a frieze *within* the tympanum area and not simply beneath it. These images, then, are brought together in a concentrated pattern as opposed to the random placement of emblems found earlier upon the Jonathan Poole stone of Wakefield. With the division of the tympanum the figures are no longer merely decorative or supportive of the dominant image. The latter shares its space with the once subsidiary emblems. The concentric circles beneath relate to the roundness of the skull. There is witty interplay between the two images as the death's-head contrasts to the flowers alive within the eternal circles. Against the stasis of the skull, the frieze offers movement: circles are placed in tension with the tipped squares, their shapes repeated by the crossed bones— another rhythmic cycle of life and death.

Mumford attempted a similar solution on the Obadiah Gill stone of 1700 standing in Copp's Hill (*Fig. 21*). Although the winged skull was again carved within the upper space of the tympanum, in this instance a band within the tympanum area does not separate it from the lower frieze. This omission further integrates images without an arbitrary demarcation of space. In the tympanum frieze geometric and organic images are combined so that the concentric circles at the center, echoing the morphology of the skull immediately above, are flanked by a symmetrical pattern of leaves moving outward in graceful curves. The circles, as cosmic symbols of angels, have their own "wings" of organic leaves, all of which parallel in design and symbolic conception the winged skull above. Surpassing the mere hints of visual unity appearing on the Mary Goose stone, the entire tympanum pattern of the Gill stone relates emphatically to the organic design of the pilasters.

Possibly the most handsome stone cut by Mumford is the Nathaniel Greenwood marker of 1684 in Copp's Hill (*Fig. 22*). Of fine, thick gray slate, precisely cut with uncompromised intent, the iconography is similar to that of the Gill stone except that in this instance Mumford replaced the simple concentric circles with a burgeoning petal motif corresponding to the Tudor rose. This vibrant image may have been an adaptation of the fan-form of the Dorcas Brakenbery stone (*Fig. 23*), cut by the Charlestown Carver in 1682, and which bears a simple but stunning shell, flower, or sun—all of which would metaphorically suggest resurrection. Bursting out of four concentric circles are three progressively

Fig. 21. The Deacon Obadiah Gill stone, 1700, Copp's Hill, Boston, Massachusetts. Slate. 22 x 22½.

Fig. 22. The Nathaniel Greenwood stone, 1684, Copp's Hill, Boston, Massachusetts. Slate. 20 x 24½.

larger tiers of "petals." Mumford, however, carved the design in full circle and shortened the petals to create a tightly organized mass. That one image may have been the source for the other lies less in their contemporaneous carving than in the underlying metamorphic impulses implicit in such motifs. Finding metaphorical similarities pointing to resurrection, the stonecarver discovered the multiple possibilities of visual metamorphosis as one form suggested another.

Although the arch above the winged skull unites the design areas of the pilasters with the central tympanum, the stonecarver generally distinguished between the winged skull and surrounding motifs by retaining structural line. Occasionally, however, such distinctions were broken by the introduction of organic motifs in near proximity to the wings of the death's-head. A son of Joseph Lamson, an eminent carver and contemporary of Mumford, cut the Charity Brown stone in 1754, located on Copp's Hill (*Fig. 24*). Not particularly pleasing in proportion, the skull is heavy and the wings bulky. Even in Boston, the winged skull was becoming a worn image by this date. (Evidence of this atrophy can be found especially in the crossed lines forming the eyebrows and nose for the skull, a slick version of an elegant use of converging lines once achieved by the Charlestown Carver.) The design, however, is not completely inert. Above the skull arch two flowers, their graceful stems growing from a leaf pattern resting upon the wings. Metaphorically they complement the winged skull and suggest both the bloom of springtime and the evanescence of life. Visually the two flowers repeat the circular form of the eye sockets, while the leaves are similar to the feathering on the wings. The capitals of the pilasters are floral pinwheels, below which are alternating leaf and gourd columns reiterating the content of the tympanum.

Despite these transformations and associations on the façade, the Charity Brown marker tends to remain analytic in its segments. Not only is the tympanum clearly demarcated from the pilasters by undecorated vertical and horizontal bands, but the flowers and leaves, regardless of their proximity to the winged skull, remain distinct and separate. The Judith Hunt stone of 1693 (*Fig. 25*), also on Copp's Hill, achieves closer integration of wings and organic elements than the Charity Brown stone some sixty years later. Above the winged skull are arched organic elements, either flowers or leaves, which, as regenerative elements, are closely related in execution to the feathering of the wings. The death's-head is no longer completely isolated from other aspects of the design.

The John Churchill stone in Plymouth (*Fig. 26*) offers a logical development of the skull's wings. Dated 1729/30, the slate, rectangular rather than tripartite in form, bears a frieze that extends the width of the stone. Centered on the

Fig. 23. The Dorcas Brakenbery stone, 1682, Phipps Street, Charlestown, Massachusetts. Slate. 16 x 20.

Fig. 24.The Charity Brown stone, 1754, Copp's Hill, Boston, Massachusetts. Slate. 31 x 26.

Fig. 25. The Judith Hunt stone, 1693, Copp's Hill, Boston, Massachusetts. Slate. 19 x 21½.

Fig. 26. The John Churchill stone, 1729/30, Plymouth, Massachusetts. Slate. 21 x 30.

frieze is a heart-shaped skull, its outline reinforced from within by a similarly shaped mouth. The heart effectively demands a reading of spiritual conversion when considered in conjunction with the death's-head. These metamorphic implications are further strengthened by the rest of the design. The extended geometric-organic pattern would otherwise constitute the wings of a conventional winged skull. Reverse spirals interspersed with broken forms that might represent feathers undulate in constant motion. Even as the geometry provides the underlying structure, it assumes a lyricism of line and movement. The spirals suggest not only the organicism of regenerative nature at the literal heart of which lies death, but also the wheels of the cherubim, their cosmic overtones transcending rational structure.

More complex than the Churchill stone, however, in its visual integration of the entire surface is the Reverend Jonathan Pierpont stone of 1709 in Wakefield (*Fig. 27*). On this masterpiece of New England carving, Joseph Lamson was able to combine his hard-earned carving techniques in mastering shallow relief with a profound conception of the entire design.[6] Its formal structure balanced against lyrical associations of its metamorphic elements created a fitting monument for this "Fruitful Christian" who "Waits the Resurrection of the Just."

Again, the conventional winged skull assumes the central position within the tympanum. It bears an organic nimbus out of which extend vines and fruits down the outer curve of each wing. The jaw rests upon an hourglass held by two figures who, with two others, carry heavy shrouds, thereby completing a tableau beneath the winged skull. These figures may be messengers of death, but they could also represent man in his nakedness, enacting his own inevi-

Fig. 27. The Reverend Jonathan Pierpont stone, 1709, Wakefield, Massachusetts. Slate. 27½ x 30.

table funeral procession. Double-lined plates of *Fugit Hora* and *Memento Mori* extend into the pilasters, which bear two handsome figures holding open books. These suggest cherubim, but they might conceivably represent the deceased divine in his gown and collar as he reads from his Bible. Each rests upon a descending column of interlocking and unfolding organic elements, creating a vibrant texture of light and movement.

Lamson was not adverse to emphasizing such peripheral figures over other aspects of the gravestone design. Whereas the Deacon John Stone marker of 1691 in Watertown (*Fig. 28*) presents a simple winged skull beneath an organic curtain, the pilasters bear ambitious images showing two views of a male figure. Each stands upon the upper portion of the pilaster, beneath which were cut what had become by this date conventional flower and leaf motifs. Both figures, with flowing hair, are in full stride, evidently rushing toward their death, as suggested by the epitaph which claims that Deacon Stone "went rejoycing / out of this world— / to the other." One is a full-face study; the other is in profile; both are naked and carry implements and emblems of death, such as an hourglass, a scythe, and arrows. The sexual implications of such instruments are supported by Lamson's depiction of the breasts of each figure and the erotic quality of the vegetative elements upon which they stand. Yet his portrayal of the figures remains skillfully ambiguous, for their sexuality not only indicates mortality (sexual knowledge associated with death after Adam's Fall), but also serves as a natural metaphor for resurrection.

The Deacon Stone marker suggests that an imbalance could result within the total design of the gravestone, the winged skull diminishing in importance as attention was turned to the pilasters. This visual deemphasis of the death's-head resulted in great measure from changing religious attitudes, but its realization in design upon the stone also took many variations dependent upon visual factors. In a work such as that for the Reverend Jonathan Pierpont, the winged skull becomes a part of the total design, diminished in importance only insofar as the subsidiary motifs are transformed for the purpose of visual integration. In subtle contrast, the Captain John Carter stone of Woburn in 1692 (*Fig. 29*) bears such magnificent pilasters of bold organic motifs and floral designs, culminating in delicately realized star-petal capitals, that the winged skull and the accompanying tableau on its tympanum appear to be of considerably less interest.

Disproportion of visual phrasing occurred if the analytic impulses of Ramist logic were unrestrained. The Thomas Bancroft stone of 1691 in Wakefield

Fig. 28. The Deacon John Stone stone, 1691, Watertown, Massachusetts. Slate. 21½ x 28.

Fig. 29. The Captain John Carter stone, 1692, Woburn, Massachusetts. Slate. 22 x 29¼.

(*Fig. 30*) in contrast to the Henry Messinger stone of 1686 in The Granary (*Fig. 31*) makes this point, even though the former bears far more striking images than the latter. The strength of the Bancroft stone lies in the Charlestown Carver's treatment of the pilasters and to some extent the frieze, which serves as a border beneath the epitaph. Unlike the winged skull, the pilasters are bold in conception and execution. The growth of petals dramatically ascends to a pair of revolving wheels. The pilaster designs are complemented by a lower border of organic forms extending from a star. This frieze grounds and unites the two pilasters, and thus serves as a complete frame for the verbal text.

With the exception of its bold lettering, the rest of the Bancroft stone is inadequate in design. The winged skull is not of sufficient proportion to command the central position on the façade; nor do the crossed bones and hourglass provide a sturdy base for the death's-head as these figures do on other stones by the Charlestown Carver. Between these motifs appear the perfunctorily cut legends *Memento Mori* and *Fugit Hora*. None of these elements exists in a unifying frieze or appears otherwise demarcated from the verbal text. Carved on the frontal plane of the stone, they are not integrated into the rest of the design. The discrete growth of an element disproportionate to other elements feeds upon the analytic impulse of plain style if unrestrained by the organizing principle of a central image. In this instance, the deemphasis of the winged skull dispersed the subsidiary elements, while a compensating unity provided by visual metamorphosis was not brought to bear on the complete design.

As on the Bancroft marker, the winged skull on the Henry Messinger stone also diminished in size and importance within the tympanum space. A sense of metamorphic possibilities, however, prevented isolated growth of single elements within the design. The death's-head hovers above what appear to be simply decorative motifs, or what might have been simply decorative motifs at one time. A fleur-de-lis is enveloped within a central heart from the bottom point of which flow leaves. The voluted lines and the lily comprise a visual pun as they become a "face" while the leaves become "wings." The heart assumes precedence in the design, anticipating the eighteenth-century demise of the winged skull which would be subsumed by heretofore ancillary figures of transformation.

Fig. 30. The Lieutenant Thomas Bancroft stone, 1691, Wakefield, Massachusetts. Slate. 18½ x 23½.

Fig. 31. The Henry Messinger, Jr., stone, 1686, The Granary, Boston, Massachusetts. Slate. 21 x 24.

CHAPTER 4

Figures of Angels

THE values of visual metamorphosis informing the imagery of the Messinger stone (*Fig. 21*) were even more strongly present on the Anna Cooper stone (*Fig. 32*), which stands undated but clearly of the mid-eighteenth century in the Woburn graveyard. One of the Lamson family carved a conventional winged skull just above the tympanum line. The wings move out and curve slightly upwards at their tips to meet leaves extending from the pilasters. A hope of resurrection, stated by the presence of the wings as well as by the organic motifs, is made even more explicit by the inclusion of a youthful looking cherub with ascendant wings superimposed directly above the death's-head. In contrast to the Kendel stone, the cherub has assumed a primary position in the design. An emblem of decay surrounded by foliated elements of regeneration, the skull remains earthbound, while the cherub rises to heaven. The Lamson carver thus dramatized the metamorphic process of death: the inevitable decay within the natural order is transcended by spiritual resurrection in the supernatural realm. Using the cherub as a metaphor for the soul of the deceased, the carver presented the process of translation from this world to the next. The analytic presentation of emblems was foresworn, since the morphological interplay between the cherub and the winged skull creates the strong associations of an implicit synthesis. Although few stones portray the translation in such graphic terms, the prevailing assumption of spiritual metamorphosis animated the widespread exchange of cherub for winged skull and established an aesthetic standard accepted and used on thousands of New England markers in the eighteenth century.

Defined in Thomas Wilson's *Complete Christian Dictionary* of 1661, cherubim were "properly, Images of men with wings and comely faces." Wilson's

Fig. 32. The Anna Cooper stone, *c.* 1750, Woburn, Massachusetts. Slate. 20 x 22.

anthropomorphic description is significant, for he claimed that the cherubim alone were visibly accessible to human beings, whereas other angels were not.[1] This distinction might seem academic, but in actuality it established a working rationale for carving otherwise unseen spiritual beings, so that the anthropomorphic terms of their definition became a metaphor for the cherubim's discourse between the two worlds.

Even so, biblical texts provided sketchy information about the appearance of cherubim, and, as a result, the stonecarver exercised greater freedom in cutting a cherub on markers than in depicting a skull. The latter was a specific emblem of mortality, representative of an event that occurred this side of the invisible world and hence within the range of empirical knowledge. Knowledge of "spiritual Things" was possible, however, according to Benjamin Keach in his *Tropologia: A Key to Open Scripture-Metaphors*, by God's "preaching them by their respective earthly *Parallels*," which inadvertently allowed, if not encouraged, visual experimentation.[2] Consequently, the metaphoric ambiguities of images as well as the metamorphic interplay of visual forms increased. Infinite possibilities were also available to the New England stonecarver from other sources, for the representation of angels possesses a long history and traverses a wide range of traditions—Judeo-Christian and pagan, classical and folk.

Cherubim, however, appear to have been the most common type of angels depicted. Prior to 1700, Samuel Sewall noted that he had ordered cherubim carved for the tops of his gateposts at his house in Boston.[3] Such angels eventually appeared even on colonial currency and were commonly used as border decoration for the printed page. Stonecarvers themselves seem to have referred to their angelic representations as cherubim. Not only the Stevens family of Newport but Henry Christian Geyer of Boston used the term.[4] According to the Old Testament, cherubim were first depicted on the Ark within the Temple. Thomas Wilson offered this description: "These were figures or representations of Angels, inclining their faces one towards the other, and touching one another with their wings, Exodus. 25. 18. The use of these was to cover, or over-shadow the *Mercy-seat* with their wings, Ibid 20. and from this *Seat* God used to speak unto *Moses*, Ibid. 22. Numb. 7. 9. Which may be applyed unto Christ, whose mediation was signified by the *Mercy-seat*."[5]

Placed in Christian terms by the then current use of the typological mode of interpretation—figures and events of the Old Testament foreshadowing those of the New—this conception of cherubim was appropriated by New England stonecarvers. A remarkably faithful description of this heavenly scene can be found on the Rebecca Georgus stone (*Fig. 33*) erected in The Granary in 1782. The epitaph cut on another marker with the same image clearly explains the iconography:

> Tell them tho 'tis an auful thing to die,
> (T'was e'en to thee) yet the dread path once trod,
> Heav'n lifts its everlasting portals high,
> and bids the pure in heart, behold their God.[6]

The quatrain contrasts the horrific experience of death with the glories of heaven for the Elect. It was this redemptive state that the stonecarver chose to portray in traditional terms. Presented are two cherubim with "comely faces," almost like those appearing on the Ark of the Covenant described by Wilson. Instead of a "mercy-seat" is an emblem more amenable to visual execution and most certainly related to the concept of God's throne—the crown of righteousness. The door-shape of the gravestone reveals the glories of the invisible world and thus expresses expectations for the visible saint. And, as befitted a Puritan saint, the scene dramatizes God's eternal glorification by His spiritual order, underscoring the lowly state of mortal man while on earth—the dark passage, suggested in the quatrain, that had to be traversed before Paradise could be attained.

The cosmic implications of the Rebecca Georgus stone were made explicit by Henry Christian Geyer on the Seth Sumner stone of 1771 in Milton, Massachusetts (*Fig. 34*). Once again appear two cherubim, carved this time, however, in profile rather than in three-quarter view. They incline toward each other, soaring through the heavens beneath a central crown. The meaning is essentially the same as that suggested by the Hopkins stone, and the iconography may have a similar, if not the same, biblical source. The cherubim hover above a curved line that can be interpreted as the earth. The arched space between is filled on either side by an anthropomorphic sun and a simultaneously crescent and full moon—both of which are surrounded by stars. Because of the extraterrestrial perspective, this view is instilled with cosmic as well as spiritual overtones. The visual rendering enhances the associations already present. According to Keach, "the Sun and Moon constantly shining do *metaphorically* denote eternal blessedness in Heaven." Moreover, since "by the Name of [Stars] illustrious and principal men are understood,"[7] perhaps an implicit visual reference to Sumner himself was intended.

Although the Sumner stone offers a discursive treatment of visual metaphors, its discrete elements are static. The quality of metamorphic interplay that is lacking is best expressed by the Love Backus stone of 1778 in Norwichtown, Connecticut (*Fig. 35*). The association of cherubim with heavenly spheres easily led to the metaphoric utilization of the sun as angel, a possibility suggested by the carver of the Backus stone. Cutting an oval sun within the center of the tympanum area, he sketched an anthropomorphic face into the encircling band, with triangular rays modulating to greater size on the outer edge. The expression on the face is joyless and suggests, so much better than many carvings do, the human realization of man's mortality. The emotion may be less concerned with gloom over death than the frustration of entrapment within mortal patterns of life.

This impression is supported, not by the facial expression alone, but by the ambiguous suspension of the image on the surface of the stone. The human implications of the face suggest the stasis of death in tension with its solar manifestations in an eternally fixed position. And the ambiguities of its immobility contrast with the unfolding elements beneath, so suggestive of wings, which in turn imply the portrayal of an angel. The six gracefully ascending and undulating forms may represent the six wings of the seraphim, which tradi-

Fig. 33. The Rebecca Georgus stone, 1782, The Granary, Boston, Massachusetts. Slate. 19½ x 30¼.

Fig. 34. The Seth Sumner stone, 1771, Milton, Massachusetts. Slate. 34 x 27½.

Fig. 35. The Love Backus stone, 1778, Norwichtown, Connecticut. Schist. 24 x 23.

tionally guard the threshold of heaven," but they also suggest leaves that open before the warmth of the sun's rays. The carving is informed, therefore, not by several metaphoric possibilities alone but by a visual metamorphosis that renders the Love Backus stone an intense icon of spiritual revelation.

It is unlikely that the carver of the stone lacked a workbench tradition, for he was close to Norwich and New London. Certainly this work does not present the conventional image of the cherub that prevailed in the Boston area, but the iconographic, metaphoric, and theological sources were generally present within the culture of the period and made such a design possible. Moreover, its skillful execution would suggest that the carver was in command of his visual intentions. The difference between the Love Backus stone and one carved in an urban area, such as the Sarah Morshead stone of 1750 in Salem, Massachusetts (*Fig.* 36), lies not in the skill of their execution or visual sophistication but in the refinement of their rendering. The Morshead stone was cut on light grey slate polished smooth; the carver flawlessly articulated the feathers of the cherub's wings, one of which was foreshortened to present a three-quarter view of its face. Its head is slightly pitched forward and covered with curls in the neoclassical manner, whereas the straight nose, clear eyes, and concise mouth provide naturalistic definition within an idealized vision.

Against the sophistication of this stone stands a rural marker cut in Bellingham, Massachusetts, for Polly Coombs, who died in 1795 (*Fig. 37*). Its iconographic similarities with the Morshead stone belie the carved rendition of the cherub this marker bears. Though superbly executed, the design upon the Coombs stone was cut within carefully chosen limits of embellishment. The carver set out a simpler problem than that involving the Morshead stone by describing a full-faced cherub symmetrically on the planar surface. Within these limits, he created a striking image of a cherub whose reticulated wings are somewhat disguised either as graceful extensions of hair or as flowing ribbons. This figure is one of joyful expectation, radiating a cheerfulness that indicates the carver's directness, at once naive and elegant. The total effect of such qualities would ordinarily suggest a rendition verging on the particularity of portraiture. There are, however, similar gravestones in the Bellingham area. Although executed freehand, these figures become a rural type of cherub, the Polly Coombs stone being the most delightful of those extant. In contrast, the design of the Morshead stone posed a more difficult carving challenge, more than ably met within the prevailing convention. A handsome marker, the Morshead stone presents a highly domesticated, eminently civilized interpretation of a cherub, whereas the Coombs stone offers a rural version of open expressiveness. Both stones have vital images, although the risks inherent in their respective formulations should be apparent. The one could have borne a worn convention, while the other could have lapsed into crude eccentricities.

The resources of urban Boston offered a wide range of imagery for the stonecarver, however restricted he was by the cultural values governing funereal conventions. The appearance, therefore, of a pagan angel such as the Dagon on several late seventeenth-century gravestones in The Granary and Copp's Hill[9] can be explained by considering numerous sources, including folklore, ancient mythology, the Bible, popular histories, and even New England's own recent past.

A mythological creature of complex origins, the Dagon assumed a variety of guises in different cultures. Among the Philistines he was a fertility god, whereas the Assyrians conceived of him as one of the judges of the underworld. Later, through etymological confusions with respect to the name, he took the form of half-man, half-fish—just as he was represented on Boston gravestones.[10] Although the Dagon was certainly a pagan deity in ancient cultures, seventeenth-century theologians interpreted him and his kind as fallen angels in order to maintain the superiority of the Christian Trinity.[11] Dagons thus indicated the fallen state of man, both in terms of his mortal sin and inevitable death, and so they appeared on New England gravestones in a visual

Fig. 36. The Sarah Morshead stone, 1750, Salem, Massachusetts. Slate. 27½ x 24¾.

Fig. 37. The Polly Coombes stone, 1795, Bellingham, Massachusetts. Slate. 26 x 16¾.

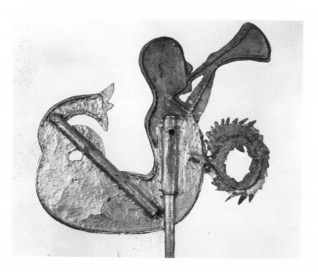

Fig. 38. Triton weathervane, lead-pewter with gold leaf, *c.* 1760, Newburyport, Massachusetts. 18½ x 15. *Courtesy of Shelburne Museum, Shelburne, Vermont.*

context that nevertheless provided the affirmative possibilities of salvation.

Since Bostonians probably did not read Milton until the very late seventeenth or early eighteenth century, after Dagons had been carved on gravestones, they would not have known of Milton's portrayal of this fallen angel in *Paradise Lost* or *Samson Agonistes*.[12] While the Bible remained the most common source for the Dagon on both sides of the Atlantic, another would have been the popular history *Purchas His Pilgrimage,* published in London in 1626. With reference to the Dagon as a pagan object of idolatry, Purchas commented that "when men are giuen ouer to themselues, then they become beasts, monsters, deuils,"[13] a judgment easily assented to by the Puritans, especially when they would recall the scandal at Thomas Morton's Merrymount during the first years of settlement in New England.

Originally Mount Wollaston, now a part of Quincy, Massachusetts, Merrymount was so named as the site for Morton and his band of profit-seekers in the Indian fur trade. Not so much for their licentious behavior (complete with the notorious maypole) but for their alleged exchange of guns and liquor for furs, the Puritans arrested Morton and quelled the potentially dangerous activity of his men. Merrymount then became known as Mount-Dagon, a derisive title indicating how the settlers at Merrymount were likened to fallen angels after their revelry.[14]

The early conflict between order and chaos soon passed into folklore. And the presence of the Dagon in popular craft is suggested by the triton with wreath horn used as a weathervane on the steeple of a countinghouse near Newburyport (*Fig. 38*). Given the literary quality of the Dagon images on the markers, however, stonecarver J. N. of Boston was most likely aware of visual images from printed sources, especially since Morton's account of his settlement had been published in Amsterdam in 1637 as *The New English Canaan*. The printer of this edition had obligingly used a cut bearing Dagons on the title page (*Fig. 39*). With an inverted triangle of copious floral elements are two Dagons, back to back, their arms interlocked and their scaly tails emerging from a single leafy ring. Erotic, actually somewhat lascivious in their posture of protruding bellies and breasts, the figures are scarcely distinguishable from the overall design.

Even though the William Greenough stone of 1693 on Copp's Hill (*Fig. 40*) differs from the title page of *The New English Canaan*, the visual properties of both designs are closely related. The woodcut is highly metamorphic, with one element transforming into another. The central mass of interlocking Dagons corresponds to the funerary urn of the gravestone designs. Organic forms found in the woodcut are transposed to the pilasters of the gravestone and encroach upon the Dagons holding the urn. Beneath the surface animation of both designs, a symmetrical structure is maintained. The baroque quality of the woodcut, however, gains a specific religious dimension of affirmation within the Puritan context, just as the Dagon, itself a pagan motif, was lent a Christian signification during the seventeenth century. Thus J. N. retained the established convention of the winged skull, which, though displaced by the Dagons and urn in the tympanum area, hovers above the primary complex, and in so doing, again emphasizes the mortality of man. Though fallen angels, the Dagons are surrounded by visual elements of regeneration, which, in conjunction with the winged skull rising from the funerary urn, suggests the resurrection of the dead.

J. N. was not the only carver to experiment with the traditional cherub. Unlike the winged skull, which offered few intrinsic variations, the cherub allowed multiple possibilities. The former was usually grounded because of its affinities to the earth as a symbol of mortality, whereas the cherub could easily and most logically be delineated in flight. Thus the Thomas Nichols stone of 1765 in Wakefield (*Fig. 41*) dramatizes Judgment Day with a flying cherub, its wings skillfully banked against the arch. Although the form resembles that of a cherub, it is certainly the angel Gabriel trumpeting the Resurrection Day command, "Arise Ye Dead." The shortcomings of this stone lie less in minor formal flaws, such as the clumsy execution of the banner, than in the carver's conception of the angel. Curiously enough, the image imparts not so much an impression of a glorious archangel, rendered with handsome mien and flowing raiment, as that of a harpy, the woman-bird of classical myth. This inadvertent impression may indicate an unwillingness on the part of the carver to forsake completely a conservative symbolic representation of the cherub so as to antic-

NEW ENGLISH CANAAN
OR
NEW CANAAN.

Containing an Abſtract of New England,

Compoſed in three Bookes.

The firſt Booke ſetting forth the originall of the Natives, their
Manners and Cuſtomes, together with their tractable Nature and
Love towards the Engliſh.

- The ſecond Booke ſetting forth the naturall Indowments of the
Country , and what ſtaple Commodities it
yealdeth.

The third Booke ſetting forth , what people are planted there,
their proſperity , what remarkable accidents have happened ſince the firſt
planting of it , together with their Tenents and practiſe
of their Church.

Written by Thomas Morton of Cliffords Inne gent , *upon tenne
yeares knowledge and experiment of the
Country.*

Printed at AMSTERDAM,
By JACOB FREDERICK STAM.
In the Yeare 1 6 3 7.

Fig. 39. Title page of Thomas Morton's *New English Canaan*, Amsterdam, 1637. *Courtesy
of The Henry E. Huntington Library, San Marino, California.*

Fig. 40. The William Greenough stone, 1693, Copp's Hill, Boston, Massachusetts. Slate. 31 x 28¾.

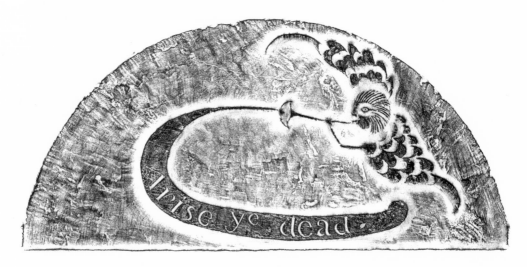

Fig. 41. The Thomas Nichols stone, 1765, Wakefield, Massachusetts. Slate. 29½ x 24⅛.

Fig. 42. The Charles Stuart stone, 1802, Peterborough, New Hampshire. Slate. 56½ x 36½.

ipate the depiction of a full angel, common in the late eighteenth and early nineteenth centuries. So, too, the frightening visage might still refer to the terrors of death itself, of negligible import in both carved and verbal statement elsewhere on the stone.

A more literal rendering of the angel Gabriel appears on the large monument for Charles Stuart in Peterborough, New Hampshire (*Fig.* 42). No longer a cherub but quite distinctly an angel, the figure is shown full-length. The wings are seen from above and appear capelike as he moves downward, trumpet held to his lips.[15] Dated 1802, the angel of resurrection flies above a classical edifice, a motif that had spread even to rural areas by the late eighteenth century. Gabriel is framed above by a rigid and symmetrical curtain from the folds of which hang two large, equally rigid tassels. An allusion to the close of life, the descending curtain itself assumes the configuration of wings, indicating thereby a vestigial undercurrent of visual metamorphosis in an otherwise static pattern of neoclassical decoration.

Although flying cherubim were not uncommon on rural gravestones, the images on the Thomas Nichols and the Charles Stuart markers suggest a cultivated and refined vision that urban carving encouraged. The execution of both images with attention paid to detail indicates restraint, readily apparent even on a stone of such ostentatious size as that for Stuart. A prototype may be found on the Masonic certificates engraved by Paul Revere. A certificate, only printed in the latter part of the eighteenth century, bears a flying angel with trumpet (*Fig. 43*). Although the stonecarver eliminated symbols such as the sun, moon, and stars, (even though they would have been consonant with the purposes of a gravestone), other elements of the Revere engraving remain. The carver elaborated upon the neoclassical edifices of the certificate and transposed the angle of the long rod carried by the Revere Gabriel to the pediment.

Despite the subject of these gravestones and the Revere engraving, Judgment Day is not envisioned in apocalyptic terms. Within the tympanum areas, the scale is small. Even in the large Stuart monument the ambience detracts from any commanding presence that the angel may have possessed. Neither violent eruption nor unmitigated doom but rather symmetry and order reign over the Judgment Day represented. Like the cherub on the Morshead stone, the acceptable pattern became domesticated, scaled down from transcendent proportions to human size.

Such is not the case with the Olive Storrs marker of 1785 in Mansfield Center, Connecticut (*Fig. 44*). Its tympanum presents a horrific image of a seraph cut deeply into the granite slab. Simple geometric floral pilasters extend into a decorative wavy band beneath the central image and suggest the flux of mortal life. The crowned seraph has a stylized, somewhat majestic, masklike visage, which evokes a sense of terror. The wings consist of six elements, slightly coiled and somewhat akin to spider's legs. These curves are repeated by two coils that turn out of the border, flanking either side of the seraph's head. Heavily carved into glittering granite, the stone image has a surface articulation in effective contrast to its immobile iconic presence. Indeed, the image is genuinely horrific, suggesting death in its apocalyptic dimensions, and belongs within a tradition persistent in New England from Michael Wigglesworth's *Day of Doom* through some of Jonathan Edwards' sermons. The spider quality of the carved image is particularly reminiscent of Edwards' effective use of the figure in *Sinners in the Hands of an Angry God.* In the sermon the spider is a metaphor for fallen man, suspended helplessly over the fiery pit by an omnipotent and angry God. Although the gravestone lacks the backdrop of Hell, it nevertheless vividly suggests at one and the same time the angel of death and man's mortality, his insignificance before the awesome experience of the eventual Judgment Day.

The image that comprises the tympanum of this large stone is at odds with the final couplet of the epitaph: "We trust her soul is now above / Where all is peace, where all is love." There is no need to doubt the family's faith in the

Fig. 43. Masonic general certificate. Engraving by Paul Revere, 1796, Boston, Massachusetts. 12¼ x 9⅝. *Courtesy of American Antiquarian Society, Worcester, Massachusetts.*

Fig. 44. The Olive Storrs stone, 1785, Mansfield Center, Connecticut. Granite. 43 x 28¼.

deceased, but the carving was informed less by a vision of love than by an intuition of the experiences prerequisite to her heavenly attainment. The forthrightness of the carving, which in no way comports with the usual platitudes, suggests a discrepancy between socially acceptable consolation and deeply felt anxieties about death.

Whereas the carver of the Olive Storrs marker remained faithful to his inner sense of death in forsaking the conventional cherub, the carver of the Ruth Conant stone of 1776 (*Fig. 45*) lacked an inner vision to control the execution of the central image. Confused about what he was carving, he superfluously included at the base of an ovoid head serrated teeth beneath a turned-down mouth. And yet the work does not lack merit. The visage, economically noted by a linear "hook and eye," is braced by wings extending horizontally from the crowned head like large leaves.[16] Although these motifs are affirmative, the expressive starkness of the head suggests the inevitability of death in life. Perhaps somewhat more benign than the Olive Storrs marker, the image is equally direct and bold as an iconic presence, a dynamic work of art despite its shortcomings.

Sheer size alone, however, would not result in a powerful design. The relatively small Nathaniel Pattin stone of South Killingly, Connecticut, is a case in point (*Fig. 46*). The grey quartz and schist slab (less than twenty inches

Fig. 45. The Ruth Conant stone, 1766, Mansfield Center, Connecticut. Granite. 36 x 24.

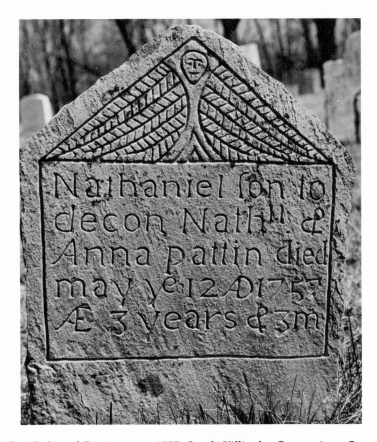

Fig. 46. The Nathaniel Pattin stone, 1757, South Killingly, Connecticut. Quartz-schist. 19½ x 14.

from peak to base) presents an exciting image of highly unusual particular properties which nonetheless reflect a common faith in the Christian resurrection of the soul. Roughly rectangular, with an angled upper line, the shape implies a classical temple façade reinforced by interior channelling following the general shape of the stone. A pediment reserved fully for the visual statement is defined by a horizontal line; the lower area contains the irregular lettering that gives the vital records of the deceased infant child.

Within the pediment thus delineated is shown a full human form, both arms upstretched against a background of lines radiating from behind the figure and moving downward toward the corner angles. The spaces between the lines are segmented by alternating cuts, optically creating ribs and feathering through which surface motion is achieved. The figure is constituted by a near-tangential meeting of two arcs; an ovoid shape denoting a head is placed within the upper divergence, while the lower area is further defined as legs by the meeting of two additional arcs.

The pattern of converging curved and straight lines, reinforced and counterpointed, is nowhere else so abstracted and essential to the effectiveness of the iconographic statement of the gravestone, with the possible exception of some early Essex County examples in Massachusetts. Although similar to the technically superior Neal children stone in its organization of the pedimental area, the substitution of a full figure, however abstract, for a naturalistic skull transforms the entire vision into one of resurrection through a series of metamorphoses. A poignant expression of mortality, the naked figure lies prostrate before God in His majesty. The transformation of the deceased is suggested by the illuminating rays that gradually become wings in combination with the arms upstretched in both supplication and ascension. In its final metamorphosis the figure assumes the guise of a cherub. As the sun strikes the rough schist, the image modulates through these possibilities. The repose inherent in the Neal children stone is complemented by the iconic motion of this relatively rude and simple marker in rural Connecticut.

Certainly not the treatment of design, but rather the kind of material available to the carver (who ably exploited it for its sensuous values) accounts for the roughness of the Nathaniel Pattin stone. On its own terms, this small stone required as much attention to detail as the more obviously refined Sarah Morshead stone, and confirms that meticulous carving was not confined to urban areas alone. The culmination of exquisite carving in a linear style occurred along the route from Bennington to Shaftesbury and then on to Arlington, Vermont. Zerubbabel Collins, from the Connecticut stonecarving family, had moved to the region from Columbia in 1778, bringing with him a basic vocabulary that he had previously worked on the rough and heavy granite material of Eastern Connecticut.

In Vermont Collins was able to employ a soft white marble that permitted delicacy of line as well as sculptural qualities. The nature of this material resulted in the transformation of basic imagery into a new sense of design. Collins continued to carve his images *on* the marble, yet in such a way that the surface is totally animated. He did not merely trace the design, but transformed the planar surface in the process. All that remains of the plain style is the boldness of a central form—a visual precept that is certainly not peculiar to plain style alone. He retained symmetry of design only so as to provide an effective substructure. Even the tympanum arch of his gravestones burgeons outward in an irregular, although balanced, curvilinear fashion. The shape has organic rather than geometric definition, since the visual interest clearly lies outside the realm of rational discourse. Collins released his imagination in a lyrical fusion of religious and aesthetic dimensions to create plastic statements of spiritual affirmation.

On the Jedidiah Aylesworth stone of 1795 in Arlington (*Fig. 47*) an oval-faced angel is grounded to the tympanum by a rectangular body.[17] Its head bears a crown that proclaims *Memento Mori*, the only didactic element, and one of the few reminders of death on a stone otherwise devoted to spiritual affirmation. The angel's face is abstract, as Collins did not attempt a naturalistic portrayal. Yet he did not ignore detail, which remains in the small coil volutes of hair above the wings, the double-lined almond eyes, and a double curve for the mouth. From the head and shoulders protrude channelled wings that are similar to the outer tympanum line. Despite the tightly organized, almost folded wing structure, there is still a strong illusion of ascension in the outward and upward movement and that quality remains in easy balance with the angel's presence on the ground.

Within the double outline of the rectangular body are circular breasts and a crescent-shaped medallion, possibly a jewelled heart, all of which suggest sexual renewal, earthly analogues for spiritual redemption. The epitaph's prophecy that the deceased "shall rise and leave the ground" is visually indicated by the cruciform position of the outstretched arms and open hands. Crucifixion and flight combine with a gesture of benediction, reflecting the "generous soul" of the youthful deceased.

The medallion on the angel's chest is repeated above its head. From that motif pairs of long, graceful leaves and flowers symmetrically descend about the arch. Thus the didactic reminder is surrounded by emblems of life. The floral pattern extends against the upward wings and gently forestalls ascension;

Fig. 47. The Jedediah Aylesworth stone, 1795, Arlington, Vermont. White marble. 34 x 25.

floral pattern extends against the upward wings and gently forestalls ascension; the thin, linear arms of the angel are given metamorphic extensions by a design similar to that above the head; the outer edge of the tympanum is punctuated by a series of flowers and leaves that create a bower for the central figure; and interplay among these elements upon the planar field of the stone creates a peaceful surface animation.

Collins' work shared the floral iconography of eighteenth-century Connecticut Valley furniture, which he most assuredly saw. In particular, the delicacy of his forms combined with their planar configuration bears a relationship with painted furniture (*Fig. 48*) [14] Collins, however, had the advantage of being able to carve his motifs, thereby lending them substance, whereas the flowers painted upon furniture were a compromise resolution of a cabinetmaker's inability or lack of desire to embellish by carving, inlay, or gesso. Collins, moreover, maintained a superb sense of structure, as the various floral elements of the Jedidiah Aylesworth stone emanate from a central mass. The contrast between the peripheral movement and the inner stillness suggests the angel's presence in a spiritual garden.

The Sarah Branch stone of 1784 in Shaftesbury (*Fig. 49*) presents a cherub with a face basically the same as that on the Aylesworth stone, though without a crown. The feathering of the wings about the face is short; then it extends outwards to create an illusion of graceful ascension. To provide here the firm structure achieved by the angel's body on the Aylesworth stone, the hovering cherub is held in suspension by a repetition of five boldly petalled flowers, their sequence interrupted by fanciful exfoliations. The combination of this garland and the organic extensions beneath do provide a firm, almost heavy base for the entire design. The stemmed leaf clusters and flowers, which are exceptionally fluid and open in their symmetry, serve as ascending accents above the cherub.

In 1794, on the Ebenezer Cole stone (*Fig. 50*), also of Shaftesbury, Collins successfully experimented with forms even bolder than those on the Sarah Branch stone. Within a similar ambience a cherub is artfully placed on a complex of burgeoning leaves perpendicular to the base. On either side stand magnificent tulips, in which line and mass are gracefully combined by the carving of a planar outline. From the tulips rise elements reminiscent of fir trees. The periphery is punctuated by flowers, and the uppermost arch is counterpointed by an embrasure of leaves. In this design the natural and the spiritual become coextensive in the "endless World" for which the quatrain of the text exhorts the living to prepare themselves.

Collins did not simply shift from bold to delicate forms, but managed to achieve an interplay between them, which is apparent on the Mary Breakenridge stone of 1792 in Bennington (*Fig. 51*). The final quatrain of the text affirms:

> Yet never let our hearts divide
> Nor death dissolve the chain;
> For love and joy were once alloy'd
> And must be join'd again.

In this sentiment, which is common to many of Collins' gravestones, the spiritual frame of reference is parallelled in the carved decoration. The text stands as a verbal figure for the synthesis that Collins was able to visualize.

Although delicate linear forms prevail, the basic composition of the Mary Breakenridge stone anticipates that of the Ebenezer Cole stone carved two years later. Collins revised the headpiece of the earlier Sarah Branch stone, and subtly recessed a nimbus for the cherub's head to sustain the structure. The cherub is

Fig. 48. Chest of five drawers, painted, 1680–1710, Connecticut. Oak, pine, and poplar. Height, 43 inches. *Courtesy of Wadsworth Atheneum, Hartford.*

Fig. 49. The Sarah Branch stone, 1784, Shaftsbury, Vermont. White marble. 41 x 26¾.

Fig. 50. The Ebenezer Cole stone, 1794, Shaftsbury, Vermont. White marble. 45 x 27½.

Fig. 51. The Mary Breakenridge stone, 1792, Bennington, Vermont. White marble. 51 x 29¾.

Fig. 52. Connecticut Valley sunflower chest, 1675–1700. Courtesy of *The Henry Francis du Pont Winterthur Museum, Winterthur, Delaware.*

here balanced above a basket of fruits and tulips, which evolve into larger, fanciful motifs reminiscent of those on the Sarah Branch marker. Since this structure risked appearing insubstantial, Collins reinforced the lower section with a pair of large sunflowers, delicately carved yet bold in mass. Long petals outlined by shorter ones radiate from a central circle and, like the tulips, correspond in style to the sunflowers carved on Connecticut chests (*Fig. 52*). Further, Collins placed on the outer edges other pairs of flowers, smaller and simpler than the sunflowers. The entire surface of the stone is modulated by these circles, which act as stabilizing punctuation for the calligraphy of the stems. Thus this design manifests an aesthetic balance between substance and line, and is, in short, an eloquent work of art, which joins "love and joy" once again.

In Attleboro there stands a slate stone (*Fig. 53*) for Hannah Tiffany, who died on August 28, 1785. A young woman married to Noah Tiffany, she lived to be twenty-four years old. The biographical particulars are perhaps more pertinent for this gravestone than for many because of the nature of its image. Within the sweep of the tympanum arch stands a chaste angelic figure wrapped

Fig. 53. The Hannah Tiffany stone, 1785, First Congregational Churchyard, Attleborough, Massachusetts. Slate. 27½ x 22¾.

in a shawl, her hands clasped at the waist in patient repose. Matching the image in its simplicity is the eloquent declaration: "I have sought & found him." The image represents both an angel and a saint, which combine to create a spiritual portrait of Hannah Tiffany. The metamorphic tensions in the relationship between angels and departed souls inevitably suggested possibilities of portraiture to the New England stonecarver.

CHAPTER 5

Portraits in Stone and Spirit

PREOCCUPATION with survival in the New England wilderness was far less an obstacle to portrait painting than was the ocean loss of a technical tradition to teach the complicated processes involved. The proper preparation of canvas, the manufacture of pigments, the mixture and application of colors—not to mention aesthetic considerations of composition and formal properties of subject matter—were difficult to learn in the absence of competent teachers. Even so, limners attempted to meet the artistic desires of Puritan society by painting likenesses, often crude but identifiable as the sitter, usually with some favorite or characterizing object at hand. From the very beginning, ministers led the way in commissioning portraiture. Thus the earliest extant woodcut done in New England is of the Reverend Richard Mather, cut by John Foster the astronomer, mathematician, and printer of Dorchester, Massachusetts. Though vanity was always a possible motive, Puritan divines had ample justification as spiritual leaders of their community for having their likenesses wrought. The most significant and comprehensive reason, however, was that oil portraits were but another means of fulfilling the Puritan need for commemoration, the rendering of a human image both for posterity and for family dynastic ambitions.

These cultural needs were ultimately grounded in religious attitudes. Unlike the Quakers, who generally rejected portraiture as well as the erection of gravestones on the grounds of idolatry, orthodox Puritans restricted their interpretation of the Second Commandment to the ecclesiastical realm. Sanction of portraiture was derived from a strong sense of spiritual vocation and sanctification upon election. Out of these values the Puritans involved themselves in worldly activity, with such discourse between the spiritual and the material providing the impulse for portraiture.

Fig. 54. Self-Portrait, by Captain Thomas Smith, oil on canvas, late seventeenth century. 24½ x 23¾. *Courtesy of Worcester Art Museum, Worcester, Massachusetts.*

Captain Thomas Smith's vigorous *Self-Portrait* of approximately 1690 is a perfect example (*Fig. 54*). Rather self-consciously but firmly seated in a three-quarter view, the Captain apparently conceived of himself as a man of the world. Although he appears comfortable in refined lace ruffles, he had partici-pated in thunderous sea battles as depicted through the conventionalized win-dow behind him. But with these earthly concerns there are the traditional spiritual emblems that also appear on gravestones. A curtain with a tassel in the background suggests the impending close of life, repeated emblematically by the skull which the Captain clasps. Lest the point not be clear, a note beneath the death's-head reiterates the visual tableau:

> Why why should I the World be minding
> therein a World of Evils Finding.

> Then Farwell World: Farwell thy Jarres
> thy Joies thy Toies thy Wiles thy Warrs
> Truth Sounds Retreat: I am not sorye.
> The Eternall Drawes to him my heart
> By Faith (which can thy Force Subvert)
> To Crowne me (after Grace) with Glory.
> T. S.

With the inclusion of the poem Smith tipped the visual balance between this world and the next to hopes of salvation.

By their very nature gravestones are biographical. Even the erection of a bare marker in the ground indicates the earthly presence of someone before. Images on New England gravestones affirmed the spiritual life of the deceased. Simply in visual terms alone, the depiction of angels in close spiritual association with the soul of the deceased led to the possibility of representational portraiture. Prior to such carving, which took hold in the latter half of the eighteenth century, emblematic portraits had been attempted. As the Colonies gained in affluence and prosperity, the stonecarver was able to borrow his iconography from the rising incidence of oil painting. This concatenation of cultural factors would suggest that money and social prominence had something to do with the commissioning of a portrait on a gravestone. The motives for carved portraiture, however, were not necessarily materialistic. Nor was the encroaching secularism in New England a prime factor. In the manner of Captain Smith and his *Self-Portrait*, stonecarvers retained spiritual values in the designs. Carved on a gravestone, a likeness of the deceased could suggest that he was literally in the world but not of it.

For important reasons, idealized portraits of Puritan ministers were occasionally cut on the stones marking their graves. The loss to the community and the church was of great concern, because a successor was often difficult to find. The death of a minister, moreover, tended to crystallize a societal belief that the spiritual mission of New England was beginning to decline. Although payment for services to the congregation had often been difficult for the living minister to obtain, upon his death a permanent memorial would be commissioned as a didactic icon to guide and inspire succeeding generations. The Reading congregation erected a superbly carved stone with a close text of eulogy for the Reverend Jonathan Pierpont (*Fig. 27*). The next step to actual portraiture was logical, if not inevitable.

The stone likeness of a deceased minister often had little to do with his actual ministerial role, involved as he was in the social and political as well as the religious life of his community. Increase Mather, for example, was active in diplomatic matters between Massachusetts Bay and England. And Cotton Mather, who delivered a wide variety of sermons, published an inordinate number of his writings, and was closely involved in the medical and natural sciences, plotted and conspired as much as he was victimized by others. As he complained in his diary, "There are knotts of riotous Young Men in the Town. On purpose to insult Piety, they will come under my Window in the Middle of the Night and sing profane and filthy songs. The last night they did so, and fell upon People with Clubs, taken off my Wood-pile. 'Tis hightime, to call in the Help of the Government of the Place, for the punishing and suppressing of these Disorders."[1] This instance is at Mather's expense, but the fact that young gazabos found occasional sport in midnight catcalls reflects the uneven communal esteem of ministers in their day-to-day engagements.

In comparison to Mather, the Reverend David Turner of the Second Church of Rehoboth, Massachusetts, had a rather quiet ministry. He came to the town in 1721 immediately after receiving a Master's degree from Harvard. Official religious controversy probably reached its peak when he signed a statement in opposition to the itinerant evangelist George Whitefield during the Great Awakening. Upon his death in 1757 he supposedly warned his successor: "Mr. Rogerson, I rejoice to find that the people are so well pleased with you and your preaching; but you must remember that, though it is 'Hosanna!' 'Hosanna!' *today* it will be *'Crucify him!' 'Crucify him!'* tomorrow." His indignant self-martyrdom becomes somewhat suspect, however, in that reputedly "his parsonage was a center for gossip."[2] The nature of this "gossip"—if indeed it was gossip—is unknown, but whether it took the form of provincial entertainment or genuine religious controversy, the situation would suggest Turner's involvement in the various intrigues of Rehoboth.

His gravestone (*Fig. 55*), however, indicates nothing of such ferment. While a conventional cherub appears on the tympanum, the pilasters bear two scenes that may have been copied from a popular catechism, "The Child's Body of Divinity" (*Fig. 56*)[3] Far superior in carving to the two crude woodcuts, the pilasters alternately portray the minister praying and meditating in his study. On the right pilaster he is seated at his desk, complete with candle and quill, behind which stands a tall pendulum clock. On the left he is praying on his knees, while light streams through the window above. A couplet beneath the epitaph corroborates these vignettes with the warning, "Watch and Pray Because / You Know Not the Hour." Though the diptych is appropriate, it emphasizes only certain aspects of the minister's role—those which, when portrayed alone, create an idealized picture of the deceased minister.

The life of the Reverend Nathaniel Rogers of Ipswich, Massachusetts,

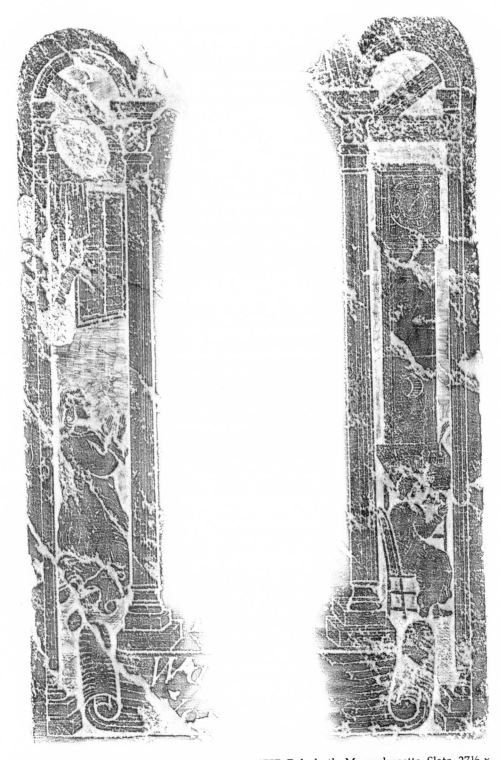

Fig. 55. The Reverend David Turner stone, 1757, Rehoboth, Massachusetts. Slate. 27½ x 24. *A.* Left pilaster, detail. *B.* Right pilaster, detail.

Fig. 56. Illustration cut from *The Child's Body of Divinity, c.* 1750. *Courtesy of The John Carter Brown Library, Brown University, Providence.*

affords another example. Upon his death in 1775 a large slate stone (*Fig. 57*) was erected bearing his likeness within an oval frame, a shape commonly chosen for portrait miniatures. Given his role and status, a portrait would not have been unusual. Perhaps his survivors were further influenced by the oil painting of Rogers' father or grandfather and that of Governor Leverett in his estate.[4] In any case, the gravestone carving succeeds as representational portraiture in well-sculpted relief.[5] The minister's gown, carefully draped to reveal innumerable waistcoat buttons, and an elaborate peruke are presented in fine detail. The naturalistic carving, however, is hardly concerned with matters of the flesh, as a reading of the epitaph makes quite clear. Just as his spiritual metamorphosis is emphasized in the vital statistics ("death translated him to the high reward of his labors"), so, too, his enumerated virtues are considered those which "mark'd the Man. . . ." In contrast, "with superior grace / The *Christian* shone in faith & heavenly zeal, / Sweet peace, true goodness, and prevailing pray'r."

Fig. 57. The Reverend Nathaniel Rogers stone, 1775, Ipswich, Massachusetts. Slate. 54 x 34.

Neither these comments nor the benign and gentle expression on his face would indicate the controversies of his ministry. The two verses would be simply extravagant, were not historical corroboration available:

> Dear Man of God! with what strong agonies
> He wrestled for his flock—and for the world!
> And like Apollos mighty in the scriptures,
> Open'd the mysteries of love divine
> And the great name of Jesus!
> Warm from his lips the heav'nly doctrine fell;
> And numbers rescu'd from the jaws of hell,
> Shall hail blest in realms of light
> And add immortal lustre to his crown.

Fig. 58. The Reverend Silas Bigelow stone, 1769, Paxton, Massachusetts. Slate. 49 x 30¼.

As the son of Reverend John Rogers, Nathaniel had joined his father in the ministry of the First Church of Ipswich in 1724/25. His selection as a replacement for Jabez Fitch was probably a political gesture, which would be characteristic of his term, although subsequent events were hardly as unanimous. Manifesting great piety, Rogers became an Edwardsian New Light and entertained the Reverend George Whitefield and other itinerant preachers in his pulpit from 1740 onward. Hence the lines upon his stone. But they give little notion of the ferment which he created, causing faction and schism among his parishioners until the Great Awakening subsided.[6] Although the congregation no doubt sincerely mourned their loss, and they had this fine monument erected (for a minister was not expected to shy away from controversial religious issues), the fact remains that, like the Turner marker, the Rogers stone minimizes earthly strife in favor of a portrait of the minister as beloved leader of his flock.

The gravestone cut for the Reverend Silas Bigelow (*Fig. 58*) of Paxton, Massachusetts, also follows the general pattern of a bereaved congregation erecting a monument to express their own great loss. The church and town were cofounded in 1767-1768, and Bigelow himself was a signer of the church covenant in September of 1767. It was understandable, then, that at his untimely death, only two years later, an epitaph was composed around the metaphor of a shepherd guarding his flock of Christians. The large, square-shouldered stone of shaley-slate was cut by William Young, and it is the masterpiece among his known works. This marker is not only a fine example of Puritan stones, but is also an acceptable variation of the Gothic *transi,* an image not generally used in New England during the seventeenth and eighteenth centuries.

The portrait of Bigelow, bewigged and clerically collared, appears above a floating bar presumed to represent the pulpit, which is supported by curved bands suggesting the sanctuary railing. From the pulpit hang large tassels, which with the church silver and other fine fabrics, were perhaps too dear for the earliest members to have obtained immediately for their house of worship. From this vantage, Bigelow addresses the congregation as he had during the two years of his short tenure: he holds the Bible in one hand and gestures oratorically with the other.

The design area was enlarged by lowering the base line of the tympanum well within the text area so that a greater space could be carved. The pilasters are crosshatched columns, the capitals of which show cherubs above orders that can be described only as dentiled. Within the border arch, comprised of double semicircles, is an interior panel also defined by a series of dentils. Like the heart of the earlier Mary Hirst stone (*Fig. 10*), the negative space creates a visual pun, offering full wings and a nimbus for the preaching minister. New possibilities, compatible with the basic interpretation, are then revealed. There is no evidence that a base for the pulpit was ever cut, even in such perishable slate as was used for this monument. The pulpit was conceived and carved only as a floating bar from which to hang luxurious tassels. These details and the visual pun would suggest that the tassels are not merely church ornaments but also those that hang from the community-owned funeral pall: the engagement of the minister being viewed is of his bodily and spiritual resurrection. The embodiment of the minister's resurrection in his public act of preaching, combined with the commemoration of the stone itself, suggests the communal hopes of salvation out of such loss.

William Young also cut the monument for the Reverend William Bowes (*Fig. 59*) of Bedford, Massachusetts, some ten years prior to the Bigelow stone. Depicting another ministerial subject, he found a special necessity not only to include an epitaph of impressions of the deceased leader distilled through a conventional rhetoric reserved for such occasions, but to fully note biographical information, since Bowes had died distant from his usual residence: "having been engaged as chaplin in the Army at [the] westward upon his Return [Bowes] was violently seized with his last illness in this place [Warren, Massachusetts] and suddenly Departed this life."

Fig. 59. The Reverend Nicholas Bowes stone, *c.* 1759, Warren, Massachusetts. Slate. 41 x 28½.

Fig. 60. The Ensign David Keyes stone, 1761, Warren, Massachusetts. Slate. 32 x 32½.

Utilizing the bold figure for the stone portrait of David Keyes (*Fig. 60*) that he had cut in 1761, which stands in the same graveyard, Young economically characterized the minister by indicating a clerical collar and scarf beneath the face. Of far greater interest than these commonplaces of role definition is the presence of chain-link armorial covering on the minister's shoulders. The recent westward campaign in which Bowes had been involved must have caught the imagination of Young and that of the bereaved survivors, who surely

Fig. 61. The Reverend Grindall Rawson stone, dated 1715, but cut in 1744, Mendon, Massachusetts. Slate. 24½ x 19¼. *Courtesy of American Antiquarian Society, Worcester, Massachusetts.*

drew parallels between the continuing Indian wars, now supported by the French, and the fate of the New England experiment. The analogies of the Christian in the wilderness had been so often repeated from the pulpit as not to have been recalled. The particular selection of the costume could well have been suggested by the sixth chapter of Ephesians, in which Christians are exhorted by Paul to take on "the whole armour of God, that ye may be able to withstand in the evil day, and having done all, to stand." He goes on to identify the various elements of armorial clothing as emblems of Christian virtues. The portrait, then, is not a representation of a possible future state of Bowes, like the rendering of Bigelow, but rather a concrete vision of the Church militant as the Christian soldier moves through the known world of temptation and strife.

One of the few gravestones that appears to capture the specific character and personality of a minister is that for the Reverend Grindall Rawson (*Fig. 61*) of Mendon, Massachusetts. Although the stone was carved *circa* 1740, Rawson died in 1711.[7] (Perhaps the decision to cut a portrait was inspired by Cotton Mather's *JustCommemorations. the Death of Good Men, Considered . . .* , Rawson among them, which Mather termed portraiture "to keep them still Present in a World, from which I am *Hastening* after them.'"[8]) Rawson had led a vigorous life. In 1680 he was invited to Mendon, but he was not ordained until 1684, a delay that had something to do with his negotiations for a proper salary. Such hard-headedness carried over into his preaching as he systematically established an incredible weekly schedule of lectures and sermons to cover all sections of the town. Not only was he a missionary to the Indians but he was also embattled against the "sectaries" of Providence. He demanded strict observance of the Sabbath by his congregation and family of eleven children. Thus his gravestone portrait is appropriate. Carved with naturalistic detail, Rawson's figure assumes a sturdy posture as he stands arms akimbo, looking upward as if to his Lord. His vigor is noted in the way his coat remains unbuttoned, strained open by his arms thrown outward at his sides to reveal the vest underneath.

The militant stance of the Reverend Rawson is matched by that of Lieutenant Nathaniel Thayer of Braintree, Massachusetts, who died in 1768 (*Fig. 62*). He is portrayed in three-quarter length as a soldier, one hand at his waist, the other firmly grasping a long staff. What appears to be a secular portrait at odds with the spiritual portrayals of ministers proves to have graphic spiritual meaning of its own. On either pilaster, leaning inward from the outer border, is an angel, presumably Gabriel, blowing a long trumpet. Sound waves, dynamically indicated by lines extending the length of the pilasters, reach a cluster of faces looking upward at the angel (*Fig. 63*). The relationship between the tympanum portrait and the tableau on the pilasters offers a profound vision. Quite clearly, Lieutenant Thayer stands awaiting Judgment Day. Like Chaplain Bowes, Thayer is also depicted as a Puritan saint, embattled in the cause of Christ. As a saint, the soul of Thayer could be awaiting its reunion with its resurrected body on the occasion of the Second Coming. The invisible saint, however, would already be united with Christ, who stands prepared to judge mortals as He reigns literally above his angels.

The eschatological implications of the Thayer stone are possibly no more remarkable than the Puritan vision of continuity between this world and the next. In The Granary a slate marker for Jabez Smith, Jr., who died in 1780, offers an excellent image embodying discourse between the two realms (*Fig. 64*). The epitaph informs the viewer that Smith was a "Lieut. of Marines / on board the Continental Ship Trumbull." Like the Thayer stone, this marker portrays Smith's vocation: carved on the tympanum is a frigate bearing the American

Fig. 62. The Lieutenant Nathaniel Thayer stone, 1768, Braintree, Massachusetts. Slate. 27 x 24½.

Fig. 63. Details of pilasters of the Lieutenant Nathaniel Thayer stone.

flag from its stern. The ship, however, which lacks sails and is "Anchor'd in the haven of Rest," becomes an appropriate metaphor for Smith's journey through life into the spiritual world.[9]

Occasionally, a family preferred to remember the deceased for his participation in the religious life of the community. In South Windsor and Tolland, Connecticut, there are stones for Matthew Rockwell (*Fig. 65*) and Joseph Lothrop (*Fig. 66*) who died in 1782 and 1788, respectively. Rockwell graduated in 1728 from Yale College, where he had studied medicine and theology. He was also a deputy in the Connecticut General Assembly for twenty-three sessions.[10] His survivors, however, chose to portray him upon his gravestone by his participation in the East Windsor church as a deacon whose major responsibility was to serve the Lord's Supper. For this reason, the Rockwell stone, and the Lothrop stone as well, bear images of communion cups and flagons upon a frieze beneath the cherub occupying the tympanum area. Heavily carved in a flat, rather deep relief, the Deacon Rockwell stone displays two flagons as a central mass flanked on the length of three beakers. This complex repeats the form of the cherub above with its upstretched wings. The Deacon Lothrop stone bears a bold asymmetrical design of a flagon standing at one end of the frieze before which extend four communion beakers. Although this discursive structure indicates the continuing presence of plain-style analysis, the dominating cherub and the foliated pilasters suggest the regenerative and essentially suprarational experience of the Lord's Supper.

With the exception of the Jabez Smith marker these portraits in stone bear explicit religious content. In contrast, the Smith marker depends upon verbal metaphor to communicate its spiritual import. The same holds true for the Dr. Thomas Munro stone of 1785 (*Fig. 67*) in Bristol, Rhode Island. If its verbal aspect is ignored, the Munro stone offers minimal religious meaning and becomes an incomplete portrait—as truncated as Thomas Smith's *Self-Portrait* on canvas would be were it not for his appended note beneath the skull. The Munro stone bears his portrait in profile from the waist upward. He wears a ruff and waistcoat, detailed in buttons, and sports a fashionable wig with a bow and pigtail. This naturalistic portrayal is seemingly reinforced by the epitaph which asserts that he "Paid his / Debt due to Nature." This incipient Deistic notion is belied, however, by an appended quatrain:

> O, Death thou hast Conquer'd me,
>   I, by thy dart am slain,
> But Christ hath Conquer'd the,
>   And I shall rise a gain.

Fig. 64. The Lieutenant Jabez Smith, Jr., stone, 1780, The Granary, Boston, Massachusetts. Slate. 31¾ x 22.

Fig. 65. The Deacon Matthew Rockwell stone, 1782, South Windsor, Connecticut. Red sandstone. 43 x 24½.

Fig. 66. The Deacon Joseph Lothrop stone, 1788, Tolland, Connecticut. Red sandstone. 45 x 23.

Within this expressly Christian context, the portrait takes on new dimensions. The doctor is not only a beneficent healer, stretching his hand outward to mankind, but also the newly risen man extending his hand to the unseen Christ. In this dual portrayal the deceased approximates the virtues of Christ by his vocation as a doctor.

Other gravestone portraits derive spiritual values from integral, although seemingly minor, aspects of the visual design itself. The marker for Mary Brown, who died in 1782, characterizes the five-year-old child as a young woman holding a branch and flower (*Fig. 68*). This discrepancy of age is largely superficial, for children were commonly dressed in small versions of adult clothes. Moreover, the carver fulfilled the family commission by engraving a variation on a pose long since conventionalized in Colonial oil portraiture. For example, John Wollaston, the itinerant portraitist, captured a likeness of Miss Elizabeth Wormsley Spottswood Carter in a very similar setting (*Fig. 69*). Beyond the social ideal, the spiritual dimensions of the carved portrait were emphasized. Indicating death at an early age, the cut rose also symbolized Christ and His

Fig. 67. The Doctor Thomas Munro stone, 1785, Juniper Hill Cemetery, Bristol, Rhode Island. Slate. 33½ x 20.

Fig. 68. The Mary Brown stone, 1782, Plymouth, Massachusetts. Slate. 23½ x 16¾.

Crucifixion, and the persistent bloom of the flower, His Resurrection. In the girl's frozen gesture exists the negated possibilities of what might have been. This likeness thus heightens the interaction between earthly and spiritual states, to vivify the contrast between mortal death and youth, the latter an analogue for Christian regeneration.

"Betsy Morton, ye Maid^n," as the Plymouth Church records poignantly list her, died at age twenty in 1790.[11] The prominent Morton family of Plymouth commissioned a gravestone portrait for Elizabeth (*Fig. 70*), who is shown in a fashionable dress with a heart locket at her throat. By placing arched roses on either side of the oval frame, the carver repeated in effect the morphology of the cherub or the earlier winged skull. Through this visual metamorphosis the carver retained traditional underlying forms while participating in the innovations of gravestone portraiture.

The markers for Mary Brown and Elizabeth Morton clearly indicate that stone portraits were not limited to public figures. From the very start the erection of gravestones had been a family affair, since the closeness of the Puritan family in life was carried over in death.[12] Although family tombs in the seventeenth century were rapidly replaced by individual markers in family areas, a preponderance of epitaphs for individual memorials note the family of the deceased, parents, a surviving wife or husband. On occasion visual attempts were made to portray an entire family. The Park family memorial (*Fig. 71*) of Grafton, Vermont, depicts the mother, Mrs. Rebecca Park, her eldest son, Thomas K. Park, Jr., as well as her thirteen infants. Erected after the mother's death in 1803, the marker was engraved in a delicate linear style rather than in shallow relief, possibly a result of the local carver's isolation from a workbench tradition. The idiosyncratic skill with which this carver executed his designs did not, however, limit the creation of a unique memorial.

A central lunette containing an image of the eldest son is balanced by two large arcs bearing an image of the mother on the right and her thirteen infants on the left. These create burgeoning peripheries that play against the interior geometry, almost exclusively comprised of abstract circular forms. The carver thus made little attempt at naturalistic portrayal. Unlike the son, whose face alone is tightly embraced by the interior dimensions of the lunette, the mother's body is included, her clothing indicated by shallow cross-hatchings. Although her elevation contrasts with the son's fixed position and so suggests upward movement as well as adulthood, she is nonetheless enclosed in a rectangle not unlike a tomb or a doorway, which, in turn, is surrounded by lightly etched leaves and vines. This elementary lyricism is better realized, however, on the opposite arc, on which the thirteen children are portrayed. An accompanying

Fig. 69. Miss Elizabeth Wormsley Spottswood Carter, by John Wollaston, oil on canvas, *c.* 1755–1758. 50 x 40. *Courtesy of The Current Company, Bristol, Rhode Island.*

Fig. 70. The Elizabeth Morton stone, 1790, Plymouth, Massachusetts. Slate. 27 x 27½.

couplet in the epitaph exhorts, "See their image how they shine, / Like flowers of a fruitful vine." The mixed metaphor makes reference not only to the sunlike forms of the children's faces but also to their delineation on the regenerative tree of life. Drawn in freehand, the trunk extends tenuous lines to the thirteen faces of the deceased, pressing outward against the tympanum border.

Although the gravestone is composed of discrete elements, an initial sense of discontinuity yields finally to the internal coherence of design. To be sure, the outer edges of each lunette are not connected and the three portraits are different; yet the interior play of line and form provides a visual totality. Circles are common to all three areas, and the vines surrounding the mother are repeated by those linking the children. The eye is attracted to the revolving motion from the children's faces to the elder brother, and then is arrested by the mother's stoic gaze. Like the thirteen infants who are depicted individually yet tied to a central vine, the marker possesses an underlying visual unity that suggests the transcendence of death and isolation in the Christian communion of spiritual regeneration.

The closeness of the Puritan family occasionally resulted in similar gravestones for husbands and wives. The marble markers for Samuel and Mary Hinckley, who died in 1798 in Brookfield, Massachusetts, bear portraits with scant sexual distinctions (*Figs. 72, 73*). The figure of Samuel Hinckley is flanked on either side by an exfoliating rose, an emblem dating back to Boston gravestones of the seventeenth century. From his shoulders emerge sinuous vines that extend upward and outward into grape clusters. Clearly symbolizing Christ, these images express the hope that Hinckley died among the Elect. Such anticipation is further reinforced by the placement of roses and, particularly, the grapes — a subtle metaphor for the wings of a cherub. By contrast, the Mary Hinckley stone is superior in conception. She stands slim and erect, the carver having achieved simplicity and chasteness of line and mass in the creation of her figure, which is shown within a bower of grapes, the clusters of which impale her, symbolically reenacting the Crucifixion. The vine descends from the overarching curve of the tympanum border into arabesques of fruit and leaves.

These two gravestones share with homecrafted crewelwork the common image of a figure beneath a bower. For example, on an eighteenth-century New England linen petticoat border a seated female was embroidered within an arch of grapevines (*Fig. 74*). Although two birds provide an element of balance, the design is essentially asymmetrical; indeed, perspective and scale have little value in this Edenic scene. In contrast, the designs on the Hinckley stones are symmetrical, the husband's marker to the point of stiffness and awkwardness. On Mary Hinckley's, however, the substructure is permeated with a quiet lyricism that matches the best work of Zerubbabel Collins in Vermont. This

Fig. 71. The Park family stone, 1803, Burgess Cemetery, Grafton, Vermont. Slate. 38 x 36½.

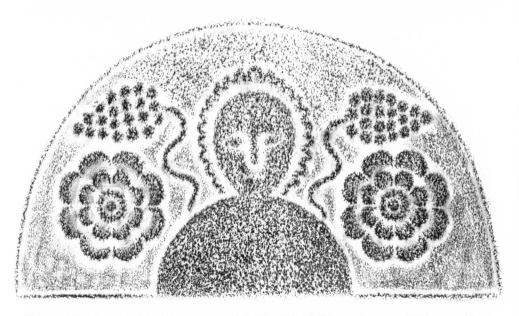

Fig. 72. The Samuel Hinckley stone, 1798, Brookfield, Massachusetts. White marble. 37 x 22⅝.

gravestone is an almost perfect manifestation of the rhetoric of plain style. A simple central figure exists within a decorative yet highly meaningful ambience. Although the stonecarver simplified the design that he shared with needle-workers, he gave the iconography a heightened poignancy and relevance through its placement in the funereal context.

Even though individual markers were erected most frequently, images of deceased husbands and wives sharing a single gravestone were not uncommon. John and Mary Pember were early settlers of Franklin, Connecticut, and after their successive deaths in 1782 and 1783, a granite monument was erected that bears a dual portrait (*Fig. 75*). Identically rendered with highly stylized, mask-

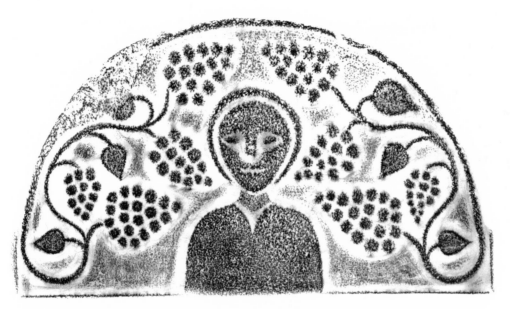

Fig. 73. The Mary Hinckley stone, 1798, Brookfield, Massachusetts. White marble. 34 x 21½.

Fig. 74. Embroidered linen petticoat border, eighteenth century. *Courtesy of Museum of Fine Arts, Boston, Gift of Mrs. Maxim Karolik.*

Fig. 75. The Mary and John Pember stone, 1783, Franklin, Connecticut. Granite. 33 x 25¾.

Fig. 76. The Lieutenant Moses and Susannah Willard stone, 1797, Charlestown, New Hampshire. Slate. 55 x 28¼.

like faces, the couple stare outward. The carver surpassed the iconographic conventions of his craft by placing the Pember figures within a bower that varies the phrasing on the Mary Hinckley stone. A fir tree both separates and joins the two figures, not only isolating them in death but also suggesting their union. The two figures are further joined spiritually by means of the flowers that curve above their heads.

In conception, at least, the realization of the same values seems to have been intended for the gravestone for Lieutenant Moses Willard and his wife Susannah (*Fig. 76*), erected in 1797 after her death. (According to the epitaph, he died much earlier, in 1756, at the hands of Indians.) In execution, however, the effect is substantially different from the Pember stone. Although the design, which includes in this instance a guardian angel or a spiritually transmuted being, was intended to dramatize the transition from this world to the next, it succeeds primarily in showing the deceased as powerful figures estranged by death.

In two related parts the work presents the restrictions of human existence culminating in death and the release afforded by spiritual resurrection. The figures, in three-quarter elevation, stand erect and face the viewer. To the extent that the vertical folds of their dress accentuate their height, they are enclosed within the restrictive arch of the tympanum border, and are further bounded and separated by tulips, the stamens of which are cruciform. Although this motif is repeated in a Trinitarian structure, the spiritual locus is to be found in the winged figure seated on the center of the arch above the two portraits of the deceased. He alone is not confined within a border, although one foot is carved within that band, possibly suggesting either his emergence from the world beneath as a spiritual metamorphosis of the deceased, or his ability to traverse the two worlds as a guardian angel, or both.

The clever placement of the angel's foot, however, brings the only movement to an otherwise static presentation. Far from dramatizing metamorphoses of the spirit, the chosen forms emphasize the stasis of death. The stiffness of the effigies is accentuated by the envelopment of their arms within their clothing, and further reinforcing their restriction is their confinement between the rigid tulips. Like the grape clusters of the Mary Hinckley stone, these flowers refer to the Crucifixion, without, however, any sense of redemption, Trinitarian overtones notwithstanding. The bower that shelters the Pembers has been replaced by a geometric band, which contributes to abstraction and harshness. Thus on the Willard stone boldness of forms describes the grimness of death, unrelieved by the regeneration of Christianity. The bold Pember figures may bear expressions of sadness too, but their ambience suggests the joy and hope possible in resurrection. The Willard stone avoids sentimentality, but it is also devoid of sentiment, the lack of which intensifies a sense of humanity estranged.

The Willard stone also stands in marked contrast to the marble gravestone erected for Elisha and Rebekah Cowles (*Fig. 77*) of Meriden, Connecticut. The carver depicted husband and wife in low-relief profile. Although the carver made little attempt at individual likeness, a sense of portraiture is suggested by his use of intersecting oval frames, reminiscent of the cameo or silhouette portraits popular at the time. The strength of this dual portrait is not to be attributed to its faithfulness to human form but rather to the inclusion of a pendant heart between the two figures. In formal terms, the heart interlocks the two ovals far better than simple intersection. Moreover, the heart, combined with the felicitous positioning of the couple, emphasizes the intimacy of marriage. Their inward turning lessens the didacticism generated by frontal display, and creates a feeling of privacy that is placed within a spiritual context by the use of the heart and the epitaph: "Heaven gives friends / Why should we complain / If heaven resumes / Our friends again." A potential sentimentality that would later permeate nineteenth-century funerary artifacts was here kept in check by a simple acquiescence to God's will.

Fig. 77. The Elisha and Rebekah Cowles stone, 1799, Meriden, Connecticut. White marble. 52 x 28.

Whereas adult portraiture was particularly geared to the religious presuppositions of the Puritans, their theological schema was inadequate to responding fully to the death of a child, and thus rendered consolation and portrayal difficult. Even Cotton Mather, with his immense store of orthodox piety, was unable to reconcile or explain to his own satisfaction the reasons and causes leading to and defining "The Special Case," as he termed the "untimely death of children" in a funeral sermon in 1689. On such occasions Mather observed that "many carry themselves under the tryal, as if, *A Death of Vertue,* yea as if, *A Death of Reason,* had therewithal befallen them." To counter this derangement, Mather offered one of his "right thoughts in sad hours" (as he had entitled the sermon) in exhortation: "But recollect yourselves, O dejected Christians, and be not like them that *Mourn without Hope* this day. Let *Bereaved* Parents be yet *Believing* Parents."[13]

The witty aphorism was inadequate, however, even for Mather, for he immediately conceded that it "is indeed very true, That this Affliction is none of the most easie to be born; the Heart of a *Parent* will have peculiar Passions working in it, and racking of it, at such a time as this."[14] Although Mather appropriated the traditional sermonic form of biblical text, derived doctrine, and application, the logical structure could not bear the weight of these intense feelings. Mather himself perceived that the "death of reason" demanded a logic beyond itself to match the "peculiar passions" of mourning parents if faith were to be sustained and affirmed. And so he engaged the congregation in an exploration of language, a quest for metaphor that would meet their needs.

Tracing through the mortality of a child, Mather portrayed him as "a *broken* Pitcher, or a *blasted Flower*," only to develop the last metaphor into "*Plants grown up in their Youth*," and so to move from an image of death to one of life. Mather ultimately sought a transcendent vision, but he admitted that "no Tongue is able to express, or Heart conceive" the comfort and beauty of children resting in Christ. No tongue indeed, for Mather's creation of a figurative language, while coherent in this particular motif, was restless and occasionally strained, so that he could only conclude, "I have done," as though exhausted in his effort, and forced to accept the biblical assurance, "Of such is the Kingdom of Heaven."[15]

Mather's silence was voiced, however, by a letter of consolation from Edward Taylor, his elder colleague on the frontier in Westfield, Massachusetts. Appended to the published sermon, the note might have been read to the congregation. In a brief passage Taylor asked that they acquiesce to the Lord's "all-disposing Providence, whereby he picks and chooses what Flowers please him best. We have nothing too sweet for Him."[16] Like Mather, Taylor quoted the standard theological position, and like Mather, he couched his argument in terms of a conventional metaphor.

However, Taylor recognized the limits of stock piety, and so suggested, "I sometimes have been refresh'd in like Cases by such Thoughts as these," followed by the final two stanzas of his personal elegy, "Upon Wedlock and Death of Children." Unlike Mather, Taylor did not strain for effect, as his language became the vehicle of faith. The movement from prose to poetry is all of a piece. Indeed, he picked up the floral image of the note and intensely modulated its verbal possibilities in his "thoughts":

> I pausing on't, this sweet refresh'd my thought,
> Christ would in Glory have a Flower sweet, prime,
> And having Choice, chose this my branch forth brought:
> Lord tak't: I thank Thee, Thou tak'st ought of mine.
>   It is my Pledge in Glory: Part of me
>   Is glorifi'd in it, now, Lord with Thee.[17]

What appeared to be a simple image informing a pithy message in the manner of the plain style becomes in retrospect energized and rendered fully complex, as flower, branch, and parent's voice reverberate in Christ. Taylor's reference to his verse as "thoughts" suggests, to be sure, that his eye was on the meaning, but also, and most significantly, that the meaning resides in the form of lan-

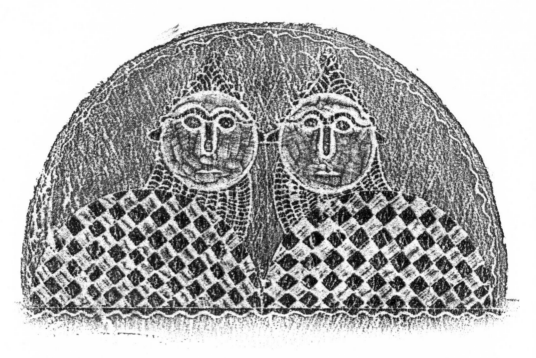

Fig. 78. The Bellows children stone, 1799, Rockingham, Vermont. Slate. 18¾ x 11¾.

guage, the suprarational configuration of which assumed the mode of meditation upon the mysteries of life.[18]

The juxtaposition of sermon, note, and verse clearly suggests the importance of symbolic expression for the Puritans. Taylor's was originally a
private elegy, but the convention was just as often made public as part of the
funeral rites. In like manner, some resolution to the questions left unanswered
by the theologians appears to have been offered on a popular level by the stonecarvers. In any graveyard there are a large number of stones erected to mark the
graves of children. Generally, these stones tend to be smaller in size and more
conservative in design than those for adults, quite possibly because the child
was not yet a visible saint, nor had he developed the importance of character
and form as a member of the community at large. Regardless, the death of a
child assumed complex dimensions that stonecarvers were sometimes moved
to articulate.

The gravestone erected for the Bellows children of Rockingham, Vermont,
in 1799 is small, measuring barely 18¾ by 11¾ inches (*Fig. 78*). But on its face
the carver expressed a complex of values that could help assuage otherwise in-
consolable grief. Lightly etched are portraits of the two children shown bundled

in their patchwork coverlets, their heads covered with what appear to be peaked, lace stocking-caps. Quite obviously, the portrayal concentrates upon the image of sleep as a metaphor for death. In depicting the children in a somewhat roused position, however, the carver suggests the possibility of spiritual resurrection. Considered in these terms alone, the image might well have been a mere euphemism for death, a sentimental cover-up for the horrors as perceived by Puritan orthodoxy on the wane. The Bellows children stone did not so degenerate. By selecting an identical vocabulary to limn both children, the carver went beyond particularized portraiture to express the universal implications of death. The figures against a blank background offer a stark statement that is reinforced by the terse epitaph:

> In Memory of
> Two Infants a Son,
> and a Daughter, of
> Elijah & Louisa
> Bellows. they Died,
> March 2th 1799.

This statement of fact is in turn followed by a brief couplet: "Sleep on sweet babes & take your rest / god cald you home he thought it best." The first line verbally echoes the visual image, while the second summarizes the laconic elements of the stone by acquiescing to God's will. In this way, through a modulation of fact and emotion, the gravestone resolves human grief without succumbing to sentimentality.

The several stones that attest to stonecarvers' solutions to the death of a mother and her child reveal a different and intense sensitivity. The theological complexities concerning the death of a child became almost intolerable when compounded by the death of the mother in the act of giving birth. However insistent the logic of Original Sin, the dual loss of mother and child revealed the work of God at its most arbitrary and unyielding, even to the most faithful and enlightened. Asked by the surviving husband to cut a marker for the common grave of his wife and child, the carvers in these instances responded in a manner that transcended the banal with a poignant simplicity of statement which balanced a matter-of-fact acceptance with the emotional upheaval of the bereaved. These mother-and-child stones fell into two categories: those that visually show the multiple deaths as iconic signs of the deceased, and those that attempt to indicate the maternal relationship, now lost to the surviving community. A visible intimacy rooted in the unique nature of the personal loss determined a visual vocabulary apprehended by the community as a means of

Fig. 79. The Mary Briant and children stone, 1724, Norwell, Massachusetts. Slate. 29 x 23¼.

alleviating otherwise insoluble religious issues. The concept of spiritual resurrection was subordinated to a primary statement that reinforced the universal human condition of motherhood at its most sorrowful.

In the first category belongs the marker that Thomas Briant of Norwell, Massachusetts, selected for his wife and twins in 1774 (*Fig. 79*). The unknown carver solicited for the work cut many stones in this area of the south shore of Massachusetts Bay in a curious combination of Jacobean total-field design and the linear carving technique so commonly used in New England. The Mary Briant stone, presenting three essentially identical crowned skulls with wings, is not unique in terms of content or emblematic vocabulary, but within these bounds it does attempt to depict the loss of the mother and her children. The shape of the skull continues the shorthand "light-bulb" configuration with dart and feathered wings protruding from behind the cranial area. Hollow and round eye sockets, triangular nose definition, and an x-row of teeth indicating the mandible area all have precedents in the established gravestone traditions of Boston to the north and Plymouth County to the south.

The remarkable aspect of this stone lies in the fact that the carver consciously disregarded his standard use of the etched pinwheel capitals upon the double-pilaster decoration and replaced these motifs with identical, albeit smaller, versions of the winged skull. Although these emblems are similar in visual and metaphoric terms, there is no complex organic relationship of Mary Briant to her twins Nathaniel and Hannah, who were eight and nine days old. The emblems for the children are removed from the central image within the tympanum area to the pilaster capitals. Subordinate to the death's-head for the mother, these emblems are discrete units, and their placement on the stone suggests the dominance of an analytic impulse characteristic of the plain-style aesthetic that held sway over Boston's gravestones of the previous century.

The Mary Briant stone attempts, nevertheless, to portray visually the deaths of the mother and her children, whereas the stone of Eastford, Connecticut, raised by Constant Hart in 1752 for his wife Sarah and son Benjamin makes no such attempt for the dual loss (*Fig. 80*). While the single pictographic visage with a pair of pigtails curving outward bears considerable charm, the son's death is noted only in the text. In much the same manner, only a tentative gesture toward portraiture was achieved on the Rebekah Clark stone of Cheshire, Connecticut, in 1785 (*Fig. 81*). Merely echoing the cherub above, the line-cut cherub placed within the text in the manner of manuscript marginalia establishes little maternal-filial bond of any but the most verbal sort.

On the marker for Betty Lane and her twins (*Fig. 82*) of Rockingham, Vermont, some sixty-seven years later in a remote area of New England, the visual statement of the relationship is modified. Here again, the images representing Betty Lane and her unnamed twins are shown as symbols of spiritual resurrection. Defined by triangularly segmented auras, anthropomorphic suns as symbols of Christ are placed together within the central arch. The epitaph unfolds the visual meaning of the images:

> Our flesh shall slumber in the ground,
> 'Till the last trumpet's joyfull sound;
> Then burst the chains with sweet surprise,
> And in our Saviour's image rise.

In contrast to the Mary Briant stone, the maternal relationship of Betty Lane to her twins is partially strengthened by the grouping of all three images within the central arch. The inclusion of a heart lightly cut beneath the central sun, presumably designating the mother, increases the quality of portraiture. This image not only alludes to the idea of the heart as the human seat of spiritual metamorphosis but also serves to suggest the person of Betty Lane. The tip of the form is not symmetrical but turned, giving a distinct impression of movement in an otherwise static presentation of resurrection.

In the same graveyard behind the Rockingham Meeting House is the Sally Morrison stone of 1799 (*Fig. 82*), which moves from the emblematic emphases of the Briant and Lane markers toward a more pronounced expressiveness of the mother and child relationship. As discrete images, the sons Jonathan and Samuel are smaller copies of the central Sally Morrison figure. Rigid and unyielding, the figures are rooted to the base line and enclosed within the tympanum. Creased, wrinkled, and almost shapeless within the heavily articulated linear outlines, age becomes irrelevant, and any anticipated spiritual sojourn is negated. Jonathan Morrison perhaps conveyed an attitude of in-

Fig. 80. The Sarah Hart and child stone, 1752, Eastford, Connecticut. Schist. 26½ x 27½.

Fig. 81. The Rebekah Clark and child stone, 1785, Cheshire, Connecticut. Red sandstone. 41 x 21½.

Fig. 82. The Betty Lane and children stone, 1791, Rockingham, Vermont. Slate. 36½ x 25½.

evitable and irrevocable loss to the stonecarver. His son Samuel was nearly two years old in 1792, and Jonathan was "one year 3 months and 26 days" in 1798. The final loss of his wife in July 1799, at thirty-three years (possibly through birth complications, although such a fact is not stated), may have encouraged this interpretation by the stonecarver.

The presence of the mother-and-child image, as shaped by the Christian tradition and embodied in the iconography of the Virgin Mary with her infant Jesus, appeared but twice during the first century and a half of gravestone carving in New England. Both examples were carved in Newport by John Stevens III while he was still a very young man. The sculptural qualities as well as the fluidity of form would indicate that Stevens carved the marker for Mrs. Mercy Buliod and her son Peter (*Fig. 84*) after the Phyllis Lyndon Stevens marker (*Fig. 85*), even though the latter is dated 1773, two years after the former. Unfortunately cut on slate of poor quality, the surface of the Lyndon stone is rough, scaled, and weatherworn. Here the figures of the mother with her newborn infant are angular, intensified by the crossed arrows adjacent. The stiffness of the mother is far more reminiscent of the limner likeness of *Mrs. Elizabeth Freake and Baby Mary* (*Fig. 86*), probably painted in 1674, than of the stone for Mrs. Buliod and her son, dated some two years earlier.

For the latter, Stevens achieved a sculptural rather than a linear effect,

Fig. 83. The Sally Morrison and children stone, 1799, Rockingham, Vermont. Slate. 33 x 25½.

Fig. 84. The Mercy Buliod and child stone, 1771, Old Common Burying-ground, Newport, Rhode Island. Slate. 29 x 22.

accentuated in part by the fluidity of forms. Thus he excluded the crossed arrows and the formal draperies from the Buliod stone and enclosed the mother and child, rendered in three-quarter profile, within a womb-like ambience. They relate to one another as part of a single mass. Only the most subtle linear extension of the right shoulder of the mother differentiates the baby's torso from the body of Mrs. Buliod. Without cluttering the small area with hands and arms, Stevens chose this manner of closeness to resolve a complicated and ambitious visual problem.

By borrowing an iconographic convention to depict a mother and child, Stevens softened the statement of loss that was explicitly and directly carved on

Fig. 85. The Phillis Lyndon [Stevens] and child stone, 1773, Old Common Burying-ground, Newport, Rhode Island. Slate. 27 x 22½. *Courtesy of American Antiquarian Society, Worcester, Massachusetts.*

two rural markers: the Mary Harvey stone of 1785 in Deerfield, Massachusetts (*Fig. 87*), and the Esther Corwin stone of 1797 in Franklin, Connecticut (*Fig. 88*). On both these stones euphemistic niceties in visual and verbal terms were eliminated to intensify the stark reality of death. All else was subordinated to the direct representation of the mother and child, side by side, in a single coffin.

In the earlier and more plainly conceived stone for Mary Harvey, a horizontal area within the definition of the tympanum is filled with a long hexagonal coffin. Completely occupying the open end of the coffin are the molded figures of Mary, the wife of Simeon Harvey, and "on her left / Arm lieth the Infant / which was still / Born." Similar to the portrayal of the physical oneness of Mercy Buliod and her son, Mary Harvey and her infant are eternally enclosed within the unyielding configuration of the grave. This simple statement implies little beyond the limits of the vocabulary used.

The starkness of the Harvey stone is matched by the marker for Esther Corwin and her child, erected some twelve years later in rural Connecticut. To be sure, the latter displays some double semicircles as cloud forms, which, by their inclusion, seem to offer some promise of salvation; but the affirmation of the stone lies elsewhere—in its achieved presence of both memorial and icon. The mother is shown cradling her infant within the open end of a coffin, the substance and structure of which are identical with the schist slab. And the

Fig. 86. Mrs. Elizabeth Freake and Baby Mary, oil on canvas by unknown painter, *c.* 1674. 42½ x 36¾. *Courtesy of Worcester Art Museum, Worcester, Massachusetts.*

Fig. 87. The Mary Harvey and child stone, 1785, Deerfield, Massachusetts. Slate. 32 x 19⅛.

Fig. 88. The Esther Corwin and child stone, 1797, Franklin, Connecticut. Granite. 31 x 23½.

image itself is highly expressive, with the left arm of Esther Corwin enveloping, as a wing, the form of the helpless child. Although the figures are not commensurate in scale with the size of the open coffin, they are, in their bulk and lack of detail, consonant with the coarse quality of the schist material. In this instance image, structure, and substance combine to create a unique monument to the intersection of life and death.

CHAPTER 6

The Unfolding of Imagery

THE introduction of winged skulls, cherubim, and portraits in seventeenth-century New England, and their subsequent diffusion throughout the next century, indicate the variety of image, phrasing, and style on Puritan gravestones. Although the three basic classes of iconography provide significant historical and cultural patterns, they are maintained only through arbitrary designation against the variegated evidence. And if the classification is confused with aesthetic worth, it is of limited value. The chronological development of the iconography does not support stone portraiture as the artistic culmination of New England stonecarving. As an eighteenth-century phenomenon dependent in great part upon changing cultural values, carved portraits were attained by the same technical skills and aesthetic concerns as those exercised in the previous century for the realization of other images and designs. Throughout this movement the metamorphic impulse took on primary importance for allowing the transmutation of central forms: images beginning as subsidiary elements within the gravestone design could assume central positioning and therefore appear as the primary statement on the stone façade.

In symbolic terms, of course, all the images used were related by virtue of their references to death and/or resurrection. Stonecarvers perceived visual similarities among the diverse forms and worked to exploit their possibilities. While the sheer variety attests in one sense to the vitality of the stonecarver's craft, the ultimate testimony lies in the quality of the gravestones carved. Although the unusual stone may be praised simply because it deviates from the normative imagery, the following works merit attention for their intrinsic aesthetic qualities. Since they range in locale and time, they do not offer a chronological history of metamorphic movement, but they nevertheless do re-

Fig. 89. The Deborah Long stone, 1678, Phipps Street, Charlestown, Massachusetts. Slate. 22 x 20.

veal that crucial process through the efflorescence of forms in the carved designs.

In the Phipps Street Burial Ground of Charlestown stands the plain tripartite marker for Deborah Long (*Fig. 89*). Cut by the Charlestown Carver, the slate stone offers a simple record of particular history. The modest but elegant calligraphy of the numeral one in the year of her death is present elsewhere on the stone by a rectangular complex of voluted hearts. This motif serves as the only decorative accent upon an otherwise empty façade beneath the epitaph. A similar arabesque can be found on the side of a seventeenth-century oak Bible-box (*Fig. 90*). Although the carving upon both artifacts has no especial spiritual signification, its function as a decorative accent certainly indicates the absence of any restriction imposed upon the stonecarver's choice of imagery.

The Charlestown Carver appropriated another motif common to furniture in carving the Cutler children stone in 1680 (*Fig. 14*). The shell, so frequently found on furniture of the Queen Anne period, and so magnificently realized on the mahogany secretary (*Fig. 91*) made by John Goddard for Joseph Brown of Providence about 1760, here served to flank the winged skull. Two years earlier, the Charlestown Carver had used the shell alone on the tympanum of the Marcy Allin stone in Malden, Massachusetts (*Fig. 92*). On both the Cutler and Allin stones, in contradistinction to the decorative treatment on the

Fig. 90. Bible-box, oak, seventeenth century. *Courtesy of Museum of Fine Arts, Boston.*

Fig. 91. Mahogany secretary, by John Goddard, *c.* 1760. *Courtesy of The Rhode Island Historical Society, Providence.*

Fig. 92. The Marcy Allin stone, 1678, Malden, Massachusetts. Slate. 18½ x 17.

Deborah Long marker, the shell assumes metamorphic value, suggesting by its form a sun or a flower, the spiritual implications of which in a funereal context would not have gone unnoticed.

From the earliest work of the Charlestown Carver, expression of the soul's mobility was visually dependent upon the presence of wings on either side of the skull or as part of the cherub. The nature of the wings used in this juxtaposition of elements resembled those of the bird—digital overlaid feathering, with central ribs providing the internal structure. The eventual presence of a whole bird, then, is hardly surprising. Since earliest times, the quickness and freedom of movement of birds have seemed to imply some mystical quality that man has interpreted to his own needs. Just as different species of birds have represented different qualities, hybrid birds such as the cockatrice and the phoenix achieved a reality as a verbal and visual convention that was concrete and readily understood among a widespread populace. In seventeenth-century New England the bird-serpent was the most prevalent hybrid on gravestones. In Boston this motif appeared only once, in a minor way, as the handles of the globe holding the lighted candle in the tableau on the Joseph Tapping stone of 1678 (*Fig. 119*). Further north in Essex County, out of a different stylistic tradition, bird-serpents were frequently carved as interlocking motifs about the central face. The Alice Hart stone of 1682 in Ipswich is an example representative of many such markers in the area (*Fig. 132*).

Not until the eighteenth century, however, were the distinguishing characteristics of a full bird shown on a gravestone. The portrait of 1767 on the Robert

Fig. 93. The Ensign Robert Cutler stone, 1761, Brookfield, Massachusetts. Slate. 27 x 27¼.

Fig. 94. The Agnes Crawford stone, 1760, Rutland, Massachusetts. Slate. 22½ x 23.

Fig. 95. The Lucinda Day stone, 1800, Chester, Vermont. Slate. 24 x 20¾.

Cutler stone in Brookfield, Massachusetts, manifests perhaps the best use of this image as a subsidiary motif (*Fig. 93*). Cut by William Young of Tatnuck, a human figure rises from a base line which is given emphasis by an organic border. In place of wings, Young substituted two birds hovering above the figure's broad shoulders. Seven years earlier he had used this device on the Agnes Crawford stone in Rutland, Massachusetts, where the birds have settled on the shoulders of the central figure (*Fig. 94*). By carving the birds in flight on the Cutler stone, Young heightened the illusion of ascension, implying that the soul of the deceased was being transported to heaven, or alternately, that the deceased had already ascended to heaven, carried there by the birds.

While retaining the bird as the soul's means of ascent, the Lucinda Day stone of 1800 in Chester, Vermont (*Fig. 95*), achieves strength in the unification of disparate conventions to illustrate salvation. Symbolizing ultimate grace, the simple form of the Federal eagle (undoubtedly derived from the limner sign-painter tradition) envelops an effigy within the heart of its belly. The statement, for all its power, is lightly engraved on the slate. The illusion of mass thus economically achieved, delicate lines indicate feathering throughout the wings and define the features within the head and beak as well as within the circular face of the effigy. Through a visual transposition of elements, the eagle's legs serve as extended arms in supplication or farewell. The allusion to the phoenix rising from its own ashes intensifies the anticipation of release from the grave. Although a recurring refrain in this area of Vermont, the last two lines of the

Fig. 96. Sundial and compass (obverse and reverse), brass, *c.* 1636. Diameter, 2½. *Courtesy of The Rhode Island Historical Society, Providence.*

Fig. 97. The Oliver Arnold, Jr., stone, 1716, Cedar Cemetery, Jamestown, Rhode Island. Slate. 29½ x 26½.

verse substantiate this metaphoric representation of the Resurrection: "When God is pleas'd to take away / A Lovely friend of mine."

Using the flight of the eagle (or even the more static representation of the winged skull), the resurrection of body and soul obviously would occur in a moment of eternity. In both its eternal and ephemeral aspects time was most often rendered as an hourglass and assigned the purpose of didactic emphasis within the working vocabulary of the stonecutter's craft. A frequent image throughout the culture, an engraving of an hourglass appears on a bronze sundial (*Fig. 96*), which, according to tradition, belonged to Roger Williams, who carried it to Rhode Island after his exile from Massachusetts in 1636. The measured moments of daily life recorded by this small dial were to pass in harmony with eternity, as the winged hourglass would suggest. Similar concepts of time, contrasting its immutability with the very mutable quality of human life, are proclaimed by the position of the hourglass above the skull within the design of the Thomas Kendel stone (*Fig. 17*). When hourglasses flank the central skull, as on the Oliver Arnold stone of 1716 in Jamestown, Rhode Island (*Fig. 97*), they visually function in place of the customary wings. Echoing the cliché "Time flies," the hourglasses wittily suggest the dual concept of time as ephemeral and yet substantially absolute. The very element which renders human life transient would also evidently offer the possibility of eternal transcendence.

With the exception of the Joseph Tapping stone (*Fig. 19*), on which time functions as a persona within an allegory, the concept of time was apparently difficult to treat visually in a satisfactory way. An early stone which used the hourglass as the central statement was that for Paul Simons (*Fig. 98*), undated but carved most likely within ten years of 1700. This gravestone in The Granary was cut in the manner of William Mumford, in which the tympanum is divided horizontally by a band with a winged hourglass appearing above and a panel of undulant leaves below. In addition to the juxtaposition of the flight of time and the transience of organic matter, there is also the triumph of eternity over ephemeral life; but the values expressed are hardly more profound than the conventional verbal warnings, and in the stone's impersonality they add little feeling or response to the deceased for whom the stone was erected.

The substitution of a winged hourglass for a winged skull was one solution for accommodating the form of the hourglass to the tympanum area, but it was no more successful than that attempted for the Naomi Woolworth stone of Longmeadow, Massachusetts (*Fig. 99*). In some ways this rural marker erected in 1761 hearkened back to the seventeenth century. Rarely since the early work of the Charlestown Carver was a gravestone so used as a compendium of mortuary emblems. Elevated vertically between the base and the arch is an hourglass, its sands very definitely exhausted. In tension with the side of the glass and braced against the upper arch, the long handle and blade of a scythe enclose the space within which stands a candle, its flame about to be enigmatically snuffed out. On the right is a cock, ambiguously alluding to Peter's betrayal and to a new day. The stonecarver made an effort to organize the various images around the central form of the hourglass, but his resolution was less integrative than atomistic, much in the analytic vein of plain style. Unlike most seventeenth-century markers, however, there is little or no hope made manifest by the traditional presence of wings, vines, fruits, or other images indicating the possibility of salvation. The power of this marker is derived from the verbal text, accentuating all the more the weakness of the imagery and its design. The epitaph is not complete, but the two lines that remain legible reinforce the closed world delineated on the tympanum: "Darkness & Death / make Hast at once."

Faced with these difficulties in dramatizing visually such a complex concept as time, stonecarvers generally retained the hourglass as a minor image. The coffin, too, had been used in a didactic decorative manner by stonecarvers in the Boston area, where, as an emblem of death, it hardly seemed promising as a major image, especially given the prevailing Christian assumptions of spiritual metamorphosis. Although the coffin remained a subsidiary image in eastern Massachusetts, it developed as an integrated and powerful central statement on gravestones located in east central Connecticut, with isolated occurrences northward into Massachusetts along the Connecticut River. All of these known stones utilizing the rigid and unyielding definition of the hexagonal pine coffin were erected after 1750.

The appearance in Connecticut and western Massachusetts of gravestones whose statements focus on the interment act itself is possibly a manifestation

Fig. 98. The Paul Simons stone, c. 1700, The Granary, Boston, Massachusetts. Slate. 15 x 18¾.

Fig. 99. The Naomi Woolworth and child stone, 1760, Longmeadow, Massachusetts. Red sandstone. 37 x 21¼.

Fig. 100. The Pember children stone, 1786, Franklin, Connecticut. Granite. 26 x 22.

of the unrestrained literal-mindedness of the rural residents. Thus the grave-stones of 1785 for Mary Harvey of Deerfield (*Fig. 87*) and that of 1786 for the three Pember sons of Franklin (*Fig. 100*) offer coffin imagery in such a way that the resting place of death is unrelieved of finality. On the Mary Harvey stone the coffined figures are laid horizontally and inclined on the right side, thereby facing the viewer in a pose of complete acquiescence to physical death. Although the three coffins designating the Pember sons are positioned vertically, there is no visual or verbal hint of possible rebirth or resurrection. The delineation of the coffins indicates the visual persistence of Ramist discourse, which informed the conventional woodcut designs for death notices in the contemporary press. This analytic impulse is further reflected by the placement of the coffins within the beginning of the text bearing the Christian names of the parents. The emblems do not exist in their own right but primarily as illustrative support of the epitaph. After the specific information of the names, ages, and dates of death of the three children, there follows the familiar short couplet of parental resignation: "Sleep sweet babes & take your rest / God called you home He thought it best."

The visual rendering of the deceased person's body—whether interred clothed, shrouded, or bewigged—could nevertheless suggest spiritual transcendence. By providing a mirror of immediate existence after death—that is, the shrouded and coffined figure—a knowable universality could possibly be stated or implied.[1] When further combined with traditional elements indicating resurrection, the coffined form takes on definite affirmative meaning, as it does on the Bridget Snow and Roswell Ensworth stones of Mansfield Center and Canterbury, both in Connecticut. These markers deal in similar ways with the theological questions of physical death and the promise of Christian resurrection by using essentially the same elements of design.

The tympanum area on the Bridget Snow stone of 1768 (*Fig. 101*) contains and controls the carved statement. Elevated vertically from the base line of the tympanum, the coffin rests in a seemingly precarious position. Flowered vines interact with the more substantial plant growth on either side of the coffin and hold its rigid shape in tension against the high outer arch. The ropelike vines achieve a delicate balance by sustaining the base of the coffin in its upright position. This structure gives the distinct feeling that the coffin would topple forward if permitted, and thus alludes to the ropes used to lower the coffin into the ground.

Despite the presence of flowered vines, both on the tympanum and along the full length of the pilasters as well, the prevailing hope of resurrection remains incomplete. The structure is unsound and tentative, especially in consideration of the epitaph verse:

> My Lover, Friend, Famil-
> iar all—Remov'd from
> Sight and out of Call,
> To dark Oblivion is retir'd
> Death or at Least [to] me Ex[pired.]

The triumph of the tomb in this case seems understood and accepted by the living poet who speaks, rather than the deceased. His lament emphasizes only the finality of death and withholds the possibility of salvation.

The problem of how to treat the vertical open coffin was more satisfactorily solved by the same, or a closely associated, carver of the Roswell Ensworth stone (*Fig. 102*) some eight years later. Here the conservative considerations regulating the outline of the gravestone have been modified to obviate the necessity of carving only within the tympanum arch and so to allow an integration of design within the total stone. The lowering of the arch, with the resultant broadening effect, permits a horizontal emphasis of the pine trees with peacocks perched in their tops facing each other above the central coffin.

Fig. 101. The Bridget Snow stone, 1768, Mansfield Center, Connecticut. Granite. 38 x 27¾.

Fig. 102. The Roswell Ensworth stone, 1776, Canterbury, Connecticut. Granite. 39 x 24.

The coils not only balance the main design but also provide relief from the rigid and solid quality of the carving technique. Then, too, the coils assume some added strength because the pilaster areas are negative panels topped by insignificant semicircles.

The shifting of the coffin into the text area results in surface integration by dissolving the traditional base-line of the tympanum. Further unity is achieved through a textual reference in which the deceased speaks directly to the viewer:

> Here in the bloom of
>   Life I lye
> To bleed & pine away
>   and die
> I warn all friends both
>   old and young
> Not to live a life as I have
>   done.

Ensworth died when he was twenty-two years old, and quite possibly his life had been less than satisfactory to his parents. Although this quatrain may well have been a conventional funereal verse for the area, its component parts were abstracted and visually articulated so that its didactic limitations are transcended. A pun on "pine" is made not only in terms of the material utilized in the coffin, illustrated above on the stone and palpably in the ground beneath, but also in terms of the carved pine trees and those in the graveyard, below both of which he was interred. The notion of physical and psychic disintegration (to "pine away") is counteracted by the growth of the trees, a traditional Christian metaphor, which take sustenance from his interred body. The visual and verbal wit central to the affirmation of resurrection is explicitly reinforced by a plea of mercy and supplication in the final two lines: "I with a smile look up to God & cry / Receive my soul that I in peace may die." Ensworth's smile of salvation is irrepressibly dramatized upon the marker itself.

As traditional symbols of Christ, vines and pine trees might understandably appear on the Bridget Snow and Roswell Ensworth stones respectively. Along with the fruited pilasters of the Reverend Jonathan Pierpont stone (*Fig. 27*) in Wakefield, Massachusetts, these motifs were drawn from the prototypical organic elements on the frieze of the Kendel stone (*Fig. 17*). Likewise, flowers have always been prominent as organic metaphors of regenerative impulse in Christian iconography. Perhaps the earliest gravestone with flowers having central importance was that cut for Ruth Carter in 1697/98 (*Fig. 115*), though here the flowers are still used in conjunction with the skeletons on the pilasters.

Fig. 103. The Thaddeus Maccarty stone, 1705, The Granary, Boston, Massachusetts. Slate. 27 x 27¼.

The Thaddeus Maccarty stone (*Fig. 103*) of 1705, also in The Granary, was the first, however, to exclude all emblems of mortality in its floral presentation.

Most likely cut by J. N., the tympanum shows a fantasy of flowers and leaves emerging from a root and stem cluster at the base. This imaginative design, realized in part by its asymmetricality, indicates with certainty a reference to crewel embroidery rather than close botanical observation or a standardized rendering derived from the stonecutter's collection of motifs. An example of crewel embroidery, an eighteenth-century bedspread from New England, reveals the stonecarver's attempt to duplicate the texture of stitch and color shadings (*Fig. 104*). The modulated depth of the carving parallels the buildup of thread and varied use of stitch such as the flat, herringbone, and bullion in rope, as well as interlaced patterns. The most striking effect, however, occurs in the articulation of leaves, whereby the greatest height rendered on the broad flat leaf is equivalent to the deepest green on the embroidered one, its lighter tones achieved upon the stone by lessening the relief.

That this particular floral arrangement was commonly known is indicated by the woodcut design for the first chapter heading of a funeral sermon for the Reverend John Cotton. Published in London in 1658, John Norton's sermon *Abel Being Dead Yet Speaketh* bears a printed embellishment (*Fig. 105*) similar in form to the embroidery and the gravestone. The woodcut, however, gives but scant illusion of depth to the various flowers and leaves, whereas the embroidery and the marker do realize a plastic effect each in its way. Although the printed illustration may have been the carver's source because of Mac-

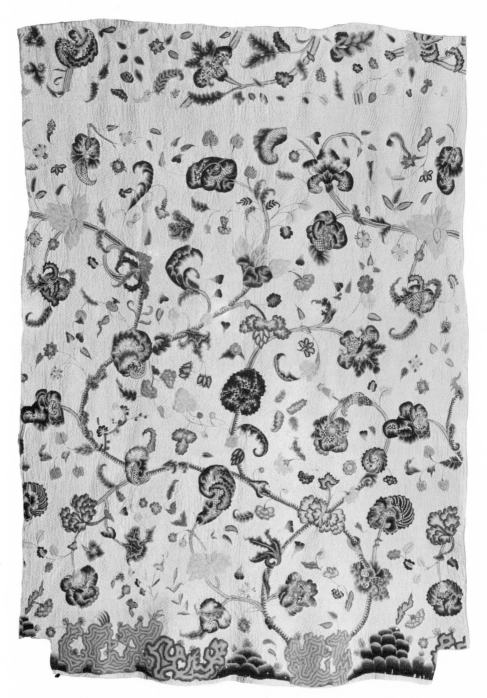

Fig. 104. Bedspread, embroidery and crewel work, New England, eighteenth century. *Courtesy of Museum of Fine Arts, Boston. Gift of Miss G. Emery.*

Fig. 105. Illustration cut for *Abel Being Dead Yet Speaketh*, funeral sermon for John Cotton by John Norton, London, 1658. *Courtesy of The John Carter Brown Library, Brown University, Providence.*

Fig. 106. The Captain Simon Sartwell, Jr., stone, 1791, Charlestown, New Hampshire. Slate 37¼ x 27¾.

carty's interest in publishing, the crewel embroidery is closer in feeling to the carving than the woodcut is. But though the embroidery is essentially decorative, the flowers in their profusion become metaphors of spiritual resurrection in the context of the funeral sermon and the gravestone.

Whereas the urban provenance of the Maccarty stone offered a relatively wide range of visual expression, the gravestone for Captain Simon Sartwell, Jr., of 1791 in rural Charlestown, New Hampshire, bears a unique floral design (*Fig. 106*). In association with an image of the human face—whether a portrait of the deceased or a soul effigy is irrelevant—the plants and blossoms suggest a popularly established optimism of Christian salvation, achieved through the known reality of physical death but with anticipation of the resurrection of body and soul.

Centered on the base of the tympanum is a firmly banded face. A pendant nose and fish-shaped eyes are the most deeply carved, the eyebrows, mouth, and hair arrangement having been but lightly engraved. Tangent on either side both to the circular band and the tympanum arch are two amorphous masses out of which emerge three curving tulip stems, the longest meeting at the apex of the arch. The blossoms are comprised of three petals with a center cross, identical to those separating the figures on the Willard stone (*Fig. 76*) in the same graveyard. The floral apex is also a threefold composite, with an additional blossom perpendicular to the base line as a joint offshoot of the plants on either side. Suspended from this complex is a cluster of grapes, the point of which rests above the head.

The bulbous elements used by silversmiths for urns and bowls seem to have little correspondence to the heavy masses on this stone. These may represent fertile clods of earth from which such tall, strong plants might gain sustenance. But whereas there is only a bit of grassy turf shown on the Thaddeus Maccarty stone, the implicit decomposition of mulch metaphorically parallels the eventual decay of the interred body. This transformation is suggested by the equality of bulk of the three masses. The rigidity of the coffinlike frame enclosing the face is relieved on the interior by the presence of leaves, which suggest the paradox of the natural cycle by which dead vegetation provides vitality for living.

The acceptance of a natural order in the lower area of the tympanum is curiously complemented by the rational simplicity of the floral construction above. The emerging stems, flowers, and leaves must react against the outer arch because of the limitations of the stone's shape. But there is no attempt to change the traditional form of the stone to allow greater freedom of design as on the Ensworth marker of Connecticut or on those stones cut by Zerubbabel Collins in western Vermont. Here, rather, carved within the strict confines of the given limitations of the prescribed shape, the flowers must defer to the arch and meet at the apex. The pressure that they exert against the arch repeats the tensions that animate the face within the bounds of the coffin. In the implicit upward movement of the blossoms, the grapes as the blood of Christ could literally raise the deceased. The mechanistic dynamics of this closed system serve as an analogue for the resurrection of body and soul.

The use of floral motifs was not always so affirmative as it was on the Mac-

Fig. 107. The Eunice Colton stone, 1763, Longmeadow, Massachusetts. Red sandstone. 37 x 22.

carty or Sartwell stones. The heavy red sandstone marker for Eunice Colton of Longmeadow, Massachusetts (*Fig. 107*), cut in 1768 in flat raised relief, shows within a sweep of clouds a scythe wielded by an undisclosed force, cutting a blossom from its rooted stem. Death appears to be a closed ending, as certain as the immediate fate of a cut flower. Although Father Time traditionally swung the scythe, his omission from the carving gives a particularly ominous feeling to the finality of death.

The image possessed a common poetic tradition in New England, extending back to Edward Taylor. In the horrific poignancy of the poem "Upon Wedlock, and Death of Children," a flower becomes the essential metaphor for Taylor's child:

> But oh! a glorious hand from glory came
>   Guarded with Angells, soon did Crop this flowre
> Which almost tore the root up of the same
>   At that unlookt for, Dolesome, darksome houre.

Following the successive deaths of his children, Taylor felt that his strength and deliverance lay in submission to the Lord:

> That as I said, I say, take, Lord, they're thine.
> I piecemeale pass to Glory bright in them.
> I joy, may I sweet Flowers for Glory breed,
> Whether thou getst them green, or lets them seed.[2]

Although the Eunice Colton stone does not offer affirmation in precisely such terms, there are indications that death does not end at the grave.

The epitaph's allusion to Job 17:11, "My days are past, my purposes are broken off," reinforces only in part the image of the cut flower upon the tympanum. Significantly, the rest of the verse " . . . even the thoughts of my heart" is not included, possibly indicating that the finality portrayed on the carving is not complete: the deceased has gained immortality, or, at the very least, mourners survive to recall her life. Likewise, the stasis of the design is relieved by the falling of the flower, a motion which suggests that death is a process rather than an immutable event. Most important, perhaps, is the stonecarver's disregard for scale—the flower, scythe, and clouds being of equal size—which here intensifies the magnitude and mystery of the event. Such rendering invests the occurrence with significance, and thus indirectly affirms the particular importance of Eunice Colton in her death.

The heart, though traditionally considered to be the seat of human emotions, appeared less frequently than floral or other organic imagery, and then it was most often a minor detail within the design. On the Elizabeth Morton stone (*Fig. 70*), for example, the figure of the deceased is portrayed wearing a heart-shaped locket. This seemingly naturalistic detail has spiritual import, to be sure, though the heart remains but one small element of the total portrait. As the form of the hourglass on the Joseph Tapping stone (*Fig. 119*) would indicate, the heart was often disguised in the design. Occasionally, however, the disguised heart was an important part of the meaning to be conveyed, as the visual pun on the Mary Hirst stone (*Fig. 10*) suggests. On the John Churchill stone (*Fig. 26*) in Plymouth and the Lucinda Day stone (*Fig. 95*) in Chester, Vermont, the heart does serve as an integral part of the structure of the primary image.

The hearts on the tympanum of the John Felt stone (*Figure 108*) in Rockingham, Vermont, were cut as a set of scales, love and mercy in balance over the soul of the deceased. Although this complex recalls the morphology of the earlier cherub and winged skull, the hearts in this instance are not the means of ascent, but rather state that judgment is imminent. The hard-edged forms, though possibly the result of the technical limitations of linear stonecutting, nonetheless suggest the proper coming together of God's reason and mercy in the salvation of the deceased: "Jesus my king did every death [un]sting."

Fig. 108. The John Felt stone, 1805, Rockingham, Vermont. Slate. 33 x 22¼.

Fig. 109. The Sarah Long stone, 1674, Phipps Street, Charlestown, Massachusetts. Slate. 26 x 27.

The use of the heart on the Felt stone can hardly be considered ancillary. Rarely, however, did this image achieve such an explicit, untrammeled prominence. For example, even on the Sarah Long stone of 1674 in Charlestown (*Fig. 109*), the outlined heart, on which the epitaph was cut, is wedged within the confines of the traditional text area. A winged skull dominates the tympanum, and the decorated pilasters remain discrete.

In contrast, the unknown carver of the Lydia Wood stone (*Fig. 110*) of 1712 in the same graveyard accommodated the tripartite gravestone to the heart. The four usually separate and distinct areas were ignored, as the deeply incised heart fills part of the tympanum, its point resting on the base line of the stone, thereby fluently distorting the pilaster columns. The resultant tablet records in Roman capitals the marriage, age, and date of death of Lydia Wood. The decorative carving that covers all the remaining areas of the face accomplishes a complete elimination of traditional divisions. The exuberant delineation of leaves and berries filling the lower areas creates an organic vitality which is reiterated in the remaining space of the tympanum. A central tulip rises from the top of the heart, its petals slightly fanning against the overriding arch. Emerging on either side from its stem are roses which, with the extending leaves, fill out the irregular space and create a Trinitarian complex. The floral profusion symbolically suggests the spiritual growth of the deceased within the heart of Christ, as she attains her ultimate conversion in heavenly salvation.

The process of transition from this world to the next, central to so many motifs and designs on New England gravestones, necessarily bore cosmic implications. The carving of suns, moons, and stars exists on the Sumner stone (*Fig. 34*), among others. With the exception of the ambiguously rising and setting sun as on the Caesar stone (*Fig. 7*), these motifs generally assumed a subsidiary position in the design. The Sarah Allen stone of 1785, in Bristol, Rhode Island, presents a variation on these cosmological designs with a fully risen sun in the central tympanum (*Fig. 111*). This anthropomorphic sun sounds his horn on Judgment Day. The lesser lights become the "Saints arising," while at the same time, the sun becomes the Son of Righteousness enacting His Second Coming for the redemption of mankind. The relationship between the sun and the lesser figures establishes the illusion of movement, but more importantly, it suggests a tendency toward allegory with a deceptive economy of means. This tendency did in some few instances lead to the conception and execution of allegorical tableaux on gravestones in New England.

Fig. 110. The Lydia Wood stone, 1712, Phipps Street, Charlestown, Massachusetts. Slate. 15 x 17.

Fig. 111. The Sarah Allen stone, 1785, East Burial Ground, Bristol, Rhode Island. Slate. 22 x 15½.

CHAPTER 7

Tableau, Allegory, and Typology

THE allegorical expression of Christian attitudes toward death cannot be considered apart from the more conventional emblematic designs on New England gravestones. The Puritan carver's use of allegory and its related forms was conditioned by the same attitudes that determined the use of emblems. The interplay, moreover, between allegory and emblem was often so fluid as to render hard distinctions arbitrary. Somewhere within a continuum between emblem and fully developed allegory lay what might be called the tableau: a dramatic scene or set piece that was not a failure of the allegorical imagination but rather a visual possibility in its own right which the carver chose to consider. Closely allied with these alternatives was the established convention of typological interpretation used primarily by ministers, who read events that occur in the New Testament in the light of Old Testament prefigurations.[1] Such analysis was certainly made accessible to the stonecarver from the pulpit. Ultimately, these modal complexities stem from the concept of metamorphosis itself —multiple meanings embodied in multiple forms provided the basis for variety and vitality in New England stonecarving.

The Puritan craving for spiritual meaning embraced both simplicity and complexity. Although the Puritans were well aware of the complexities wrought by the inevitable changes of human experience, they passionately sought a simple sign, which was never forthcoming. Tensions caused by a conflict between frustrated anticipations of absolute knowledge and an awareness of transience and illusion lay at the center of their religious sensibilities. On an abstract level, then, the emblems used were concise and simple enough in meaning to satisfy their needs for absolute value. Gravestone iconography when reduced to its literary dimensions is therefore clearly limited in scope.

The complexities of gravestone art become apparent, however, when the emblems are considered in the context of their carved design. The act of cutting forms to embody ambiguous meaning had little to do with inept carving ability, particularly when such metamorphoses were reinforced by consciously conceived formal patterns.

As an obvious consequence, the total pattern of imagery on the gravestone created an artifact of extensive symbolic representation, intended to express the hopes of the living for the departed soul released through death. With these visual possibilities allegorical expression was generally superfluous. Nevertheless, stonecarvers did not exclude an occasional tableau, allegory, or typological rendering from their repertoire of set patterns appropriate for gravestones. Such ventures were not always artistically successful, nor were they even necessarily superior to the dominant emblematic conventions. Like all the others, these gravestones have to be judged individually on their artistic merits, but as a group they bear a certain cultural significance for New England stonecarving. Although gravestones with allegories were few in number and hence numerically insufficient to counter notions that Puritan symbolism was "crabbed and narrow," as one literary critic would have it,[2] this group indirectly emphasizes the complexities of those gravestones that best worked out of the emblematic tradition. Such a contention becomes all the more meaningful when the aesthetic values of the gravestones in the allegorical mode are surveyed.

Although little increase in technical skill or exercise of imagination was required to draw a full skeleton from the simple skull as an emblem of death, broadsides offered frequent examples for such transformations by the stonecarver. The introduction of the skeleton presented not simply an emblematic variation on the expression of mortality but important new possibilities of movement, with dramatic action as well. Whereas the winged skull existed as a symbolic complex, the skeleton could serve as a character within the extended narrative of allegory. Such presentation, however, was but one modulation of the image, as stonecutters treated it not only as a simple emblem, but also as a set figure within a tableau. The specific context in which the image appears identifies the visual mode of expression, as a reading of the following markers will demonstrate.

The William Sinclear stone (*Fig. 112*) of 1753 in Spencer, Massachusetts, suggests the pitfalls of facile classification. Most likely derived from a woodcut, the image is that of a reclining skeleton with one leg outstretched and the other raised, on which rests its extended hand. This pose within a low-vaulted arch reveals a rather macabre yet witty insight into the grave. The static quality of the imagery would indicate a simple emblematic treatment on the part of the stone-carver. Close examination, however, reveals that the Sinclear stone does not offer merely an emblem of death, a didactic reminder of man's ultimate end. The imagery engages in understatement, creating an austere vision that partakes of tableau.

Actually, the Sinclear marker improves upon the image of the skeleton drawn from the body of English funeral broadsides, particularly that of 1691 for George Cokayn (*Fig. 113*).[3] The latter is cluttered with subsidiary emblems that disperse the visual impact of the skeleton, which, in turn, is awkwardly drawn. By comparison, the carver of the Sinclear stone carefully worked within the narrow space he afforded himself, or had available, on the tympanum. He emphasized the horizontal lines of the bones and cleverly distorted the rib cage to give an upward-flowing curve to the skeleton's torso, which rests against a "pillow." While the skeleton comfortably occupies its space, the enveloping vault evokes a sense of subterranean confinement. These very slight tensions look toward the Second Coming, when the grave would be opened, affording reunion of body and soul before Christ.

In contrast to the Sinclear stone, the marker erected some eight years earlier in 1745/46 for Thomas Faunce of Plymouth is a nearly perfect tableau (*Fig. 114*). Its façade presents a world created as a set piece in the realm of art. The stonecarver's success, without resorting to large scale (the stone measures 32 by 22¼ inches), testifies to his graphic power. A skeleton, its visage unfortunately or perhaps ironically marred by time, arrogantly sits upon a winged hourglass, with one arm outstretched, grasping a scythe. The skeleton assumes a regal attitude: death is a king whose reign extends over time.

Death's dominion, however, is not absolute. The central image of stasis, its horrific nature undiminished, is surrounded by motifs of movement and change. Dramatically suspended above the skeleton is a burgeoning shell, which may serve as a crown for the skeleton; but its relationship to the sea suggests a more powerful symbol of eternity than the winged hourglass. The superior position of the shell metamorphically suggests the sun, indicating Christ's victory over death. That the skeleton's right arm meets a cascade of leaves implies that death does not exist in isolation, but is indeed part of the natural process over which the spiritual power of Christ reigns. Organic motifs notwithstanding, the overriding impression of the Faunce stone is one of immobility. In bringing together stylized elements that tend to interact conceptually rather than visually, the stonecarver successfully created an apocalyptic vision frozen upon slate.

Near the close of the previous century (in 1697/98), the Boston artisan J. N.

Fig. 112. The William Sinclear stone, 1753, Spencer, Massachusetts. Slate. 14¼ x 19¾.

Fig. 113. Funeral broadside for George Cokayn, 1691. *Courtesy of British Museum, London.*

Fig. 114. The Thomas Faunce stone, 1745/46, Plymouth, Massachusetts. Slate. 32 x 23¼.

Fig. 115. The Ruth Carter stone, 1697/98, The Granary, Boston, Massachusetts. Slate. 27 x 28¼.

organized the Ruth Carter stone in such a way that the total structure resembles a tableau, even though its façade retains the standard tripartite divisions. These structural ambivalences notwithstanding, the stone achieves its visual impact through subtle qualities of surface movement. An awareness that J. N. boldly transposed elements to areas from those traditionally designated initiates a sense of visual interaction. In a conscious aesthetic decision, he shifted organic motifs from the pilasters to the tympanum: the covered urn which he had previously placed between two Dagons is then replenished with a flower. But at the same time he retained the familiar symmetrical pattern of leaves that profusely overflow from the urn on either side. Implicit in the general form of the floral arrangement is that of the conventional winged skull, a palimpsest that relates to the side panels.

On the pilasters J. N. carved two differently posed skeletons standing on pedestals. The figure on the left indirectly faces the viewer. The right leg is extended forward to the edge of the platform while the left arm is bent at the elbow across the sternum—a posture which suggests that the skeleton is about to step out of the slate façade. Although J. N. was unable to resolve the problem of carving the skeleton on the right in perspective (since the definition of the legs is decidedly awkward), the crossed legs give an illusion of movement as the figure turns away from the viewer and raises one hand in departing gesture.

These motifs surround the plain text, which emphasizes the remains of the deceased ("HERE LYETH BURIED / Y^e BODY OF / RUTH CARTER"). Complementing this statement of fact are the interacting images. The movement of the skeletons suggests even the transience of bones, just as their erect stance posits the hope of some ultimate resurrection from the grave. The panels are subordinate to the tympanum, on which organic profusion defines the life process as change and growth. The skeletons are thus part of this natural regeneration, an analogue for spiritual resurrection determined by the central image of the lily symbolizing Christ.

A year later the carver of the Timothy Lindall stone (*Fig. 116*) in Salem, Massachusetts, reiterated the graphic ambiguities inherent in the Ruth Carter stone. Although the slate façade has an allegorical dimension, as distinct personae interact conceptually and visually, the structure remains discrete in format and hence indeterminate in presentation. While a well defined outline unites the three arches at the top of the marker, the panels are left open to heighten the illusion of communication. Instead of a floral centerpiece on the tympanum the carver used a cherub, its wings outstretched as though to embrace the panel figures. On the left, there is a standing skeleton, its pelvis lightly braced against the text panel and its hollow gaze directed toward Father Time, who appears on the right. Carved in profile, this robust figure marches, or floats, toward the skeleton. Death and eternity, the structure suggests rather tentatively, appear to vie for the remains of the deceased, as hope of spiritual resurrection presides over the inevitable contest. But as the organization of the façade fails to create a vigorous sense of struggle, the dramatic impact of allegorical presentation is lacking.

Such possibilities were more fully realized by the Rebecca Gerrish stone of 1743 (*Fig. 117*) and the Rebecca Sanders stone of 1745/46 (*Fig. 118*), both cut by William Codner.[4] Standing almost side by side in King's Chapel, the two markers present similar narratives: a standing skeleton and a winged male figure

Fig. 116. The Timothy Lindall stone, 1698/99, Salem, Massachusetts. Slate. 20 x 23½.

Fig. 117. The Rebecca Gerrish stone, 1743, King's Chapel, Boston, Massachusetts. Slate. 16 x 30.

Fig. 118. The Rebecca Sanders stone, 1745/46, King's Chapel, Boston, Massachusetts. Slate. 17¾ x 30½.

flank a lighted candle; in turn, vegetation grows upward from the pilasters and penetrates the tympanum area. A simple reading would suggest that Death, in the familiar form of the skeleton, attempts to extinguish the flame, which is representative of human life, while Father Time watches.

Such a reading, however, scarcely considers the subtle visual ambiguities posed by each stone. The presentation of figures on the earlier marker, that cut for Rebecca Gerrish, is loosely structured, thereby muting the dramatic possibilities of the narrative. Nevertheless, there are some contextual advantages, for the characters are distinctly portrayed in their respective roles. The skeleton, one hand delicately touching the flowers, bridges the central space by leaning forward so as to apply the snuffer carefully over the flame. Father Time, in flowing robes, proffers an hourglass to indicate the final moment. His other hand is raised in assent rather than admonition. He seems also to emphasize the moral implications of the situation. As if to heighten the dramatic import of the scene, Codner scored the slate background, creating an atmospheric flow around the participants.

Codner redressed the lack of the dramatic in his second effort, the Rebecca Sanders stone. Though some background scoring is retained, the drama arises in the confrontation between the two figures. The skeleton, rearing backward and grimacing, attempts to extinguish the flame of human life, and Father Time leans forward to fend off the efforts of Death. His free hand clutches an hourglass, here less a didactic emblem than an aggressive weapon. Codner, moreover, in emphasizing the wings of Father Time, sought to underscore the eternal prospects of the deceased. No longer are Father Time and Death viewed as grandiloquent figures, posturing in a stylized, declamatory manner. If somewhat less graceful, and far less domesticated, both personae are powerfully structured, ready for combat. Significantly, the skeleton (as on the Thomas Faunce stone) sturdily clutches the luxuriant vines that emerge out of the pilasters, replete with corn, leaves, flowers, and acorns. Once again, death becomes a part of the natural process in all its abundance, whereas Father Time is independently stationed—part of the supernatural realm.

Insofar as Puritans were ambivalent about the role of Father Time, such attitudes were basic to their conception of time in its human and eternal dimensions.[5] That is, if the passage of time were emphasized, then Father Time might well be man's adversary, hastening him to his death; but representing eternity, the figure would oppose mortal death and transport the deceased to heaven rather than leave him in the grave. The ambiguities that Father Time inevitably embodied were still present on the two markers cut by Codner near the middle of the eighteenth century, even though these refer to the concerns of the previous century. The Charlestown Carver had cut, in 1678, the Joseph Tapping memorial (*Fig. 119*), also standing in King's Chapel. This splendid slate stone was probably the original source for Codner's later efforts. The Charlestown Carver, in turn, found his source from an engraving in Francis Quarles' popular emblem book *Hieroglyphiques of the Life of Man* (*Fig. 120*), published in London in 1638.[6]

The Charlestown Carver probably had Quarles' book at hand, because the engraving and the stone image are similar enough to suggest a direct copy. In both, a skeleton is about to snuff out a lighted candle, while Father Time stands behind the figure of death. There are few differences between the two versions. The Charlestown Carver, for example, omitted both the sun and the sundial present in the engraving. He replaced the dial with a vertical scythe as a structural element for the background, and instead of an urn-base for the candle, he used a globe with elaborate handles in the shape of birds' heads. Despite these variations, the Joseph Tapping stone offers an emblem that is hardly crude but rather a minor triumph of the Charlestown Carver's skills as he successfully transposed the tonal gradations of an engraving into flat, linear planes on slate.

The vitality of the Charlestown Carver's image is derived in great measure from the confrontation between Death and Time. Just as Quarles' emblem hardly indicates conflict, his poetic commentary suggests that Time and Death work more or less hand in hand. Death, however, is slightly impatient when he declaims, "Time, hold thy peace . . . I surfeit with too long delay."[7] The Charles-

Fig. 119. The Joseph Tapping stone, 1678, King's Chapel, Boston, Massachusetts. Slate. 28 x 28½.

town Carver seized upon this hint of conflict in the poem as the solution by which to depict the skeleton braced back against Time, who solidly holds his ground and, reinforced by the elevated scythe, restrains Death's attempts to snuff the candle.

The Charlestown Carver only implied this significant difference between the image on the Tapping stone and that in the emblem book—a difference that he more fully explored in the John Foster stone (*Fig. 121*), cut three years later in Dorchester. Here the elements of the engraving are retained only in the

Fig. 120. Engraving from *Hieroglyphikes of the Life of Man* by Francis Quarles, London, 1638. *Courtesy of British Museum, London.*

Fig. 121. The John Foster stone, 1681, North Burial Ground, Dorchester, Massachusetts. Slate. 23 x 23.

personae. The fenestral limitations are removed, and the scene is thrust into the arch of the tympanum; the two figures assume the same stance, this time as recognizable antagonists; and the skeleton continues to brace itself against Time, though in a posture exaggerated by its bony stride. Close examination reveals that the Charlestown Carver originally intended to place the skeleton's anterior leg behind that of Time, who would thereby have gained greater leverage of restraint. But in order to give Death the advantage, the skeleton's leg was recut in front. To be sure, this pose simply reaffirms that which was presented in the original engraving and in the Tapping stone as well, and it suggests a vestigial ambivalence in the conception of the Charlestown Carver. There are other differences, however, that indicate his preference for depicting a struggle. The skeleton on the Foster stone has relinquished its dart so as to grasp the handles of the globe. In turn, Time does not hold an hourglass merely as a didactic accessory, but he pushes it against the skeleton's rib cage in an effort to delay the inevitable end.

There are other important differences between the Tapping and Foster stones. The latter for example, is crude but dynamic in the sheer technics of carving. Though the Charlestown Carver was certainly capable of achieving elegant forms, as the Neal children stone definitely shows, the discrepancy between the Tapping marker and the Foster stone may have resulted from his failure to have the engraving at hand as a guide. Such an explanation would also account for his adjustments of the skeleton's posture. But if the Charlestown Carver was forced to work from memory, he fell back upon his own powerful pictorial skills, boldly increasing the size of the globe and shortening the candle to maintain an appropriate height. Without the restraints of a graphic model, he was free to visualize the relationship between Time and Death to his own liking. His freehand rendering lent a new formal vitality to his slightly modified conception of the allegory.

Allegory was regularly appropriated from English sources, though the appropriations were usually adapted to New England. With the Tapping stone the Charlestown Carver first contended with problems of transposing an allegorical statement which appeared within the pages of an emblem book to the surface of a slate marker. This transposition required structural solutions of a pictorial as well as of a technical nature. He resolved these problems in much the same way as on the Neal children stone (*Fig. 16*), if not, indeed, more satisfactorily. The magnificent winged skull of the latter was supported by lightly etched columns which transformed the entire front into a temple facade. Although the columns were conceived in a Gothic rather than a classical manner, essentially the same structure served the Tapping stone. Possibly more sure of

himself after his earlier experiment on the Neal children stone, he firmly incised the columns, which provide the setting for the allegory of Time and Death.

Having established a solid framework for this drama, the Charlestown
Carver then accommodated the new subject material to what were becoming
the established phrases of New England funerary art. In the upper area he continued to work out of a hierarchical and discrete logic conditioned by the principles of plain style, achieving, nevertheless, visual and conceptual correlations
between the two major areas of the stone. The hourglass above the skull relates metaphorically to the allegory and repeats the emblem held by Time. To
make the meaning clear, the glass is balanced by the two aphorisms, *Fugit Hora*
and *Memento Mori,* thereby establishing a verbal relationship with the allegory.
The winged skull rests above a frieze, which in its elements repeats the foliated
spandrels of the arches. The upper area of the Tapping stone is at once outlined
and framed by scrolls, the convolutes of which suggest the coextension of the
natural and the eternal.

Whereas the Tapping stone was a *tour de force* of pictorial adaptation, the
same allegory was particularly suited to John Foster, whose life and death the
stone illuminates. A young man of substantial achievement when he died, his
loss was keenly felt by the Boston community. A printer of almanacs, a mathematician, and an astronomer, Foster in his vocations made the use of the allegory appropriate. The metamorphic quality of the earth and sun, life and death,
death and resurrection, was reinforced elsewhere by the anagram "I Shone
Forth," drawn from Foster's name and supplemented by elegies that invoke
images of the sun and other heavenly spheres as vivid metaphors of Foster in
his resurrected state."

The Tapping and Foster stones stand as the best realizations of allegory in
New England during the seventeenth and eighteenth centuries. A related form
of symbolic discourse stimulated few carvings. Only three stones still standing
in southern New England permit a typological interpretation. One reason for
the rarity of this kind of design might lie in the intellectual — indeed, cerebral —
nature of such an interpretation. Stonecarvers, nevertheless, must have been
familiar with the standard types of the Old Testament that prefigured the fulfillment or antitype of Christ in the New, if for no other reason than that they
were accustomed to this kind of scriptural exegesis at the meetinghouse.

Typology, moreover, was not only a means of biblical analysis but also a
way of perceiving the world. In a meditation prior to participating in the Lord's
Supper, Edward Taylor exclaimed:

> The glory of the world slickt up in types
> In all Choise things chosen to typify,
> His glory upon whom the works doth light,
> To thine's a Shaddow, or a butterfly.
> How glorious then, my Lord, art thou to mee
> Seing to cleanse me, 's worke alone for thee.
>
> The glory of all Types doth meet in thee.
> Thy glory doth their glory quite excell:
> More than the Sun excells in its bright glee
> A nat, an Earewig, Weevill, Snaile, or Shell.
> Wonders in Crowds start up; your eyes may strut
> Viewing his Excellence, and's bleeding cut.[9]

Taylor's particular typological mode of knowledge had its roots in the Puritan's ascription of spiritual values to the phenomena of experience. Taylor suggests in his meditation that everything becomes a "Shaddow" or type which has its source in Christ. In the final analysis, typological perception became for him a means of creating poetry for the glory of God.[10] The poet could treat even the most ostensibly insignificant phenomena of this world—"A nat, an Earewig, Weevil, Snaile, or Shell"—as proper material for his poetic creation of spiritual value. The dichotomous analysis of type and antitype provided a structure for the poem: typology thus afforded an exegetical analogue for the poetic conceit.

Although typology may have been particularly suited to poetry, the intrinsic nature of typological interpretation created problems for the stonecarver in the presentation of such themes. The complexity of determining pictorial form became all the more acute in the consideration of typology itself. Typology would require the visual identification of both terms in the analysis. The depiction of Christ the antitype belonged probably outside the pale of sanction. Not only was there the risk that the stonecarver might be visualizing God, and hence breaking the Second Commandment, but he also might be engaging in "Papish" activity by cutting crosses on markers. (There were, to be sure, many crosses upon New England gravestones, but they were generally a circumspect part of the design.)[11] These proscriptions were to militate against a widespread use of visual typological interpretation.

The Sarah Swan marker (*Fig. 122*) of 1767, in the East Burial Ground of Bristol, Rhode Island, makes a typological statement that is only partly visualized. Foliate pilasters guide the eye to the Edenic scene carved in shallow relief on the tympanum. Standing with arms akimbo, Adam and Eve face the viewer

Fig. 122. The Sarah Swan stone, 1767, East Burial Ground, Bristol, Rhode Island. Slate. 25 x 19.

from either side of the Tree of Knowledge. The serpent winds down the trunk to proffer the fruit to Eve, who, with Adam, stands frozen and about to make the human gesture of acceptance.

Immensely popular, Adam and Eve in the Garden illustrated children's primers and catechisms and appeared on embroidery, firebacks, and various other artifacts. A piece of crewelwork done by Mary Sarah Titcomb about 1760 (*Fig. 123*) shows Adam and Eve in nearly the same pose as that on the Sarah Swan stone and that on an iron fireback from Essex County, Massachusetts (*Fig. 124*), which was made some ten years later. Each of these artifacts, products of different crafts, portrays essentially the same scene, though the emphases and the ultimate expressiveness are different. The needlework, in its reliance on color, offers a fanciful Eden. The impending doom is only suggested by a dog chasing a deer, as disharmony begins to enter the Garden. The 1770 fireback gives prominence to the horrified expressions on the faces of Adam and Eve, for which its dull colors are appropriate. That Adam rather than Eve is shown here about to eat of the apple signifies imminent expulsion. Like the monochromatic fireback, the Sarah Swan stone emphasizes the supposition

Fig. 123. Adam and Eve, crewel on linen, Mary Sarah Titcomb. *c.* 1760, Newport, Rhode Island. *Courtesy of Wadsworth Atheneum, Hartford.*

Fig. 124. Iron fireback, dated 1770. *Courtesy of The Essex Institute, Salem, Massachusetts.*

that death entered the world at the moment of Adam's sin, and thus it stands in sharp contrast to the colorful innocence of the crewelwork Eden.

Neither the fireback nor the crewelwork, however, possesses the theological dimension that the Sarah Swan stone offers through its typological reference. In his *Christian Dictionary* Thomas Wilson determined that "The former *Adam* is called the first *Adam*, and Christ the last *Adam*, because the former was a type of the latter." Having posited the type and antitype, he elaborated further: "Either the first man so called, being great parent, root and head of all mankinde, deriving into them as his branch and members, sin and death . . . or else, Christ

Jesus, the root, head, and beginning of all the elect and believers, unto Whom he conveyeth in this life, his righteousness by imputation, and his Spirit or Grace by infusion; and in the life to come, perfect glory both to soul and body."[12] The scene in the Garden described on the gravestone bears such a meaning, which is made verbally explicit by the quotation from Corinthians I engraved upon the background: "For as in Adam all die, even so in Christ shall all be made alive." Visually corroborating the affirmation of the New Testament, an anthropomorphic sun shines forth from the tympanum border. Death and resurrection assume the rhythms of spiritual metamorphosis as the New Testament fulfills the Old.

The large red sandstone marker erected in 1797 for Eliakim Hayden in Essex, Connecticut (*Fig. 125*), bears the same typological reference to Adam in the epitaph. The carved design, however, offers a different type—that of Noah and his ark. Wilson again explained the image: "Noah's Arke did figure Christ his Church, whereinto they that enter by faith, are saved from the flood of Gods wrath; of which grace Baptisme (the answerable type) is the sign and seal." The Hayden stone presents the only design extant in New England that offers a complete typology. In the bottom half of the design is Noah's ark adrift upon the flood waters. Flying against a cross background is a dove returning with a branch as a sign of land: Christ obviously offering salvation from Adam's Original Sin. Above the tableau are two eyes, possibly the eyes of God, which, according to Benjamin Keach, are metaphors for "his most exact knowledge" as well as "his providential *Grace* and divine benevolence to Men."[13]

The design of the Hayden stone is cut within an oval, the top part of which is the outer arch of the tympanum. The interior border of the typology itself resembles a heart, supported thematically by the presence of the ark, which may, according to Wilson, "signify the heart of a godly person."[14] While copied, in all likelihood, from a woodcut that appeared in popular catechisms for children, this ark was skillfully carved, exploiting the sandstone texture with patterns of linear scoring.[15] In the cross above the ark flies a dove with its olive branch. The ark and the cross are type and anti-type: the Old Testament symbol and the New Testament, prefiguring the salvation of Christ within the church. The design offers an integrated structure that balances each element of the typology.

Whereas the Hayden stone clearly spells out all the terms of its typology, the Charles Bardin stone (*Fig. 126*) of Newport, Rhode Island, does not. It remains somewhat ambiguous in meaning, yet open to typological interpretation. Cut on blue slate of fine quality by John Bull in 1773, this marker is, if nothing else, a prime example of virtuoso carving skill. Like the carver of the Hayden stone, Bull probably copied the central image not from a crude woodcut but most

Fig. 125. The Eliakim Hayden stone, 1797, Essex, Connecticut. Red sandstone. 43 x 24.

Fig. 126. The Charles Bardin stone, 1773, Old Common Burying-ground, Newport, Rhode Island. Slate. 37 x 28¼.

likely from a mezzotint, a popular graphic form available in the colonies in the eighteenth century. Though the mezzotint itself would have provided fineness of detail for the stone design, Bull's technical skill was the final determinant of the excellence that characterizes this marker. Rising above stylized clouds or a turbulent sea is a bearded figure in flowing robes. His left hand beckons across the waves, while his right gestures in restraint. Enclosing this powerful scene is an arch consisting of interwoven bands, at the centers of which were cut stylized Tudor roses, commonly used on silver.

This patriarchal figure may have been a metaphorical allusion to Charles Bardin himself, whose death notice in *The Newport Mercury* of June 7, 1773, emphasized his role as head of the family.[16] Ludwig, however, has identified the carved image as the "one direct representation of God the Father" on New England gravestones.[17] But despite the obvious European iconographical tradition, the figure on the tympanum is most logically interpreted as an Old Testament prophet—especially in consideration of the cultural values of colonial New England. Even in cosmopolitan Newport prior to the Revolution the sanctions against the representation of God would still possess a strong legacy from Puritan attitudes of the previous century. The figure may otherwise represent Moses (without the traditional horns) parting the Red Sea to lead the chosen people into the Promised Land. Two mutually consistent typological interpretations of Moses are available. In either case, the overarching roses suggest the emblematic presence of Christ to reinforce a typological reading of the central image.

Bull might have been aware of the Mosaic class of typological interpretation because of a manual on baptism published in Newport by the Reverend Samuel Wilson in 1772, a year prior to the date of the Bardin stone. In this manual the Reverend Mr. Wilson discussed baptism in terms of the Old and New Testaments, Moses and Christ. His quotation from Corinthians corroborates the visual ambiguities of the image on the Bardin stone: "I would not that you should be ignorant, how that all our fathers were under a cloud, and all passed through the sea, and were baptized unto Moses, in the cloud, and in the sea."[18] Moreover, a popular resurgence of Mosaic typology occurred before the Revolution as a means of uniting the colonists against the English King. At the behest of a citizens' committee in Boston, for example, James Allan published in 1772 a poem characterizing the King as Pharaoh from whom the colonial Israelites had been delivered across the Atlantic Red Sea.[19] These political fulminations surely would have reverberated to Newport and John Bull.

The religious dimensions of typological interpretation, however, would certainly have taken precedence on the gravestone. In Wilson's *Christian Dictionary* emphasis on the moral law of Moses—particularly the moral law graven upon the stone—suggested the hardness of man's heart as an obstacle to performing the law.[20] In this view, Moses becomes a type similar to Adam, whereas Christ becomes a contrasting antitype. The gravestone, then, is almost a literal depiction of the original Mosaic tablets and emphasizes the punishment of death visited upon man by God for his failure to obey the Covenant of Works.

In the *Tropologia*, however, Keach preferred to emphasize the affirmative aspects of Moses, who becomes a savior of his people: "He was appointed by God and sent to deliver all the *Israel* of God from the cruel Bondage of Satan, and heavy Oppression and Burthen of Sin." In even more specific reference to the Bardin stone, "*Moses* led *Israel* through the Red Sea: Christ leads his Church through a Sea of Tribulation." Elements of this comparison become typological in meaning as well. Thus Keach claimed that "the miraculous *Passage* of the *Israelites* through the Red Sea . . . was a Type of Gospel-Baptism." In turn, baptism is related to death. "Burial precedes the Resurrection, or raising of the dead Body to a State of Immortality," just as "the Immersion of the Party baptized, precedes his Emersion, or coming out of the Water; which symbolizes or answers to two things: 1. The Resurrection of Christ, 2. Our rising again to Newness of life."[21]

Aware of many if not all of these explicit allusions, a contemporary viewer of the Bardin stone would have understood the carving as a dramatization of the death and resurrection of Charles Bardin. Moses parting the waters of the Red Sea becomes Christ engaged in the sacrament of baptism. The new life for the Israelites anticipates the new life in Christ. The carving of a type literally points to the antitype of Christian salvation after death. Ultimately, the Bardin stone comes full circle in its cultural implications for New England. As an individual member of the community, Bardin was thought to have reenacted the experience of the first settlers. By his migration from London, his settlement in Newport, his eventual death, and his presumed resurrection, he represented the mission of the Puritans to the New World as self-proclaimed Israelites in search of the Promised Land. Far from engaging in a pastiche of some chance mezzotint, Bull made secondhand visual sources a locus of compelling cultural values. By conceiving of the individual deceased in his rites of passage as a recapitulation of New England history, Bull worked in the best tradition of gravestone carving — providing memorials of the dead for the living.

CHAPTER 8

The Icons of Essex County

Within the framework of John Bull's restatement and striking affirmation of early cultural ideals, stonecarving by the middle of the eighteenth century had undergone many transformations since the early attempts of craftsmen during the seventeenth century. One pattern of change originated in Essex County, Massachusetts, and then spread westward to Harvard and southward to Norwichtown, Connecticut.[1] The characteristic iconic qualities of early Essex County gravestones were, however, greatly attenuated in this move. Indeed, by the eighteenth century the Harvard stonecarving family of Jonathan Worster had recast the Essex County imagery into neoclassical designs. A similar transformation took place in Norwichtown, where the imagery assumed explicit cosmological dimensions. All these changes were the result of interacting visual and religious values of a metamorphic nature.

Among the earliest examples of any sort of decorative stonecarving in this country are four large diorite stones found in Byfield, Massachusetts.[2] Of these four stones, which were probably used as thresholds or doorstones before 1650, one bears a crudely incised image of a face, presumably female because of the curvilinear markings indicating the hair (*Fig. 127*). This heavy slab is thought to have been a bridal gift at the marriage of John Dummer. It might have been decorated by the local miller, who would have had at least a rudimentary knowledge of stonework, as he had to sharpen millstones. But more important than this supposition is the fact that similar motifs appeared again in Essex County on gravestones dated a generation later. The Mary Hart stone of 1689 (*Fig. 128*) in Ipswich bears a similar image, for example. Perhaps another stonecarver who had been exposed to the same visual conventions in England had come to this country.

Fig. 127. Doorstone, *c.* 1636–1640, Byfield, Massachusetts. Diorite. 31 x 44 x 15. *Courtesy of Smithsonian Institution, Washington, D. C.*

Both the Byfield doorstone and the Mary Hart gravestone might be characterized as primitive, insofar as primitive means crude, but this crudeness of execution was largely a condition of wilderness technology. For instance, the Reverend Zachariah Symmes stone (*Fig. 129*) of Haverhill, dated 1711, has a carved surface that appears no more refined than that of the Hart stone, yet it bears an epigraph in Latin, which accentuates the rough imagery all the more. Even so, Essex County gravestones do not support the view that early New

Fig. 128. The Mary Hart stone, 1689, Ipswich, Massachusetts. Slate. 22 x 20.

Fig. 129. The Reverend Zachariah Symmes stone, 1711, Bradford, Massachusetts. Schist. 26 x 25¼.

England technology was too crude to express the values of European civilization. Although the image on the Symmes stone is not so finely carved as the earlier work of the Charlestown Carver, consciously espoused cultural and religious values of the period superseded technical limitations or ill conceived conventions in determining the style of the Essex County markers.

In his history *Of Plimouth Plantation* William Bradford asserted that the band of Pilgrims whom he governed wanted "the churches of God [to] reverte to their anciente puritie, and recover their primative order, libertie, & bewtie."[3] Bradford and others sought the primal in Christianity, a return to first principles to be achieved by stripping away that which was superfluous and hence corruptive of the original order. This restoration did not entail the destruction of society and its institutions so that they might be replaced by life in nature: to the Pilgrims and Puritans alike, the natural man was unregenerate, the son of Adam; his salvation would come through the Covenant of Grace, an agreement between man and God that lay at the heart of cultural purification. This process involved the idea of transformation of culture, not its destruction.

Some twenty years after Bradford wrote his history, the gravestones of Essex County reaffirmed this quest for the primal. The stonecarvers produced an art form that attempted to create as directly as possible the felt spiritual realities intrinsic to death and resurrection.[4] These artifacts were not idols to be worshipped, nor did they catalyze a mystical response in the viewer. Rather, the stones as carved evoked an aesthetic response that was fused with the faith involved. The power of the Puritan's symbolizing imagination, intensified by his spiritual faith, transformed the stone into a new reality as a sculpted object. The artifact did not simply present an image carved upon the surface to dramatize spiritual possibilities. Instead, the image was carved out of the stone surface, which was at one with it, so as to be the anticipated reality for the deceased and hence confirm the faith of the community. Here was an instance when signs were not discovered but created out of an available tradition, and the creation generated an aesthetic intensity that was the reality they sought.

The allied art of carving furniture suggests the cultural pervasiveness of a style which was put to particular use with regard to the gravestone. Thus the early cabinetmakers, advertised as turners or joiners, carved decorative motifs on the seventeenth-century furniture of Essex County in a manner that bears strong affinities with the gravestones of the area. The similarities between gravestones and family chests in particular suggest that these artisans plied their respective crafts out of a set of images and a carving style common to their experience and drawn from their English heritage. An example of such affinities can be seen on an oak chest attributed to Thomas Dennis of Ipswich (*Fig. 130*). Even though the planar surface is primarily flat rather than molded, the exfoliations of the design are not carved upon a frontal plane that would then be distinguishable from the motifs of the design; rather, the carved pattern *is* the articulated surface: wooden substance and floral design are fused in the plastic dimension of a carved object.

Dennis carved his own family deedbox (*Fig. 131*), which indicates some of the ways this style would evolve on eighteenth-century chests and some Essex County gravestones.[5] The differences between the two panels on the front of the box are primarily of degree. The guilloche on the lower drawer is tightly organized into a unit of sculpted relief, as the rosettes are defined by their encircling bands. And though the upper section is, in contrast, a flat pattern carved on the surface, the planes created by recess and relief still interact spatially by virtue of arabesques. Because the front is clearly segmented horizontally, however, the carved areas cease to comprise the frontal plane, as on the family chest, and simply become a part of the surface area. The upper section of the deedbox forecasts the geometric motifs that would appear on Essex County chests toward the close of the seventeenth century. But of additional importance, this geometrical tendency suggests a structural diffusion that would also characterize eighteenth-century Essex County gravestones.

Representative of early gravestones in Essex County, the Reverend Zachariah Symmes marker of Haverhill and the Alice Hart stone of Ipswich (*Fig. 132*), dated 1682, share a carving style and selection of motifs with contemporaneously crafted chests. Both gravestones focus on an abstract central face: holes bored for the eyes are enclosed by double incisions which meet in a vertical line to represent the nose. This abstraction notwithstanding, the face is conceived as an oval mass in shallow relief and is locked into an arch created by the buttressing of curvilinear forms. The entire design of both stones is tightly structured, much in the manner of the Essex County chest. The pilasters of the Symmes stone resemble, albeit rather crudely, the floral base of the motifs which comprise the outer panels of the chest previously noted (*Fig. 130*). In addition, the rosettes on the capitals of this gravestone are similar to those on the deedbox and are structured in the same manner within a plain continuous band (*Fig. 131*).

The furniture of seventeenth-century Essex County, however, remained as decorative house-furnishing, although both utilitarian and representative of economic status, whereas the gravestone, because of its distinctive function, gave explicit meaning to the motifs and even to the style itself. The essential character of these markers is corroborated by a local funeral elegy in which rational structure coexists with the intuitional quality of metamorphic motifs.

Fig. 130. Seventeenth-century Essex County chest, of oak and pine, carved and painted, attributed to Thomas Dennis of Ipswich, Massachusetts. *Courtesy of Museum of Fine Arts, Boston. Gift of J. Templeman Coolidge.*

Fig. 131. Dennis family deedbox, oak, seventeenth-century, owned by H. Ray Dennis.

Fig. 132. The Alice Hart stone, 1682, Ipswich, Massachusetts. Schist. 22 x 20.

In 1681 the Reverend Joseph Capen of Topsfield wrote an elegy for John Foster which is interspersed with erudite allusions that presuppose a cerebral response on the part of the reader. Yet, at the same time, "Still what's to come we dread," Capen admits. Through a primal fear of the unknown, he has recourse only to suprarational faith, reflected in his use of metaphoric transformation:

> Yea, though with dust thy body soiled be
> Yet at the Resurrection we shall see
> A fair Edition and of matchless worth,
> Free from Errata, new in Heaven set forth:
> 'Tis but a word from God the great Creatour,
> It shall be Done when He saith *Imprimatur.*[6]

Through the play of language, the word of the poet anticipates the Word of God.

Impulses of similar intensity characterize Essex County gravestones. The image on the Alice Hart stone, for example, is a variation on the general morphology of the winged skulls crafted by the Charlestown Carver in the Boston area, although the particular style began in Haverhill, Massachusetts.[7] Possibly even more than the winged skull, this image anticipated the cherub that would become prevalent in the eighteenth century. The interlocking elements embracing the face suggest wings, though they are birds as well, given the intersecting lines that imply beaks. These abstract shapes remain ambiguous, however, for they also call to mind worms or serpents.

Corroborative visual evidence is not conclusive, although the combined bird-serpent image appears as a minor motif in the allegory contemporaneously carved on the Joseph Tapping and John Foster stones (*Figs. 119, 121*). Literary

sources of iconographic meaning that were available at the time are more help-
ful in establishing this visual ambiguity as a deliberately conceived motif on
the Essex County stones. Benjamin Keach maintained that "Christ calls himself
a [Worm] with respect to his debased state, and the extream contempt to which
he was exposed in the World." And Thomas Wilson, in his *Christian Dictionary,*
claimed that a serpent indicated not only Satan (as one might expect) but also
a "good Christian, using godly discretion to avoyd the evils intended him by
others." Following Wilson's assertion that the wisdom of the serpent is highly
desirable, Benjamin Woodbridge used this hybrid metaphor to characterize
John Cotton upon his death in 1652. Because of his scholarly yet humble nature,
Cotton was at first "A simple Serpent," but was then further qualified as a
"Serpentine Dove, / Made up of Wisdome, Innocence, and Love." The combined imagery eulogized the complete man, but then this was consonant with
the theology offered by a popular conversion tract in 1684: "Christianity allows
you as much of the Serpent as of the Dove; the Dove without the Serpent is
easily entangled, and the Serpent without the Dove is venemously hurtful; the
head of the Serpent, and the heart of the Dove, make up the best and the most
blessed composition."[*]

Based upon these verbal clues, the pattern of meaning provided by the
stones themselves completes a convincing interpretation. Thus, on the Alice
Hart stone, the hitherto abstract ornimorphic elements would emerge as a dove,
following the literary designation, and symbolize the Holy Ghost. At the same
time, the worms would suggest the decay of death, while the serpent would
point to Adam's sin and punishment in the form of mortality, which itself was
viewed as a transitional process. Equally important, the face of the deceased is
suspended to indicate simultaneously the embrace of death and decay as well as
the spiritual reunion with Christ through the Holy Ghost. The nature of the
design dramatizes the metamorphoses imposed by physical death and spiritual
resurrection, while the carving style evokes a concretized presence as stone
material.

The Alice Hart stone offers perhaps the most intense expression of death
and resurrection among Essex County stones. In the following century, however,
this iconic quality decreased in intensity. By 1705, the Sarya Wicom marker of
Rowley, Massachusetts, indicated a relaxation of structure and concomitant
iconic values (*Fig. 133*). Although the pilasters retain the interlocking tulip
motifs that culminate in pinwheels on the capitals, the images on the tympanum
area have become identifiable as discrete though interrelated elements. The
crowned face now separates the heads of the two birds. These figures have lost
some of their original ambiguity and are more easily interpreted as birds rather

than as worms or serpents by virtue of an increased curvature. Decorative forms paraphrasing the bird images help to distinguish the design from the material. There is, moreover, an introduction of well defined negative space that also demarcates image from stone.

In 1714/15 the carver of the Richard Goss stone in Ipswich (*Fig. 134*) extended the tympanum base-line to present a discursive structure. The birds were diminished in size and relegated to either extreme of the tympanum. On each side of the face the carver introduced bold rosettes, simplified variations of those on the capitals. These motifs are geometrical, and foreshadow the rational structures that would later fully emerge. In the meantime, the design of this marker falls somewhere between mere surface carving and iconic presence. The elements are thinly banded, thereby emphasizing the negative space, while the circular repetition suggests the embrace of the face by spiritual forces.

Eventually, as the structure of this basic design continued to loosen, the iconic quality threatened to evaporate. For the Nathaniel Knowlton stone of 1726 in Ipswich (*Fig. 135*) the carver retained the three circular forms from the earlier Goss marker. He was unable, however, to fill successfully the large space that remained. Thus the three circles are no longer contiguous and so fail to lend solidity to the structure. The area above the face is occupied by a stylized crown of coil volutes that awkwardly extend around the rosettes and resemble lattice-work. Though these coils are ostensibly disposed rationally, the excessive repetition creates a counterproductive baroque effect. Then, too, the carver failed to mirror the double coils beneath the face. The final admission of structural failure is indicated by the vertical line on which the face is balanced.

Total loss of the iconic dimension is apparent on the Jonathan Pickard marker of 1735 (*Fig. 136*) in Rowley. Suspended in the center of the tympanum there is a circular face, implicitly held in tension by cantilevered coil volutes. But once again the structure of the design is subverted by the slack composition of the coils. The expansive background makes the image seem insubstantial and eradicates any vestigial iconic qualities.

The trend from iconic presence to surface image, along with an increased reliance on geometrical forms, did not preclude the possibility of successful designs. For example, the marker for the Reverend Joseph Capen (*Fig. 137*), who died in 1725, is a blend of metamorphic values and geometric structure that recalls his elegy for John Foster. Geometric rosettes, simplified variations of those on the pilasters, serve to support the face. Although lightly etched tendrils balance the head, the entire design is strongly composed and emphasizes the metamorphic interplay among the rosettes and the face. Equally bold is the design carved in 1740 for Joseph Little of Newburyport (*Fig. 138*). In this in-

Fig. 133. The Sarya Wicom stone, 1705, Rowley, Massachusetts. Slate. 21 x 21¼.

Fig. 134. The Richard Goss stone, 1714/15, Ipswich, Massachusetts. Slate. 20 x 20½.

Fig. 135. The Deacon Nathaniel Knowlton stone, 1726, Ipswich, Massachusetts. Slate. 38 x 30.

Fig. 136. The Lieutenant Jonathan Pickard stone, 1735, Rowley, Massachusetts. Slate. 29 x 24½.

Fig. 137. The Reverend Joseph Capen stone, 1725, Topsfield, Massachusetts. Schist. 37½ x 25½.

stance, the standing figure is secured by large pinwheel rosettes. Subsidiary coils provide a peruke around the outer perimeters of the rosettes and occupy the spaces on either end of the base. Thus the static figure that stands at the center is surrounded by linear movement.

The successful transformation of iconic expression was achieved by Jonathan Worster, followed by his son Moses, both of whom worked out of Harvard, Massachusetts. These stonecarvers appropriated the motifs that were conventional on Essex County stones and developed them in a manner that had previously been only implied. The Jonathan Pickard stone of 1735 had already freed the central face from its surrounding motifs. And as early as 1726, the Elizabeth Wade stone (*Fig. 139*) of Ipswich displayed the overarching coil volutes that later would be further dispersed on the Pickard market. It was Jonathan and Moses Worster, however, who realized to perfection the means of implied disposition of elements found on early eighteenth-century Essex County stones. The father may have cut the Jacob Danforth stone (*Fig. 140*) of Billerica in 1754, while Moses cut the Samuel Green marker (*Fig. 141*) of Lexington in 1759. In these instances, the Worsters' preference for finely grained dark slate contributed to their precise delineation of motifs. Generally, the gravestones of Rowley and Ipswich had been schist, much coarser than slate, but the selection of material was not the sole factor in the transformation. The Worsters' sense of harmonious balance based upon geometric proportions was the most important determinant toward a precision of means. Ultimately, theirs was a rational aesthetic that dominated, and hence transformed, the intuitive iconic quality of seventeenth-century Essex County gravestones.

As a consequence, the precise placement of motifs on the Samuel Green

Fig. 138. The Captain Joseph Little stone, 1740, Newburyport, Massachusetts. Schist. 33½ x 30.

Fig. 139. The Elizabeth Wade stone, 1726, Ipswich, Massachusetts. Slate. 29 x 26.

Fig. 140. The Captain Jacob Danforth stone, 1754, Billerica, Massachusetts. Slate. 39 x 29½.

Fig. 141. The Samuel Green stone, 1759, Lexington, Massachusetts. Slate. 33½ x 28.

stone altered their conventional meanings. Moses Worster improved upon the abstract features of the face by enlarging the eyes and lengthening the nose so as to fill the circle. He also supplied depth to the slightly ovoid empty eye sockets. The total effect was to increase the mystery of death. His abstract rendering of the face and its surrounding motifs, however, created a new ambience for this mystery. At the same time that Worster retained the characteristic circular form of the face, he added a lower point and so resolved an earlier problem on the Jonathan Pickard stone. The pointed "chin" effectively replaced the cantilevered coils on the latter and balanced the face within the total surface design. Circular repetition and variation became the structural principle of rational harmony. Death, nonetheless terrifying, falls within the scheme of universal, almost mechanistic forces. Although the ambience forecasts the rational world-view postulated by Deists during the Revolutionary period, the total design corroborates the theological values of revealed and natural religion preached by the Reverend Charles Chauncy of Cambridge prior to the middle of the eighteenth century. The mysteries of God remained inviolate in His natural universe, the workings of which could be discovered through science, a promise fulfilled by the new physics of Newton and disseminated through the ubiquitous almanac.[9]

In Connecticut the iconic expression of Essex County gravestones developed in two major ways. One can be seen on the Esther Barrows stone (*Fig. 142*) of 1716 in Mansfield Center. The original bird-serpent configurations have been completely domesticated and reduced to decorative elements, the forms of which only vestigially function as wings. A simple geometric sequence of semicircles serves as a decorative band beneath the tympanum and down the side panels.

The phrasing of the primary statement had become simply one more convention in the repertoire of Connecticut stonecarvers.

The other development of Essex County traditions was by far the more significant in light of the beautiful markers cut by Benjamin Collins in Norwichtown and its environs. In Mansfield Center, on the Exercise Conant stone (*Fig. 143*) of 1722, the stonecarver under whom Collins is thought to have served an apprenticeship reinterpreted the geometric motifs originally articulated on the eighteenth-century Essex County stones.[10] (The concentric squares on the pilasters constitute another borrowing from Essex County chests.) The compass-drawn rosettes on the pilasters, and the burgeoning coil volutes surrounding the face and repeated on the frieze beneath, were appropriated by the Collins Master and later used to near perfection by Collins himself.

Although Collins borrowed many iconographic conventions, he was most certainly an innovative craftsman and a self-conscious artisan, as his signature on at least one gravestone indicates. He varied the exterior form of the gravestone by defining the tripartite division of arches as a design on the stone surface itself. While some of his stones were sliced with triangular peaks, others have a curved top that embraces the width of the stone in a broad arch. This new shape would serve well for his thematic considerations. Ultimately, however, the measure of Collins as an artist lay in his ability to transfigure traditional forms in vital ways.

The cherub on the Deacon Thomas Leffingwell stone of 1733 (*Fig. 144*) in Norwichtown controls the curvilinear movement of the total design, and so provided the basis for future departures. From behind the clearly banded oval face feathered wings emerge and follow the downward curve of the arch. The face itself is supported by a series of curved lines that flow smoothly into the pair of coils in the frieze beneath. Within the space between the divergent coils Collins carved a heart, the spiritual seat of man, dominated by the angel above and the flux of nature on either side.

The Leffingwell stone was cut in the traditional tripartite shape except for a slight peak at the height of the arch. One year later, in 1734, Collins deliberately exploited this irregularity by slicing a triangular top for the Abigail Huntington stone (*Fig. 145*), also of Norwichtown. He then incised the tripartite shape on the granite surface, with the central arch tangential to the sides of the outer triangle. At the peak he cut a form that suggests the boughs of a tree, conceivably a symbol of Christ. However appropriate the image and its meaning may have been for funerary art, Collins misgauged its visual value for this particular work. In hierarchical terms Christ might well appear above a cherub, but the nonspecificity of the motif renders it superfluous, a mere decoration.

Fig. 142. The Esther Barrows stone, 1761, Mansfield Center, Connecticut. Granite. 45 x 26.

Fig. 143. The Exercise Conant stone, 1722, Mansfield Center, Connecticut. Granite. 26 x 21¼.

Fig. 144. The Deacon Thomas Leffingwell stone, 1733, Norwichtown, Connecticut. Granite. 26 x 25¼.

Fig. 145. The Abigail Huntington stone, 1734, Norwichtown, Connecticut. Granite. 27½ x 21½.

The failure of such an addition may be attributed to Collins' willingness to experiment with traditional forms. That attempt notwithstanding, he implemented many new possibilities on the Huntington stone which later he further developed on other markers. By cutting the arches on the stone surface itself, Collins achieved a new means of structural unity. The central arch, anchored by rosettes, firmly encloses the cherub, which resists such restraint, as indicated by the upward cast of its feathered wings. By lowering the features of the face Collins slightly altered the perspective to further suggest the illusion of ascension.

As though playing a variation on the late seventeenth-century gravestones cut by William Mumford in Boston, Collins placed the cherub within a total pattern that was geometric rather than organic. The result was a blend of spiritual and rational values. The cherub still occupies the central area of the design and dominates the heart on the frieze beneath. But Collins lent equal visual emphasis to the frieze, which was made more complex than that on the Leffingwell stone, by adding rosettes within the circles created by the curves. Whereas Worster suggested that human death was a mystery within a rational universe, Collins reasserted the centrality of spiritual values subject to rational interpretation. This metaphysical view is further strengthened by the presence of the heart within the total pattern. Its association with both the angel and the frieze implies that man is a composite of the spiritual and the rational, a creature whose dualities are not mutually exclusive but interpenetrative.

In 1735 Collins carved the Deacon Christopher Huntington stone (*Fig. 146*), also erected in Norwichtown. He cut this massive granite slab in the tripartite form. Almost a yard wide, the broad tympanum arch is bound by two large capitals. With this marker Collins demonstrated his ability to treat rough stone material with commensurate bold forms. Not simply a carver who could etch complex geometry on the stone's surface, he was also capable of carving forms out of the stone appropriate to its textures. Articulated in shallow relief, the design exists as part of the imposing material.

The total effect of this carving achievement was to invigorate the forms that Collins had used on the earlier Leffingwell and Abigail Huntington stones. On the Christopher Huntington marker the domination of the cherub is all the more remarkable in light of the large rosettes on the pilasters and bottom border. The strength of the cherub lies in its rendering, not in its position in the design. From the circular definition of the cherub's face, with its proportionate features, radiate the molded feathers of its wings. The plastic delineation creates a pulsating motion that attracts the eye and creates the ambiguous illusion of the cherub as sun.

Cosmic identification of the cherub requires in large part an intuitive

Fig. 146. The Deacon Christopher Huntington stone, 1735, Norwichtown, Connecticut. Granite. 35 x 48. *A*. Tympanum, detail. *B*. Right pilaster, detail.

acquiescence to its modeled properties, which—in contrast to the flat, planar carving that verges upon sunken relief on the rest of the stone—emphasize the tympanum area by texture. Collins himself must have eventually perceived the solar implications of this cherub, for ten years later he cut two stones that bear explicit cosmic images of the sun, moon, and stars. The excellence of these stones was achieved through the use of a linear carving technique that effectively cast surface details in relatively intricate geometric patterns.

Thus for the Hannah Huntington stone of 1746 (*Fig. 147*) in Norwichtown Collins used a granite slab with a broad top and inwardly slanting sides on which he again carved the traditional outline to serve as a structure for his design. The all-inclusive arch of the stone itself unifies and reinforces a representation of the cosmos. Centered on the frieze is a semicircle containing images of the sun, the moon, and stars. On either side and above there are paired rosettes in a sweeping network that encloses the cherub. As a result the tympanum repeats the semicircle of the heavenly spheres.

Further visual relationships are established on the surface by the geometric rendition of the cherub. The angular rays of the base for the oval face and the sharply articulated feathers alternately cut in sunken relief combine to create an image of the sun. Fully risen, the sun symbolizes resurrection and serves as a spiritual analogue for the rational and mechanistic emblems of the physical universe contained in the orb below. The geometry integrates the total design and so suggests that the invisible realm is characterized by the same rational powers which are perceived in the material world.

On either side of the semicircular complex of cosmic motifs are leaves and tendrils with clusters of grapes. Though these figures clearly have Christian connotations, their lyrical rendering is hardly consonant with the geometrical style and its implications. Their exclusion from the undated Zeryiah Buckingham stone (*Fig. 148*) in nearby Columbia would indicate that Collins carved the Buckingham marker before the Huntington stone, and not after, as one might expect. An increasing complexity from the Thomas Leffingwell marker ten years earlier to the Abigail Huntington stone would suggest a similar progression from the Buckingham stone to the Hannah Huntington marker. Collins' artistic consciousness at work accounts for the visual complications, which are not necessarily of consistent aesthetic worth.

The Zeryiah Buckingham stone is superior to the Hannah Huntington marker, although the internal structures are essentially identical. Working with fewer elements on the Buckingham stone, Collins economically set the enlarged cosmic emblems within a decorative arch that unites the rosettes on the frieze. By varying the rosettes, Collins made the simple geometry of forms itself the unifying force of the design. The Buckingham stone, a work of polish and restraint, shows Collins' skills at their best.

Differences among these various styles are significant for what they reveal, not only about changing religious values over a period of sixty or seventy years, but also about the craft of stonecarving itself. Seventeenth-century Essex County stones appear to have been carved under the domination of a strong communal sense of religious values. Other factors came into play with Moses Worster and Benjamin Collins. Worster ceased carving in his father's manner in 1772, when he adopted a conventional cherub from the Boston area.[11] He was quite obviously affected by fashionable styles, which he allowed to dictate to

Fig. 147. The Hannah Huntington stone, 1746, Norwichtown, Connecticut. Granite. 42 x 38¾.

Fig. 148. The Zeryiah Buckingham stone, *c.* 1746, Columbia, Connecticut. Granite. 36½ x 32.

his carving. As a provincial carver he may not have been certain of his own tastes, but most likely economic necessities forced him to switch to a new but hackneyed style that would sell. In submitting to the demands of the market-place, Worster exercised the priorities of entrepreneurial craft over art. Collins, on the other hand, in signing some of his gravestones and certainly in experimenting with gravestone forms, indicated his awareness of artistic individuality, which, however, was not always realized with the best judgment. Although his occasional lapse was hardly so detrimental as Worster's, both artisans exhibited the limitations dictated by stonecarving as a craft. The values of business and art were not necessarily opposed, but they generated ambiguities made all the more complex because they were oftentimes not recognized by the stonecarver. These craft tensions were most clearly revealed in the work of three generations of a stonecarving family in Newport, Rhode Island.

CHAPTER 9

The John Stevens Shop
of Newport

THREE generations in the John Stevens Shop cut gravestones of a quality and range of design all but unsurpassed by other stonecarvers. A continuity of craft tradition accounts for the integrity of their carvings as well as the maintenance of workbench skills. Without an enduring sense of the past to temper changing tastes, however, the vitality of their work diminished near the close of the eighteenth century. Over the course of that century the work produced by the Stevens Shop reveals not only the strengths and weaknesses of a commercial craft engaged in the creation of funereal art, but also the crucial problems facing early American artists as they attempted to elevate their work from the status of craft to fine art. Therefore, the Stevens Shop can serve as a model to provide an understanding of both the development of New England carving as well as the issues confronting artists in the young Republic.

The first John Stevens emigrated from Oxfordshire, England, to Boston, where he presumably added the craft of carving gravestones to his trade in stonework—one that would appear heretofore to have primarily involved mill-work. In 1705 he moved to Newport and opened his shop on Thames Street, which has been its location up to the present day. His son John II, an apprentice in the shop, fully assumed and enlarged the business after his father died in 1736. John Stevens III, born in Newport around 1753, also worked in the shop as a young man and continued the business after the second John's death in 1778.

This youngest Stevens was in close touch with the sophisticated tastes of Newport prior to the Revolution, just as he was aware of the funereal conventions established by his grandfather and carried on by his father. However, he was unable to accommodate innovation with tradition in some important commissions—lapses that can be attributed only in part to his youth. Such failure of vision was caused primarily by his growing awareness of the artist's role as distinct from that of the entrepreneurial craftsman. His orientation was imbued with paradoxes and ironies that were less idiosyncratic than cultural. Only a shop as successfully established as that of the Stevenses could have fostered the development of the youngest carver's artistry, his awareness of which, however, as it turned out, would vitiate the very craft itself. Further, his heightened self-consciousness as an artist did not enhance his work, but rather turned him away from craft values and traditions. The logic of fine art had neither the essential strength nor the appropriate cultural conditions to develop its own course. At the same time, his early period of experimentation came to a close with the economic burdens placed upon his business by the post-Revolutionary depression in Newport. Caught between an incipient sense of fine art and an economically vulnerable craft, the achievement of John Stevens III exemplifies the tension between art and culture in early America.

The Stevens Shop maintained a series of daybooks (four of which are extant), recording the daily transactions of an active enterprise. The earliest book, begun by the first John Stevens, bears the handwriting of all three generations and contains cost-accounting records interspersed with poems, fables, epitaphs, and lists of books favored by the youngest Stevens. More than the business notations, these entries are a significant index of the aesthetic and religious attitudes shared and modified through time by this family of craftsmen, and thus they reveal the cultural mainsprings of craft activity in the shop.

On the opening page of the first daybook is a lengthy poem entitled "On the Divine Uses of Musick." Entered in 1727 by John Stevens II, the poem is addressed to music but applies to other arts as well. And the very fact that the second Stevens would include it in a book primarily used to record day-to-day business matters discloses what he considered to be the relationship of his craft to God. Indeed, these verses became an appropriate proem for the artistic development of the shop over the course of the eighteenth century. That other songs expressing other values eventually took its place only accentuates its original validity if not its vitality.

The collective "we" of the narrator establishes a communal orientation that extends to the creative process. The individualized artist, whom the youngest Stevens would later stress in protoromantic fashion, is subordinated here to the social act of singing a hymn to God:

> We sing to The whos wisdom form'd
> The curious organ of the Ear

> And Thou who gave'st us Voices Lord
> Our grtefull Songs in kindness hear
>
> We'll say in fact who is the Spring
> of Lawful Joy and harmless mirth
> Whos boundless Love is fittly cald
> The harmony of Heaven and Earth
>
> Theas Praises Dearest Lord aloud
> Our Humble sonets shall Rehere
> Which Ritly tun'd are Ritly still'd
> The MUSIK of the Universe.[1]

Their song is directed to the Lord, at once the source and the audience of their singing. Mortal song spiritually attuned becomes universal music.

Aware of the "Vulgar use" that has often characterized music, the narrator promises a music for "nobler Joys":

> thus we poor mortals still on Earth
> will Immitate the Heav'enly quires
> and with high notes above the Clouds
> We'll send men with more Rais'd Desires.
> and that above we may be shure
> when we come their our Part to know
> whilst we live here att Home and Church
> We'll Practis singing oft Below.[2]

As the spiritual goals of music take on an aesthetic dimension, the very process of creativity becomes praise to God. An affirmation of the spiritual necessarily involves an affirmation of the artistic. The joys of heaven are reflected by the joys of earthly music.

Probably both the elder Stevenses assented to the attitudes in this poem, which is all the more important given its implications regarding their craft of gravestone carving. In his sermon on *Christian Calling*, John Cotton had asserted that "A true believing Christian, a justified person, he lives in his vocation by his faith."[3] "On the Divine Uses of Musik" reiterated Cotton's views insofar as a craft vocation involved the exercise of art. Stonecarvers were called upon to depict visually the spiritual hopes of the survivors for the deceased. Their earthly efforts affirmed the faith of the living toward the invisible world in much the same way that their songs were prelude to "Heav'enly quires." The eldest Stevens' magnificent carving on the Mary Carr stone of 1721 (*Fig. 12*), just seven years prior to the entry of the poem, offers this sense as the birds on the lower frieze serve as analogues for the spiritual realm of the cherub above.

The transmission of craft skills and the business of the shop itself from generation to generation encouraged the persistence of such values during the latter part of the eighteenth century, even in the grandson. This continuity is clearly evident in the account book, which is full of orthodox pieties that the youngest Stevens most certainly read. In written form these crystallize and thus idealize the attitudes that were supposed to govern family behavior. In addition to a wide selection of stock epitaphs that were utilized on New England gravestones, the account book contains "A Dialog between a Man and a Toade," which is significant for its religious sentiments: "If that in sin thou Dyest [exclaims the toad, evidently feeling unduly belittled] / Death will not Eand thy Shame and misery / When thou hast Boath felt & Seean / Loathsum toad like me youl wish you'd Bean."[4] With a thinly disguised Calvinism the dialogue reiterates a vision of man from the previous century. Equally important are the book lists of John Stevens III, who in 1767 claimed to have read widely, including many religious tracts by ministers ranging from Benjamin Colman to Isaac Backus. These entries all point to the concern for religious matters in the lives of those who ran the shop.

The grandson also absorbed the transformational values characteristic of New England stonecarving from its beginnings, and so continued to work in the traditions established by his grandfather and father. The qualities of visual metamorphosis manifested in the carvings on the gravestones appeared as well in the account book in conjunction with a garbled rhyme (possibly composed by the youngest Stevens himself, but most certainly recorded in his hand). The narrator bewails earthly entombment without a gravestone:

> . . . alas poor I
> That left behind no bosom friend
> To Erect a Stone for such an end
> To [tell] my Name my birth or Who
> That in full bloom I maried too . . . .[5]

Although the kindest way to describe this verse is as a forerunner of the advertising jingle, its inclusion in the account book is significant. Aware of conventional phrases in writing epitaphs, John Stevens III grasped the metaphor "full bloom" to draw a flower with an extensive leafy stem (*Fig. 149*) in the right margin. Just as the verse was derived from an elegiac tradition, so the grandson's sure and graceful sketch had as its model the linear floral motifs so masterfully carved by his grandfather and his father on the pilasters of gravestones. The drawing is far too casual to have been a formal pattern such as those for lace or embroidery designs penned on parchment (*Fig. 150*); but its association with

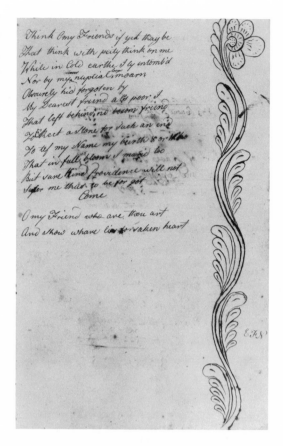

Fig. 149. Drawing, *c.* 1766, from *John Stevens: His Book, 1705. Courtesy of Esther Fisher Benson.*

the poem suggests the presence of a sensitivity that allowed the youngest Stevens to engage in an intuitive discourse between verbal metaphor and visual delineation.

Unlike the hymn of his father and grandfather, the poems entered by John Stevens III exhibit a decided streak of sentimentality, which he was not always able to restrain in carving gravestones. Foreshadowing the romantic attitudes of the nineteenth century, his sentimentality was simply one manifestation of an artistic sensibility diverging from that of preceding generations. Thus, during 1766, on the eve of his creative efforts in stonecarving, he recorded "A New Song":

> My Time, Aye Muses, was happily spent,
> When Phebe went with me wherever I went;
> Ten thousands sweet pleasures I felt in my Breast:
> Thure never fond Shepherd like Colin was blest,

Fig. 150. Embroidery pattern for needlework, parchment, before 1720. *Courtesy of Museum of Fine Arts, Boston. Gift of Mr. and Mrs. John R. Remensnyder.*

> But now she is gone, and has left me behind,
> What a marvellous Change on a sudden I find?
> When things were as fine as could possibly be,
> I thought twas the Spring; but alas! it twas she.

Inevitably, the poor shepherd cannot live without his love, and threatens to die, but not without offering fair warning to others: "Take heed, all ye Swains, how ye love one so fair."[6] The shepherd's advice, however, has no genuine substance, and his warning is remote from the didactic legend *Memento Mori* that appeared upon many seventeenth-century gravestones.

Whatever its deficiencies, the poem is nonetheless important for its expression of neoclassical values that would also inform many of the designs cut by the youngest Stevens. In a pastoral mode, the poem reflects an idyllic world inhabited by Colin the shepherd, Phebe his love, and the Muses. In contrast to his grandfather and father's hymn, sung to the Lord, Stevens' shepherd addresses himself to the Muses. And this classical allusion to specific deities of art as opposed to the orthodox God of Christianity is a major indication of Stevens' departure from both his father and his grandfather. (This does not mean, however, that John Stevens III was any less orthodox in his personal religious orientation; but a separation of religious orthodoxy from his art is part of the subsequent relegation of art to a special sphere as fine art, distinct from everyday life.) The reference to the Muses suggests a heightened awareness of the artist's role, and it certainly reveals a different sensibility from his predecessors' which, when applied, would modify traditional gravestone emphases.

With the loss of Phebe, the shepherd discovers, "When things were as fine as could possibly be, / I thought twas the Spring; but alas! it twas she." The pathetic fallacy exists in terms of art, for Colin exclaims, "Her Voice in the Concert, as now I have found, / Gave every thing else its agreeable Sound." The fathers' hymn sang of God's glory in the universe, whereas the shepherd sings to Phebe, whose own song transfigures nature. The poem's celebration of man the creator indicates the nascent efforts of the grandson to assert his identity as an independent artist, later shown by the signing of some of his gravestones.

When the first John Stevens cut the Mary Carr stone of Newport in 1721 (*Fig. 12*), he had rapidly progressed in technical proficiency from the Oliver Arnold stone (*Fig. 97*) of Jamestown, Rhode Island, just five years earlier. Insofar as the design was etched on the surface rather than carved in shallow relief, the Arnold stone is indeed somewhat crude. Stevens did not yet have control of the skills that are evident in the carving on the Mary Carr stone. Despite these limitations, his substitution of hourglasses for the conventional wings of the skull indicates a perception of metamorphic possibilities. Moreover, the particular notation made of the turnings on the glasses' stands foreshadowed the exquisite articulation of line in his later work.

That the Mary Carr stone was neither an isolated nor an exceptional example of the first Stevens' achievement is confirmed by the Nathaniel Bosworth marker of Bristol, Rhode Island (*Fig. 151*). Although dated 1690, the stone was probably cut in 1726, ten years before Stevens' own death.[7] Without a lower border the Bosworth marker lacks the total surface integration that characterizes the Mary Carr stone. Stevens compensated for this omission in the detailed phrasing on the pilasters and the use of a cherub independent of tympanum restraints. While the Mary Carr stone has a fantasy of intricate leaf patterns ascending the pilasters, which are topped with petalled rosettes, the Bosworth stone has pilasters crowned with exfoliating petals, the stems of which bear leaves alternating with a variety of field flowers (*Fig. 151 B, C*). The

Fig. 151. The Deacon Nathaniel Bosworth stone, 1690, First Congregational Churchyard, Bristol, Rhode Island. Slate. 26½ x 22¼.

stone was intended to be set with the base of the text level with the ground so that the flowered stems in their apparent growth would provide an analogy to the hovering cherub, its wings carved to create an illusion of flight.

The first Stevens' fond use of flowers and birds firmly established a shop tradition enthusiastically carried on by John Stevens II. The Thomas Pelham slabstone (*Fig. 152*) of 1724, in the Governor Arnold Burying Place of Newport, bears the Pelham coat of arms on the upper portion, while the lower contains the epitaph, its fine lettering commensurate in size to the whole, and spaced accordingly to create a surface articulation of visual and verbal pattern. Roses carved in each corner not only serve as decorative accents but also define the dimensions of the slab. Yet the outstanding features of this work are the imaginative adaptations that surround the coat of arms. A bold envelopment of leaves gives the shield a heart outline, the top of which is dominated by a large peacock. The circular unfolding of the tail, reminiscent of a sunburst, reinforces the interpretation of the peacock as a dual symbol of immortality, perpetuating the deceased individual as well as the family line. Stevens' sense of form and meaning overcame an awkward depiction of the body of the peacock as an eagle.

The second Stevens' success in treating coats of arms was not limited to the Pelham slabstone. The Sarah Harris stone of 1723 (*Fig. 153*) shows the formal three-bird shield mounted on a floral background, its delicate arabesques matched by the curvilinear leaves which culminate in flowers on the pilaster capitals. By 1726, on the William Harris marker (*Fig. 154*), Stevens had removed the birds from their rigid stations within the shield to a more graceful setting which integrated the birds within a leaf design. Perhaps taking a cue from his father, John Stevens II restored a cherub to the tympanum. With its floral pilasters the William Harris stone thus approximated the design of the Mary Carr stone five years earlier. In 1729, for the Job Harris stone (*Fig. 155*), John Stevens II continued to use the cherub, but in this instance he placed the birds in a charming fruited bush. The designs on the William and Job Harris stones developed logically from the family shield used for the Sarah Harris marker as well as from Stevens' innovative carving of coats of arms and crests.[8] At the same time, Stevens might well have been encouraged by the informal treatment of motifs used by needleworkers. A bedcover embroidered by Elizabeth Swann Brewster of Roxbury is but one example of such free but delicately balanced imagery (*Fig. 156*).

The second Stevens' apparent willingness to perceive the values of other crafts seems to have been sensed by his son. Thus the youngest Stevens appropriated the Madonna-and-child image that also informed the seventeenth-century oil portrait *Mrs. Elizabeth Freake and Baby Mary* for his stone portrait of

Fig. 152. The Thomas Pelham slabstone, 1724, Governor Arnold Burying Ground, New-port, Rhode Island. Slate. 6 ft. x 3 ft.

Fig. 153. The Sarah Harris stone, 1723, North Burial Ground, Providence, Rhode Island. Slate. 24½ x 19.

Fig. 154. The William Harris stone, 1725/26, North Burial Ground, Providence, Rhode Island. Slate. 25¼ x 23.

Fig. 155. The Job Harris stone, 1729, North Burial Ground, Providence, Rhode Island. Slate. 27¾ x 24¼.

Fig. 156. Embroidered bedspread by Elizabeth Swann Brewster of Roxbury, Massachusetts, eighteenth century. *Courtesy of The Connecticut Historical Society, Hartford.*

Fig. 157. The Captain Nathaniel Waldron stone, 1769, Old Common Burying-ground, Newport, Rhode Island. Slate. 36½ x 28¼. *A.* Tympanum. *B.* Right pilaster, detail. *C.* Base, detail.

Mercy Buliod and her child in 1771 (*Fig. 84*). As a young man scarcely in his teens and working in his father's shop, John Stevens III introduced fashionable portraiture as well as neoclassical motifs to the funerary art of the shop. He carved three gravestones during this early period that merit especial consideration: the stone of 1769 for Captain Nathaniel Waldron (*Fig. 157*); the stone of 1771 for Hannah Byles (*Fig. 158*); and the stone of 1775 for Jonathan Wyatt (*Fig. 159*). Essentially, all three stones bear representational portraits of the deceased, their faces modeled in three-quarter view. Further, all three markers firmly establish Stevens' ability to carve fine detail. Finally, these gravestones indicate Stevens' own concerns with relating neoclassical values and contemporaneous portraiture.

Perhaps the most fanciful of the three is Stevens' portrait of Hannah Byles. In the foreground and to the right an hourglass with its sands definitely exhausted is carved on the frontal plane of the tympanum. Gazing at this symbol of mortality, the figure of Hannah Byles stands to the left within the tympanum perspective. With her hair falling in waves, she wears a stola, just as Stevens no doubt imagined the classical mode illustrated by contemporary engravings of antiquities. The wings clearly suggest her immortal state as she looks back to the moment of death.

For the portrait of Jonathan Wyatt, Stevens chose to clothe the figure in contemporary dress. The detailed rendering of Wyatt's peruke is matched throughout by a close attention to clothing, particularly buttons, collar, and

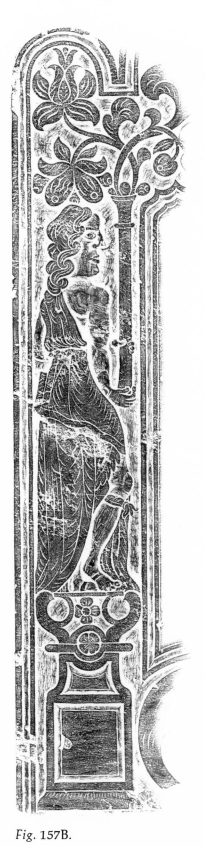

Fig. 157B.

Fig. 157C.

Fig. 158. The Hannah Byles stone, 1771, Old Common Burying-ground, Newport, Rhode Island. Slate. 24 x 25¼.

Fig. 159. The Jonathan Wyatt stone, 1775, Old Common Burying-ground, Newport, Rhode Island. Slate. 24 x 21.

cravat. In the place of wings are the Tudor rose and thistle of Scotland. While these emblems suggest Wyatt's familial ties with the mother country, they also have traditional Christian meaning, for the rose symbolizes Christ, and the thistle "is put for one of no power or strength."[9] Wyatt, powerless in death, is given new life by Christ.

The most ambitious portrait that John Stevens III carved appears on the stone for Captain Nathaniel Waldron. As completely detailed as the figure of Wyatt, Waldron stands at the center of the tympanum. Instead of a rose and thistle, pairs of crossed arrows confine the figure. Above and behind him is a descending curtain with tassels. These surrounding conventions announce the close of Waldron's life, but such signs of mortality are only a part of the larger pattern of regenerative motifs. Emerging from long torch standards held by two stola-clad women on either pilaster, an erotic (in conception, if not in actuality) bower of flowers and fruits vaults the arch and envelops the figure of the mortal Waldron. The ecclecticism of the stone, comprised as it is of traditional funerary emblems, organic elements, and neoclassical figures, is further increased by the exotic creature centered on the lower border, again probably taken from a bookplate or similar woodcut.

The career of John Stevens III resembles that of Moses Worster in one respect: early during the decade of the 1780s, he too quit his individualistic efforts at carving and began to produce conventional cherubim for his customers. Unlike Worster, however, Stevens III did not change his art because of the prevailing fashions—after all, he *had* provided Newport with fashionable designs—but rather because he was forced to increase production out of economic necessity. Despite the curtailment of originality, he had adequate opportunity to develop his talents. And, unlike Benjamin Collins, John Stevens III enjoyed a youthful period in his father's shop when he was relatively unpressured by the marketplace.

The youngest Stevens was no doubt also influenced by the carving of John Bull, who, by this time, had returned to Newport and resumed his old trade.[10] After the carving of the superb Charles Bardin stone (*Fig. 126*), Bull chose to cut a multitude of flat, planar cherubs, their sentimentality exaggerated by unruly locks of hair carefully arranged. On the Elizabeth Sisson stone of 1774 (*Fig. 160*), however, he reverted to straightforward didacticism and presented an angel uncompromised in stance. Starkly beautiful and unambiguous, it validated the persistence of seventeenth-century form. The full range of Bull's sensibilities and technical achievements was demonstrated in the carving of the highly expressive Benjamin Wyatt stone of 1767 (*Fig. 161*). As Ludwig has noted, "It is

Fig. 160. The Elizabeth Sisson stone, 1774, Old Common Burying-ground, Newport, Rhode Island. Slate. 35¼ x 31½.

Fig. 161. The Benjamin Wyatt stone, 1767, Old Common Burying-ground, Newport, Rhode Island. Slate. 29 x 26¾.

certainly one of the most moving images in all New England. The sorrowing eyes seem to express a universal grief in the mortality of man, a grief only partially tempered by the conception of the immortality of man's soul. Surely, this stone reflects the observation of Jonathan Edwards that men who love the beauty of this world are slow to exchange it for the joys of the next.'"[11] The sidelong glance and sensuous lips of the cherub are literally and metaphorically cut off from this world by a relentless scythe that points to a drained hourglass. The image exquisitely dramatizes the eternal gulf between the visible and invisible worlds.

Substantial differences between Bull and the youngest Stevens are only too apparent. Not only was Bull the superior technician, he was also more capable of innovation within the visual traditions of New England stonecarving. Stevens III certainly utilized funereal conventions, but, with the sole exception of the Mercy Buliod stone, he did not achieve Bull's depth of human statement. The portrait of Jonathan Wyatt, for example, remains standing as a fashion plate rather than as a profound blend of contemporary and traditional values. The Nathaniel Waldron stone was an ambitious effort, but nonetheless a composite of uncontrolled elements. Significantly enough, the bower vaulting the arch of the tympanum echoes the elegiac lines for John Davenport in 1742:

> The sacred Man is to his Shape convey'd
> On Cammomile his asking Temples laid;
> Here Roses, Honey-Suckles, Jessamine
> In beauteous Arches o'er the Champion twine.[12]

Insofar as these genteel lines by a lady poet are distant from seventeenth-century New England elegies, they approximate the poetic tastes of John Stevens III as well as the domestication of his portraiture.

The immediate source of the grandson's gentility and its concomitant values was his clientele. As a good businessman he attended to their tastes, since craft economics demanded that the consumer be heeded. In John Stevens III, however, the traditional craft values had not been sufficiently inculcated for him to accept new pictorial tastes successfully. In this respect he may have been too young to have been fully attuned to the historical values that Bull was able to express. While all three Stevenses were artists, the youngest's self-consciousness as artist stressed individual assertion and an inclination for innovative ideas equated with current fashions—at a time when he was still learning the traditions of the shop. Although he rapidly acquired the purely technical skills, these could not compensate for his inexperience and inability to feel deeply the values of the past.

At the same time, the demands of an entrepreneurial craft would not allow him to separate completely the role of artist from that of craftsman. The fault did not lie entirely with the craft itself, for both the older Stevenses consciously exercised aesthetic values in harmony with a thriving business. Since John Stevens III was unable to relinquish gravestone carving to become a sculptor, his only alternative was to remain in business, either promoting conventional designs to meet the exigencies of production or catering to fashionable tastes as an occasional outlet for creativity. That these latter commissions sometimes succeed testifies to his talent shored against a divided sensibility.

The economic aspect of gravestone carving—the interaction between artisan and client providing the essential cultural nexus—had initially determined the resultant artistic values. The quality of the work produced depended upon the balance that the craft could sustain between innovation and tradition. The bold failures of the grandson indicate a faltering equilibrium. Nevertheless, in overall performance, the John Stevens Shop of Newport represented New England stonecarving at its best during the eighteenth century. The family took a full measure of creativity in their attempts to work imaginatively out of traditional forms. Their achievement illuminates the internal dynamics of New England gravestone carving: the necessity for an aesthetic consciousness combined with a sense of the past, transmitted through the institution of craft.

The Gravestone Considered: Toward an American Art

A limner of portraits was in one sense more fortunate than his fellow-craftsman the gravestone carver, for if a limner were sufficiently talented, he could forsake the trade of sign painting and devote all his time to commissioned portraiture. And, if his aspirations were higher, he might have been able to negotiate travel and study in Europe, where history painting was viewed as the estimable achievement. Both Benjamin West and John Singleton Copley, in accord and sympathy with European taste, deemed history painting far superior to portraiture. Among the arguments offered, there was always present the implication that portrait painting somewhat demeaned art by virtue of the entrepreneurial relationship between sitter and painter. History painting was not only fraught with lofty moral sentiment but also liberated from the commercial pressures of craft, and was thereby elevated to the status of fine art.

The distinctions between fine art and craft were not so readily apparent to the gravestone carver in colonial New England. To be sure, the transition from limner to portraitist was not easy either. As Copley indicated in his letters to his stepbrother Henry Pelham, even simple materials were difficult to come by in the Colonies.[1] Consequently, to the limner the absence of instruction must have been all the more formidable an obstacle. Yet once he perceived certain rudiments of portrait painting, his new-found art had the advantage of being considered among the fine arts, and even higher than the lowest form of painting, a status reserved for the landscape. Because neither the distinct function of the gravestone nor its economic status could be ignored, the carver, in contrast to the limner, was closely identified with his craft. If there was little opportunity to transform the craft and its utilitarian nature to a fine art, there was apparently even less opportunity to become an independent sculptor. Henry Christian Geyer, for example, was sufficiently aware of his role as an artist to advertise the plaster-casting of animals and busts along with his gravestones. But these products were probably some of the first examples of American *kitsch*, in part a result of trade pressures dictating Geyer's sense of art in terms of what would sell.[2]

In addition to these difficulties, the absence of church or court patronage must have been felt by colonial artisans, even though they probably accepted the withdrawal of the former from art as a given condition. The unwillingness of Puritan congregations to commission religious art for their churches and the lack of government support created a cultural vacuum for aspiring artists in New England. Still, the loss of even minimal court patronage was perhaps inevitable, given the distance between the English crown and its colonies, and should not be attributed to supposed Puritan attitudes of anti-art. Within these limitations the craft nature of gravestone carving should not be discounted or underestimated. The institution of a somewhat informal craft structure provided the transmission of aesthetic values and techniques from carver to carver, from town to town, from generation to generation. And this structure had further significance in that it increasingly drew patronage from the rising mercantile classes.

Derived from the same cultural context, stonecarving and limner portraiture have significant parallels. Consonant with the early limners' lack of teachers in the art of oil painting, that which characterizes New England gravestone carving as peculiarly American was the initial absence of a workbench tradition, preventing the wholesale importation of craft values and skills from Europe. This discontinuity, however, established the craft of stonecarving in New England with its own visual development drawn from a basic European iconography. Thus the absence of sculptural relief in a baroque style does not define New England gravestones as primitive. As crude as many gravestones are, the craft was not without its own art, just as portraiture remained art despite its proximity to limner status. This point cannot be stressed enough, given twentieth-century tendencies, then just emerging in eighteenth-century New England, to dissociate art from craft. Within a craft structure the art of stonecarving at its best resulted in the creation of many gravestones that possess an exciting aesthetic dimension, undiminished if not enhanced by its particular cultural function.

Cast as art within a craft framework, gravestone carving provides many insights into the Puritan culture of New England. First and foremost, the conception of Puritans as iconoclasts must be revised or qualified. Strictures against art were reserved for the ecclesiastical realm alone. In the civil realm art was not only allowed but encouraged to exist, overcoming the general Protestant suspicions of art so long as it served cultural needs without assuming the aura of art for art's sake. The qualifications offered by Samuel Mather and Samuel Willard are corroborated by the visual designs on the gravestones. The commonality of motif and treatment in all crafts further verifies the widespread creation of art in Puritan culture.

The manner in which gravestones served the needs of the Puritans sheds light upon the general function of art within their culture. A Puritan was supposed to manifest restraint and moderation in the face of death in the family lest his spiritual love for God be superseded by a profane love for mortals.[3] With such imperatives Puritan funerals provided one form of emotional restraint and release. A ritualized activity that was socially approved allowed a proper outlet for the emotions under stress. Thus, with respect to a monument for the deceased, the Puritan hired a professional artisan to express that which was inchoate in himself. In turn, the carver appropriated visual conventions that were socially acceptable, and through the designs, he articulated that which was either inexpressible or, if expressed, uncontrollable. In this way the carver achieved a crucial aesthetic distance for the surviving family and community. Nondiscursive and symbolic, art would orchestrate those profound feelings released by the event of death in spiritually affirmative ways (including the didactic, to be sure), but beyond didacticism art would celebrate the community's past made visible for the future.

Gravestones, then, did not exist as an unconscious mystical outlet for what has been thought of as a repressive and repressed cultural group. On the contrary, gravestone carvings appeared in the latter part of the seventeenth century to meet openly articulated needs. The very existence of gravestones with their designs — the carving and erection of which were scarcely surreptitious activities — attests to cultural needs and served as their open fulfillment. The designs were cut to create a sense of the past insofar as cultural models were necessary to restore a flagging sense of spiritual mission in the New Canaan. Along with the histories, elegies, and biographies, gravestones served to dramatize the hopeful possibility of Christian resurrection, affirming the deceased by the faith of the living, and thereby confirming the faith of the living as well. Gravestones were therefore a popular art at every social level of early New England.

The intense desire of the New England Puritans for spiritual metamorphosis — expressed in religious terms by their emphases upon conversion and their retention of the two transformational sacraments, baptism and the Lord's Supper — was further articulated in the ritual surrounding death, the final passage and hoped-for conversion to the realm of heavenly saints. Along with the verbal metaphors of transformation in the elegy and the funeral sermon, the gravestone expressed spiritual metamorphosis in visual terms. Visually equivocal forms in deliberate patterns of interplay dramatized on stone the spiritual resurrection of the deceased.

With these preoccupations New England stonecarvers accommodated and modified European sources. An image that appeared in an emblem book took on new modulations when placed on the tympanum of the John Foster stone of 1681. Utilizing the emblem tradition, the allegory of Time and Death was adapted specifically to the life, death, and hopeful resurrection of the Dorchester printer. Some ninety years later, in 1773, John Bull could assume a typological interpretation of Christ and Moses for the Charles Bardin stone of Newport. An essentially scriptural exegesis out of a medieval tradition was transformed in the New England context as a reiteration as well as a reaffirmation of the Puritan's migratory experience to the New World—a conceptualization that was peculiarly American on the eve of the Revolution.

In order to achieve these transformations, a fusion of aesthetic sensibility and religious faith was required. The realization of a visual metamorphosis in carving further required the correlation of forms: their synthesis within a total design upon the stone façade. The earliest stonecarvers of the seventeenth century rendered the available motifs according to the analytic presentation of the plain style. This linear articulation of motifs was akin to the exegetic unfolding of scriptural metaphor in a plain-style sermon according to the dictates of Ramist logic. While an adherence to analytic design countered the synthesis of visual forms, the possibilities of metamorphosis were gradually perceived and articulated on a symmetrical structure. From the late seventeenth century throughout the eighteenth, gravestone carvers modulated their designs between these polarities of analysis and synthesis, and however the designs were modulated, their presentation of images has merely an apparent simplicity that conceals a complexity of means—possibly the most creative legacy of seventeenth-century Puritan plain style.

In the end, the gravestones remain. Their designs affirmed the lives of the Puritans. Their art was the point, after all.

The Epitaphs

THE gravestone epitaph traditionally gave biographical information about the deceased, but it often included theological and philosophical observations and just as frequently even petty or humorous comment or personal moral exhortation. This appendix records all the epitaphs found on the gravestones discussed in this study. The verbal material is given with the visual to facilitate a complete reading of the artifact. Orthography and length of line have been copied as closely as possible, but no attempt has been made to reproduce the carved text in facsimile.

Fig. 7. The Caesar stone, dated 1780, but probably recut in facsimile during early twentieth century, North Attleborough, Massachusetts.

> In memory of
>
>   CAESAR
>
> Here lies the best of slaves
>
> Now turning into dust;
>
> Caesar the Ethiopian craves
>
> A place among the just.
>
> His faithful soul has fled
>
> To realms of heavenly light
>
> And by the blood that Jesus shed
>
> Is changed from Black to White

Jany. 15, he quitted the stage

in the 77th year of his age.

1780.

Fig. 8. The Captain Hezekiah Stone stone, 1771, Oxford, Massachusetts.

In Memory of Capt. Hezekiah

Stone Who Departed this Life

July $\overset{e}{y}$ 18th, 1771 in the

61st, year of his Age.

Ben$\overset{e}{a}$th this Stone Deaths Pri∫∫ner Lies

The Stone Shall move the Pri∫ner Ri∫e.

Fig. 9. The Joanna Buckley stone, 1716/17, Copp's Hill, Boston, Massachusetts.

HERE LYES BURIED

$\overset{e}{y}$ BODY OF M^{rs}.

JOANNA BUCKLEY

WIDDOW TO M^R. JOSEPH

BUCKLEY AGED 54

YEARS & 9 M^o. DEC^D.

MARCH $\overset{e}{y}$ 4th. 17 16/17

Fig. 10. The Mary Hirst stone, 1717, Copp's Hill, Boston, Massachusetts.

HERE LYES $\overset{e}{y}$ BODY OF

MARY HIRSST WIFE TO

HINDREH HIRSST DAU^R

OF JAMES BILL &

MEHITABL HIS WIFE

DIED NOV^R $\overset{e}{y}$ 23

1717

IN $\overset{e}{y}$ 37 YEAR

OF HER AGE

Fig. 11. The Captain Jonathan Poole stone, 1678, Wakefield, Massachusetts.

MEMENTO TE ESSE MORTALEM C·$\overset{e}{y}$ 2

FUGIT HORA

HERE LIES $\overset{e}{y}$ BODY OF CAPT,

JONATHAN POOLE WHO DEC^{D}.

IN $\overset{e}{y}$ 44 YEAR OF HIS AGE

1678

FRINDS SURE WOULD PROVE TO FAR UNKIND

IF OUT OF SIGHT THEY LEAVE HIM OUT OF MIND

& NOW HE LIES TRANSFORM'D TO NATIVE DUST

IN EARTHS COLD WOMB AS OTHER MORTALS MUST

IT–S STRANGE HIS MATCHLESS WORTH INTOMB–D SHOU$\overset{LY}{LD}$

OF THAT HIS FAME SHOULD IN OBLIVION DY

Fig. 12. The Mary Carr stone, 1721, Old Common Burying-ground, Newport, Rhode Island.

Here lyeth

the Body of

Mary the Wife

of John Carr,

Dyed Sep$\overset{r}{:}$ $\overset{e}{y}$

28$\overset{th}{:}$ 1721: in $\overset{e}{y}$

21$\overset{st}{:}$ year of her age

Fig. 13. The Thomas Drury stone, 1778, Auburn, Massachusetts.

MEMENTO MORI

Here Lyes interr,d the

Remains of ^{Mr} Thomas

Drury, who departed

this life Nov$^{r.}$ 3^{d} 1778 in

the 59th year of his age.

READER

Death is a debt to nature due

which I have paid & so muſt you.

Fig. 14. The Cutler children stone, 1680, Phipps Street, Charlestown, Massachusetts.

HERE LIES THE CHILDREN OF JOHN AND MARTHA CUTLER

FUGIT HORA

JOHN CUTLER	MARGRET CUTLER	MARGRET CUTLER
AGED 3 WEEKS	AGED 9 WEEKS &	DIED MARCH Y^{e} 8
DIED MAY Y^{e} 18	3D DIED FEBR^{Y} Y^{e} 18	1677
1676	1680	

Fig. 15. The Joseph Farnum stone, 1678, Copp's Hill, Boston, Massachusetts.

JOSEPH FARNUM

AGED ABOUT 30

YEARS DEC$^{D.}$ NOVE^{R}

y^{e} 30 1678

ULTIMA SEMPER EXPERANDA DIES

HOMILAE DICIQUE BEATUS

ANTE OBITUM NEMO

SUPREMAQUE FUNERA DEBIT

[In anticipation of the last day, one ought always to speak blessed words and things before death and final rites.]

Fig. 16. The Neal children stone, *c.* 1678, The Granary, Boston, Massachusetts.

THE CHILDREN OF ANDREW & MELICEN NEAL

TEMPUS EDAX, RERUM

ELIZABETH NEAL	ELIZABETH NEAL	ANDREW NEAL
AGED 3 DAYES	AGED 2 WEEKS	AGED 18 MONTHS
DEC^D 1666	DEC^D JUNE $\overset{e}{y}$ 12	DEC^D
AS ALSO $\overset{e}{y}$ BODY OF	1671	
HANNAH NEAL IS		
HERE INTER'D		

Fig. 17. The Thomas Kendel stone, *c.* 1678, Wakefield, Massachusetts.

FUGIT   HORA
MEMENTO TE ESSE MORTALEM

UPON $\overset{e}{y}$ DEATH OF THOMAS KENDEL
HERE IN $\overset{e}{y}$ EARTH IS LAYD ON OF $\overset{e}{y}$ 7 OF THIS CHURCH FOUNDATION
SO TO REMAIEN TEL $\overset{e}{y}$ POWRFUL VOICE SAY RIS INHERIT A GLORI^s
                                        HABITATION
A PATARN OF PIATI & LOVE & FOR PEACE HERE WE MOURN & MOURN WE MOUST
BUT NOW ALAS HOW SHORT HIS RACE TO SE, ZION STONS LIK GOLD NOW LAYD
                                        IN DUST

Fig. 18. The William Hescy stone, 1689, Wakefield, Massachusetts.

MEMENTO FUGIT HORA
MORI

HERE LYES THE BODY OF
LI^{E}UTENANT WILLIAM
HESCY AGED ABOUT 70
YEAR DECEASED THE 30 OF
MAY 1689

Fig. 19. The Rebekah Row stone, 1680, Phipps Street, Charlestown, Massachusetts.

MEMENTO MORI   FUGIT HORA

HERE LYES BURIED $\overset{e}{Y}$ BODY

OF REBEKAH ROW WIFE

OF ELIAS ROW AGED

ABOUT 54 YEARS WHO

DEPARTED THIS LIFE 24 DAY

OF FEBRUARY 1680

Fig. 20. The Mary Goose and child stone, 1690, The Granary, Boston, Massachusetts.

HERE LYES $\overset{e}{Y}$ BODY OF

MARY GOOSE WIFE TO

ISAAC GOOSE AGED 42

YEARS DEC^{D} OCTOBE^{R}

$\overset{e}{y}$ 19th 1690

Here lyeſ alſo ſuſana

gooſe $\overset{e}{y}$ 3^{d} aged 15 m^{o}

died auguſt $\overset{e}{y}$ 11th 1687

Fig. 21. The Deacon Obadiah Gill stone, 1700, Copp's Hill, Boston, Massachusetts.

HERE LIETH BURYED

$\overset{e}{y}$ BODI OF OBADIAH

GILL DEACON OF $\overset{e}{y}$

NORTH CHURCH IN

BOSTON AGED 50

YEARS DECEASED

JANUARY $\overset{e}{y}$ 6 1700

Fig. 22. The Nathaniel Greenwood stone, 1684, Copp's Hill, Boston, Massachusetts.

HERE LYETH INTERRED

Y^e BODY OF NATHANIEL

GREENWOOD AGED 53

YEARS DEPARTED THIS

LIFE JULY THE 31

1684

Fig. 23. The Dorcas Brakenbery stone, 1682, Phipps Street, Charlestown, Massachusetts.

HERE LYETH Y̊ BODY OF

DORCAS BRAKENBERY

WIFE TO JOHN BRAKENBE^{RY}

AGED 16 Y^{RS} DEC^D JULY 25

1682

Fig. 24. The Charity Brown stone, 1754, Copp's Hill, Boston, Massachusetts.

Here lyes ẙ Body of

Mrs CHARITY BROWN

Confort to M^r·

JOHN BROWN

Who Departed this Life

April ẙ 13th AD 1754 in

ẙ 31st Year of Her Age

Fig. 25. The Judith Hunt stone, 1693, Copp's Hill, Boston, Massachusetts.

HERE LYETH BURIED Y^e

BODY OF JUDITH HUNT

y^e WIFE OF THOMAS HUNT

AGED ABOUT 38 YEARS

DEPARTED THIS LIFE Y^e

18 OF OCTOBER 1693

$\overset{e}{y}$ DAUGHTER OF CAP^T

WILLIAM TOREY

OF WAYMOUTH

Fig. 26. The John Churchill stone, 1729/30, Plymouth, Massachusetts.

HERE LYES $\overset{e}{y}$ BODY

OF MR JOHN

CHURCHILL WHO DEC^d

FEB^{ry}. $\overset{e}{y}$ 25th DAY

1 7 2 9/30

IN $\overset{e}{y}$ 39th YEAR

OF HIS AGE.

Fig. 27. The Reverend Jonathan Pierpont stone, 1709, Wakefield, Massachusetts.

MEMENTO   FUGIT

MORI   HORA

The Reuerand Mr JONATHAN PIERPONT

Late Pastor of The Church of Chris^t

in Redding For The Space of Twenty

years Aged 44 years Who Departe^D

This Life The Second Day of JVNE 1709

A Fruitful Christian, And a pastor Who

Did good to all, and lov'd all good to do:

A tender Husband; and a parent Kind:

A Faithful Friend, Which Who, oh! Who can find

A preacher, that a bright Example gave

Of Rules he preach'd, the Souls of Men to ſave

A PIERPONT All of this, here leves his dust,

And Waits the Reſurrection of the Just.

Fig. 28. The Deacon John Stone stone, 1691, Watertown, Massachusetts.

HERE LYES THE BODY OF

DEACON JOHN STONE WHOS^E

LIFE WAS MUCH DESIRED &

WHOSE DEATH IS MUCH

LAMENTED AGED ABOUT 55

YEARS HE WENT REIOYCING

OUT OF THIS WORLD IN-

TO THE OTHER THE 26 DAY

OF MARCH 1691

Fig. 29. The Captain John Carter stone, 1692, Woburn, Massachusetts.

MEMENTO   FUGIT

MORI   HORA

HERE LYES $\overset{e}{Y}$ BODY OF

CAP$\overset{t}{.}$ JOHN CARTER

AGED ABOUT 76

YEARS DECEASED $\overset{e}{Y}$

14 OF SEPTEMBER 1692

Fig. 30. The Lieutenant Thomas Bancroft stone, 1691, Wakefield, Massachusetts.

MEMENTO MORI FUGIT HORA

HERE LYES THE BODY

OF LIEUTENANT

THOMAS BANCROFT

AGED 69 YEARS

DECEASED $\overset{e}{y}$ 19 OF

AUGUST 1691

THE MEMORY OF $\overset{e}{y}$ JUST IS BLESSED

Fig. 31. The Henry Messinger, Jr., stone, 1686, The Granary, Boston, Massachusetts.

HERE LYETH BURIED

$\overset{e}{y}$ BODY OF

HENERY MESSINGER JUNIER

AGED 32 YEARS 2

MONTHS & 17 DAYES

DECEASE^{D} NOVEMBER

y^{e} 17   1686

Fig. 32. The Anna Cooper stone, *c.* 1750, Woburn, Massachusetts.

Here Lyes Buried

The Body of

ANNA COOPER

Aged 45 Years who

departed This Life

.   .   .

Fig. 33. The Rebecca Georgus stone, 1782, The Granary, Boston, Massachusetts.

Here lies

Mrs. REBECCA GEORGUS

.   .   .

Fig. 34. The Seth Sumner stone, 1771, Milton, Massachusetts.

Here lies Buried the Body, of

M^r. SETH SUMNER,

who died Novr. 11.th 1771

in the 61st Year of His Age.

Lament me not as you paſs by,

As you are now, so once was I;

As I am now, ſo muſt you be;

All Flesſh is Mortal you may se.

Fig. 35. The Love Backus stone, 1778, Norwichtown, Connecticut.

In memory of M^{rs}

Love Beckus who died

the 29th of Decem

1778 in the 68th

Year of her Age

Fig. 36. The Sarah Morshead stone, 1750, Salem, Massachusetts.

This Stone Perpetuates

the Memory of

MAD^M. SARAH MORSHEAD

who died Decr. 25th

1750

Aged 67

Fig. 37. The Polly Coombes stone, 1795, Bellingham, Massachusetts.

In Memory of

Miſs Polly Coombe^s

of Bellingham; who

expired on y^e, 16.th of

Nov. 1795 in the 25.th

year of her age.

Reader attend: this state

will soon be thine.

Be thou in youthful health

Or in decline;

Prepare to meet thy God

.   .   .

Fig. 40. The William Greenough stone, 1693, Copp's Hill, Boston, Massachusetts.

HERE LYETH BURIED

ye BODY OF CAP^T

WILLIAM · GREENOUGH

AGED ABOUT 52 YEAR^S

DEC^D AUGUST ye 6.^{t}

1693

Fig. 41. The Thomas Nichols stone, 1765, Wakefield, Massachusetts.

Arise   ye dead

In Memory of

Mr THOMAS NICHOLS

who exchanged worlds

in the month of april 1765,

Aged almoſt 83 years

Fig. 42. The Charles Stuart stone, 1802, Peterborough, New Hampshire.

ERECTED,

in memory of

Mr. CHARLES STUART,

who died 13, Octr 1802,

in the 57 year of his age,

Farewel vain world; as thou hast to me,

Dust & a shadow; those I leave with thee,

The unseen vital substance I resign

To Him that's substance, life, light, love, divine.

Stat sua cuique dies; brevis

& irreparabile tempus.

[The final day comes for everyone; time is short and irretrievable.]

Fig. 44. The Olive Storrs stone, 1785, Mansfield Center, Connecticut.

In Honour & to the memory

of Mrs Olive Storrs the

amiable & virtuous consort

of Mr Benjamin Storrs

who departed this Life

Feby 24th 1785 in $\overset{e}{y}$ 29th

Year of her Age.

While yet alive her virtue shind,

The product of a pious mind;

We trust her soul is now above

Where all is peace, where all is

love

Fig. 45. The Ruth Conant stone, 1766, Mansfield Center, Connecticut.

The Remains of

Mr.^s Ruth Conant

Consort to the

Honble Shubael

Conant Esqr Who

Departed this

Life July ye 27th. A D

1766 Ætatis

Suae 46

Fig. 46. The Nathaniel Pattin stone, 1757, South Killingly, Connecticut.

Nathaniel son to

decon Nath^{ll} &

Anna pattin died

may ye 12 AD 1757

Æ 3 years & 3 m

Fig. 47. The Jedediah Aylesworth stone, 1795, Arlington, Vermont.

mementomori

In MEMORY OF

Mr Jedediah Aylesworth. Son of Mr Abel

& Mrs Freelove Aylesworth of Arlington.

who died March the 18th AD 1795.

Aged 16 Years. 6 Months. & 9 Days.

This youth tho Young was lov'd by all

By old & young by great & small

His generous soul his obliging way

Amongst his acquaintance bore their sway

But death that conquerer bow'd his head

And now he lies among the dead

Yet he shall rife & leave the ground

. . .

Fig. 49. The Sarah Branch stone, 1784, Shaftsbury, Vermont.

IN MEMORY

of Mrs. SARAH BRANCH,

the Amiable Confort of Mr.

AMASIAH BRANCH: Who

died Auguft the 2nd 1784,

In the 41 ft Year of her Age.

Yet never let our Hearts divide,

Nor death diffolve the Chain;

For love and Joy were once alloy'd

And muft be join'd again.

Fig. 50. The Ebenezer Cole stone, 1794, Shaftsbury, Vermont.

IN MEMORY OF

Ebenezer Cole Efq. who died

March 22nd 1794, in the 82nd

Year of his Age

You fee the place where I am laid,

Death is a debt that muft be paid;

And as by.me you find it true,

And time will prove it fo by you.

Let not your time then run to wafte,

In vain delights to pleafe your tafte:

But for an endlefs World prepare,

For time is fhort you muft be there.

Fig. 51. The Mary Breakenridge stone, 1792, Bennington, Vermont.

IN MEMORY OF

Mrs. Mary Breakenridge, Daugh-

ter of Lieu^t WILLIAM HENRY

and Mrs. ISABEL his wife, the

Lovely companion of Capt.

James Breakenridge. She died

July 28th 1792 in the 30th

year of her age

Yet never let our hearts divide

Nor death dissolve the chain;

For love and joy were once alloy'd

And muft be join'd again.

Fig. 53. The Hannah Tiffany stone, 1785, First Congregational Churchyard, Attleborough, Massachusetts.

I have fought & found him

SACRED

To the Memory of

M^{rs}. HANNAH the

wife of M^r. NOAH

TIFFANY fhe Died

Aug^{ft}. 28th 1785

in the 24th Year

of her Age

My loving friends as you pass by

.   .   .

Fig. 55. The Reverend David Turner stone, 1757, Rehoboth, Massachusetts.

In Memory of

the Reverend M^r

DAVID TURNER

Paſtor of the Second

Church in Rehoboth,

who Departed this

Life on $\overset{e}{y}$=9th Day of

August AD 1757 in

$\overset{e}{y}$ 63 Year of his Age

Watch and [Pray] Because

You [Know] not the hour

Fig. 57. The Reverend Nathaniel Rogers stone, 1775, Ipswich, Massachusetts.

In   Memory of

The REV. NATHANIEL ROGERS who was

more than 47 years, a faithful & beloved

Paſtor of the firſt Church & Congregation in

this place: Colleague the firſt 18 years with

his venerable Father, the REV. JOHN ROGERS of

precious memory, whoſe duſt lies near: Alone

in office after, until death translated him to

the high reward of his labors. He slept in

Jesus May 10th: A.D. 1775 Æt 74.

A mind profoundly great, a heart that felt

The ties of nature, friendship & humanity;

Distinguished wisdom, dignity of manners,

These mark'd the *Man*: but with superior grace

The *Christian* shone in faith & heavenly zeal,

Sweet peace, true goodness, and prevailing pray'r

Dear Man of God! with what strong agonies

He wrestled for his flock—and for the world!

And like Apollos mighty in the scriptures,

Open'd the mysteries of love divine

And the great name of Jesus!

Warm from his lips the heav'nly doctrine fell;

And numbers rescu'd from the jaws of hell,

Shall hail him blest in realms of light unknown,

And add immortal lustre to his crown.

Fig. 58. The Reverend Silas Bigelow stone, 1769, Paxton, Massachusetts.

Here lyes the body of

the Reu^d, Mr SILAS

BIGLOW ^{Who}was Ordained

over the Flock of Chrift in

Paxton oct^r 21th AD 1767

he died Nov^{r} ^{16th}AD 1769 Ætat

31 a man of an Excelent

Spirit in whom Dwelt

the Sincere Chriftian

and real Frend much

Beloved by his kind peop^{le}

in Life and his Death

Greatly Lemanted

Fig. 59. The Reverend Nicholas Bowes stone, *c.* 1759, Warren, Massachusetts.

Here lyes interred the

Remains of the Rev^{d}: M^{r}

NICHOLAS BOEWS

Late Paſtor of the Church

of Chriſt in Bedford: who

having been e^{n}gaged as

chaplain in the Army at [the]

weſtward upon his Retur[n]

was violently seized with

his laſt illneſs in this place

and suddenly Departed

this life Dece^{mr} 12th A:D 175[?]

in the 50th year of his a[ge]

Fig. 60. The Ensign David Keyes stone, 1761, Warren, Massachusetts.

HERE LYES INTERR'D

THE REMAINS OF

ENS$^{,\text{n}}$ DAVID KEYES

WHO WAS BORN

SEPT' 1th 1729 &

DIED OCT$^{.\text{r}}$ 8th 1761

Fig. 61. The Reverend Grindall Rawson stone, dated 1715 but cut in 1744, Mendon, Massachusetts.

Here Lyeth Interr'd

the Body of the Reverend M^{R}.

GRINDALL RAWSON

The late Faithfull & Learned Pastor

of the Church of CHRIST In MENDON

who Dyed Feb^{ry} y^{e} 6th 1715

and Interd 6 Days into ye 57th Year

of his Age. Deceaſed the 35

Year of His Miniſtry.

The Memory of ye Just is BLeſsed.

Fig. 62. The Lieutenant Nathaniel Thayer stone, 1768, Braintree, Massachusetts.

In memory of Lieu^{t}

Nathaniel Thayer who

Died Decr 28

1768 aged

59 Years

Bereft of my Companion Dear:

O found in Comfort far nor Near:

My Lonely state drove me from Home:

& here I met [Jesus?] ſolemn Tomb.

Fig. 64. The Lieutenant Jabez Smith stone, 1751, The Granary, Boston, Massachusetts.

Anchor'd in the haven of Reſt.

In Memory of

JABEZ SMITH Junr,

Lieu^{t}, of Marines

on board the Continental

Ship Trumbull;

born in Groton,

State of Connecticut,

Auguſt 31. 1751;

departed this Life in Boſton,

June 28. 1780.

Aged 29 Years.

Fig. 65. The Deacon Matthew Rockwell stone, 1782, South Windsor, Connecticut.

In memory of Deac^{n}

Matthew Rockwell

who Died March y^{e}

28th AD 1782 in ye 75th

year of his Age.

If piety and learning mete

It can secure us from ye grave

we see our faithful teachers laid

on common level with ye slave.

Fig. 66. The Deacon Joseph Lothrop stone, 1788, Tolland, Connecticut.

In memory of

 Deacon

Joseph Lothrop

who Died May ye 6th

1788 in y^{e} 68th

year of his Age.

His virtue aught

A monument . . .

But underneath this stone

His ashes lie.

Fig. 67. The Doctor Thomas Munro stone, 1785, Juniper Hill Cemetery, Bristol, Rhode Island.

Here Lies Inter^d

y^e Remains of D,^{r,}

Thomas Munro

who Paid his

Debt due to Natur^e

Septem$^{br;}$ 12,^{f} 1785

in y^e 55^f Year of

   his age.

O, Death thou haſt Conquer,d me,

   I, by thy dart am ſlain,

But Chriſt hath Conquer,d the,

   And I ſhall riſe a gain

Fig. 68. The Mary Brown stone, 1782, Plymouth, Massachusetts.

In Memory of

Mary Brown Daughter

to Robert Brown &

Mary his wife who

Expir'd on Sep:^{r} 27th

AD 1782 Aged 5 years

1 Month & 14 Days.

Sleep ſilent Dust till Christ our Lord

The Omnipotent, will speak the word.

Then Soul & Body both will ariſe

To endleſs joys above the Skies.

Fig. 70. The Elizabeth Morton stone, 1790, Plymouth, Massachusetts.

To

the Memory

of

Mifs ELIZABETH MORTON

who departed this Life

May ye 21^{ft}. AD 1790 in y^e

20th year of her age.

Fig. 71. The Park family stone, 1803, Burgess Cemetery, Grafton, Vermont.

In Memory of

Thomas K. Park Junr

and thirteen Infants,

Children of Mr.

Thomas K. Park and

Rebecca his wife.

In Memory of Mrs.

Rebecca Park wife of

Mr. Thomas K. Park,

who Died Septr 23^d

1803 in the 40th year

of her age.

Youth behold and fhed a teer,

Se fourteen children flumber here

Se their image how they fhine,

Like flowers of a fruitful vine.

Behold and fe as you pass by -

My fourteen children with me lie,

Old or young you foon must die,

And turn to dust as well as I.

Fig. 72. The Samuel Hinckley stone, 1798, Brookfield, Massachusetts.

In Memory of

Mr. Samuel Hinckley

who died December

24th 1798

aged 67 years.

Fig. 73. The Mary Hinckley stone, 1798, Brookfield, Massachusetts.

In Memory of

Mrs. Mary Hinckley

wife of Mr,

Samuel Hinckley

who died January

28th 1798

aged 64 years

Fig. 75. The Mary and John Pember stone, 1783, Franklin, Connecticut.

In Memory	In Memory of
of Mrſſ, Mary	Mr, John Pem-
Wife to M^{r},	ber who Died
John Pember	Jan, 20th 1782
Who Died	in ye 86th, year
April 17 1783	of his Age.
in y^{e}, 86th year	
of her Age.	
Remember	Time swiftly
Death	Paſſes.

Fig. 76. The Lieutenant Moses and Susannah Willard stone, 1797, Charlestown, New Hampshire.

Erected in Memory of

Lieu^{t}. Moſes Willard and M^{rs}

Suſannah his Wife, Who

Were firſt Settlers of this

Town; Whoſe boddys are

interd here; He, was Killed

by the Indians June 16th 1756

In the 54th. year of his age;

And fhe departed this Life

May 5th 1797 In the 88th year

of her age

what rendered their lives remarkable

was their being bereft of two of their elder

daughters, by the Indians, one of whom had

her family with her, and continud in

captivity till after his death.

Fig. 77. The Elisha and Rebekah Cowles stone, 1799, Meriden, Connecticut.

Erected to	Alfo of
the Memory	Mrs.
of Mr	REBEKAH
ELISHA	wife of
COWLES	Mr. ELISHA
who died	COWLES
Nov 23d AD	who died
1799 Æ	Aug 15th AD
50 years	1785 Æ
	30 years

Heaven gives friens

Why should we complain

If heaven refumes

Our friends again.

Fig. 78. The Bellows children stone, 1799, Rockingham, Vermont.

In Memory of
Two Infants a Son,
and a Daughter, of
Elijah & Loviſa
Bellows. they Died.
March 2th 1799.

ſleep on ſweet babes & take your rest
god cald you home he thought it best

Fig. 79. The Mary Briant and children stone, 1724, Norwell, Massachusetts.

HERE LYES Y^{e} BODY
OF M^{rs} MA·RY BRI·AN^{T}
WIFE OF M^{R} THO·MAS
BRI·ANT WHO DYED
NO·UEMBER THE 30th
1724 AGED 39 YEARE^{S}
& IN HAR ARMS DOTH
LYE Y^{e} CORPS OF TWO
LOUELY BABES BORN
OF HAR 8 DAYS BE·FOR^{e}

HAR DEATH ONE A SO^{N}
NATHA^{niel} DYED Y^{e} DAY
BEFORE HAR A DAUGH^{tr}
NAM^{eED} HAN^{NAH} DYED A FEW OUR^{S} AF^{ter} HAR

Fig. 80. The Sarah Hart and child stone, 1752, Eastford, Connecticut

HEAR LIES Y^{e} REMAINS OF

Mrs SARAH HART WIFE

TO Mr CONSTANT: HART

WHO DI^e d MARCH Y^e

12th 1752 IN Y^e 26th

YEAR OF HUR AGE &

BENJAMIN HART THAIR

SON WHO^s BEARTH &

DEATH WAS ON Y^e 4th

OF MARCH 1752

Fig. 81. The Rebekah Clark and child stone, 1785, Cheshire, Connecticut.

In Memory of

Mrs REBEKAH wife of

Mr AMASA CLARK

who died *March* 6th. 1785.

In the 26th. Year of her Age

Alſo

their *CHILD* who died

in Infancy.

Death is a debt

To nature due

Which we have paid

And so muſt you.

Remember us when

we are turned to duſt.

Fig. 82. The Betty Lane and children stone, 1791, Rockingham, Vermont.

Sacred, to the Memory of

Mrs.. Betty Lane: Who Died

June 22nd, 1791 In the 34th

year of her Age. & alſo her

Twins, one ſtill-born, the others

age 3 days.

Our fleſh ſhall ſlumber in the ground,

'Till the laſt trumpet's joyfull ſound:

Then burſt the chains with ſweet ſurprize,

And in our Saviour's image riſe.

Fig. 83. The Sally Morrison and children stone, 1799, Rockingham, Vermont.

In Memory of Mrs,

Sally Morriſon wife of,

Mr, Jonathan Morriſon.

who Died July 26th 1799

being 33 years of Age.

Samuel Morriſon Died

1792 Aged, one year.

11 months & 23 days.

Jonathan Morriſon Died

1798 Aged one year 3

months & 26 days. Sons

of Jonathan and Sally

. . .

Fig. 84. The Mercy Buliod and child stone, 1771, Old Common Burying-ground, Newport, Rhode Island.

IN MEMORY of

MERCY the Wife of

Mr LEWIS BULIOD

who died Auguſt

the 12th. A.D. 1771 in

the 39th. Year of her Age.

In Memory alſo of Peter

their Son who died Aug.^{ſt}

the 19th. 1771 aged 14 Days.

Cut by John Stevens Jr.

Fig. 85. The Phillis Lyndon [Stevens] and child stone, 1773, Old Common Burying-ground, Newport, Rhode Island.

IN MEMORY of PHILLIS

a late faithful Servant of

JOSIAS LYNDON Eſq.^r

  and Wife of

ZINCO STEVENS

who died March 9th. A.D.

1773 Aged about 27 Years

Alſo PRINCE their Son who

died March 22.^d 1773 aged 2 M.^o

  & 27 Days.

Life how Short Eternity how Long!

Fig. 87. The Mary Harvey and child stone, 1785, Deerfield, Massachusetts.

In Memory of

Mary the Wife ^{of}

Simeon Harvey

who Departed thi^s

Life Decembr 20th

1785 In 39th year ^{of}

Her age on her left

Arm lieth the Infan^t

  which was ſtill

    Born.

Fig. 88. The Esther Corwin and child stone, 1797, Franklin, Connecticut.

Sacred to $\overset{e}{y}$, Memory of M^{rs}

Esther $\overset{e}{y}$ Wife of M^{r}, $Edwar^{d}$

Corwin, with her Infant

Who Died August 20th

1797 Aged 31 years

.   .   .

Fig. 89. The Deborah Long stone, 1678, Phipps Street, Charlestown, Massachusetts.

HERE LIES $\overset{e}{Y}$ BODY OF

DEBORAH LONG AGED 18 Y^{RS}

DEC^{D}: $FEBR^{Y}$: 28 1678

Fig. 92. The Marcy Allin stone, 1678, Malden, Massachusetts.

$MAR^{c}Y$ ALLIN WIFE

TO JOHN ALLIN AGED

35. Y^{rs}. DEC^{D} IN JANUARY

1678

Fig. 93. The Ensign Robert Cutler stone, 1761, Brookfield, Massachusetts.

IN MEMORY OF $ENS:^{n}$

ROBERT CUTLER WHO

WAS BORN APRIL 30th

1728. DIED APRIL 11th

1761.   READER

REMEMBER Death

Fig. 94. The Agnes Crawford stone, 1760, Rutland, Massachusetts.

IN MEMORY OF M$^{rs.}$

AGNES CRAWFORD

WIFE OF Mr Aaron

Crawford WHO

DEPARTED THIS

LIFE DECEM^{r}, 19th 1760

AGED 82 YEARS

Fig. 95. The Lucinda Day stone, 1800, Chester, Vermont.

In Memory of Mrs.

Lucinda Day who Died

March 22nd 1800 Aged

24 years; wife of

Mr. Stephen Day.

Why should I mourn what can I ſay

why should my thoughts repine

When God is pleaſ'd to take a way

A lovely friend of mine.

Fig. 97. The Oliver Arnold, Jr., stone, 1716, Cedar Cemetery, Jamestown, Rhode Island.

Here lyeth the body

of Oliver Arnold, y^{e}

son of Oliver Arnold

and of Phebe his Wife

aged 22 years and

departed this life

April the 24th 1716

Fig. 98. The Paul Simons stone, *c.* 1700, The Granary, Boston, Massachusetts.

HERE + LYETH + BURIED

$\overset{e}{y}$ BODY   OF

PAUL   SIMONS

AGED about 33 YEARS

DEPARTED THIS LIFE

. . .

Fig. 99. The Naomi Woolworth and child stone, 1760, Longmeadow, Massachusetts.

In Memory of

$M\overset{RS}{...}$ NAOMI;

Wife of $M\overset{R}{.}$

RITCHARD –

– WOOLWORTH

who died aug,^{ft}

$22\overset{d}{,}$1760, aged 39

Years; alfo IOSEPH

their son died

the Same Day

aged 6 days.

Darkness & Death,

make Halt at once.

. . .

Fig. 100. The Pember children stone, 1786, Franklin, Connecticut.

In memory of

three   Sons

of Mr.   Jacob

and Mrs.   Lydia

Pember, Philaſter died

Feb^r, 10th 1773 in his 6th Year

Philaſter 2^d died ſept 10th

1780 in his 4th Year

Jacob died July 30th 1786

aged 13 months

Sleep sweet babes & take your rest

God calld you home He saw it best

Fig. 101. The Bridget Snow stone, 1768, Mansfield Center, Connecticut.

May ye 30, A D: 1768

Departed this Life M^{rs}

Bridget Wife to M^r

Ebenezer Snow in y^e

37th, year of her Age

My Lover, Friend, Famil-

iar all — Remov'd from

Sight and out of Call,

To dark Oblivion is retir'd

[Dead] or at Leaſt me Ex[pired]

Fig. 102. The Roswell Ensworth stone, 1776, Canterbury, Connecticut.

In   Memory

of M^r.   Roſwell

Enſworth   ſon to Capt

Jabez &   Meheta–

bel Enſworth   he died

may 11th 1776 in $\overset{e}{y}$

22^{d} year of his Age.

Here in the bloom of

life I lye

To bleed & pine away

and die

I warn all friends both

old & young

Not to live a life as I have

done.

I with a ſmile look up to

God & cry

Receive my soal that I in

peace may die.

Fig. 103. The Thaddeus Maccarty stone, 1705, The Granary, Boston, Massachusetts.

HERE LYES $\overset{e}{Y}$ BODY

OF THADDEVS. MACCARTY

AGED 65 YEARS, &

6 MONTHS DESESED

IVNE.$\overset{e}{Y}$.18.1705

Fig. 106. The Captain Simon Sartwell, Jr., stone, 1791, Charlestown, New Hampshire.

In Memory of

Capt Simon Sartwell, J^{r}.

Who died May 30th

1791 In the 43rd,

year of his age.

How I lie Buried, deep in Duſt,

My Fleſh, ſhall be thy Care,

Theſe Withring Limbs, with the I truſt,

To raiſe them, bright and fair.

Fig. 107. The Eunice Colton stone, 1763, Longmeadow, Massachusetts.

In Memory of

M.ᴿ.ˢ. EUNICE

Daughter of

M.ᴿ. GEORGE &

M.ᴿ.ˢ. EXPERIENCE

COLTON

Who died

Oct.ᵇ.ʳ. 15.ſᵗ. 1763

In the 29.ſʰ. YEAR,

Job 17:11 My days

are past my purpoſes

are broken off

Fig. 108. The John Felt stone, 1805, Rockingham, Vermont.

Jeſus my king did every death on ſting

In Memory of Mr. John

Felt who Died April

The 19 1805 in the 23

Year of his age Son to Mr

Eliphalet and Ione Felt

Be bold and ſe as you pas by

As you are now ſo once was I,

As I am now so you muſt be

Prepair for death & follow me.

Fig. 109. The Sarah Long stone, 1674, Phipps Street, Charlestown, Massachusetts.

SARAH LONG,

WIFE TO ZECHARIAH

LONG, AGED 38 YEARS

DECEASED JULY

THE 3

1674

Fig. 110. The Lydia Wood stone, 1712, Phipps Street, Charlestown, Massachusetts.

HERE LYES $\overset{e}{Y}$

BODY OF LYDIA WOOD

WIFE TO JOSIAH

WOOD AGED 74

YEARS DIED NOVEM^R.

Y^e 25th 1712

Fig. 111. The Sarah Allen stone, 1785, East Burial Ground, Bristol, Rhode Island.

Saints arifing

M^{rs}: Sarah, wife

of M^r: James

Allen, & Daugh'^{tr}

of M^r: James

Diman & Anna

his wife: Died

July 29th 1785. in

ye 23^d Year

of her Age.

Fig. 112. The William Sinclear stone, 1753, Spencer, Massachusetts.

HERE LYES THE BODY O[F]

Mr WILLIAM SINCLEAR WH[O]

DIED JULY THE 4th. 175[3]

AGED 77 YEARS

HE WAS BORN IN *IRELAN*

IN THE COUNTY OF *DOWN* IN Y[E]

PARISH OF *DRUMBLOO*, HE LIV'D

IN *NEW-ENGLAND* 24 YEARS

Fig. 114. The Thomas Faunce stone, 1745/46, Plymouth, Massachusetts.

Here lyes buried

the Body of

M.^{r} ThOMAS FAUNCE

ruling ELDER of the first

Church of CHRIST in

PLYmouth deceaſed FEB.^{ry}

27th. An: Dom. 1745/6 in

the 99th. Year of his Age

The Fathers, where are they;

Bleſsed are the dead who

die in the LORD.

Fig. 115. The Ruth Carter stone, 1697/98, The Granary, Boston, Massachusetts.

HERE LYETH BURIED

Y^{e} BODY   OF

RUTH CARTER

Y^{e} WIFE OF

THOMAS CARTER

AGED ABOUT 41 YEAR^{s}

DECEASED JANUARY

Y^{e} 26   1697/8

Fig. 116. The Timothy Lindall stone, 1698/99, Salem, Massachusetts.

SANCTORUM MEMORIA SIT BEATA

[Blessed be the memory of the Saints.]

HERE LYETH BURIED

Y^{e} BODY OF

MR TIMOTHY LINDALL

AGED 56 YEARS

& 7 M^{O} DECEASED

JANUARY Y^{e} 6

1 6 9 8/9

Fig. 117. The Rebecca Gerrish stone, 1743, King's Chapel, Boston, Massachusetts.

HERE LIES BURIED

THE BODY OF

M^{rs}. REBECCA GERRISH

.   .   .

Fig. 118. The Rebecca Sanders stone, 1745/46, King's Chapel, Boston, Massachusetts.

Here lyes Interr'd

the Body of

Mrs REBECCA SANDERS

.   .   .

Fig. 119. The Joseph Tapping stone, 1678, King's Chapel, Boston, Massachusetts.

FUGIT   HORA

MEMENTO   MORI

JOSEPH

TAPPING   VIVE

AGED 23   MEMOR LOETHI

YEARS   FUGIT HORA

DEC^D DEC^R [Live mindful of death; time flies.]

$\check{Y}$ 20

1678

TEMPUS ERAT

Fig. 121. The John Foster stone, 1681, Dorchester, Massachusetts.

THE

INGENIOUS

Mathematician & printer

MR JOHN FOSTER

AGED 33 YEARS DYED SEPT^R 9TH

1681

———

April, 1681.

I.M. ASTRA COLIS VIVENS; MORIENS, SUPER ÆTHERA *FOSTER*
SCANDE, PRECOR; COELUM METIRI DISCE SUPREMUM.
J.F. METIOR, ATQUE MEUM EST: EMIT MIHI DIVES *JESUS*
NEC TENEOR QUICQUAM, NISI GRATES, SOLVERE.

[Increase Mather: Living thou studiest the stars; dying, mayest thou, Foster, I pray, mount above the skies and learn to measure the highest heaven.
John Foster: I measure it and it's mine; the Lord Jesus has bought it for me; nor am I held to pay aught for it but thanks.]

Fig. 122. The Sarah Swan stone, 1767, East Burial Ground, Bristol, Rhode Island.

CORIN:^S   Vears 22

CHAP. XV   ſo in Chriſt

For as in   Shall all be

Adam   made aliv^e

all die, even

Hear lies the Body

of SARAH, daugh -

- ter of EBENEZER

& MARGARET SWAN,

who depáted this

Life Apr: ẙ 17 AD 1767

  Aged 20 years

behold! O friend & Spend one thought on me.

ſee what I am, & what you all

        [muſt be

Fig. 125. The Eliakim Hayden stone, 1797, Essex, Connecticut.

In Memory of

Mr. ELIAKIM HAYDEN

who died Feb 8th.   1797

Aged 50 Years.

As in Adam, all mankinde

Did guilt and Death derive

So by the Righteousness of Christ

Shall all be made alive.

Fig. 126. The Charles Bardin stone, 1773, Old Common Burying-ground, Newport, Rhode Island.

In Memory of

CHARLES BARDIN

Eſq.^{r}

was born in LONDON

July 13th: A:D:1700 and

died June 3^{d} A:D:1773

JB

Fig. 128. The Mary Hart stone, 1689, Ipswich, Massachusetts.

HEAR LIES MR^{S}

MARY HART y^{e}

WIFE OF REF^{T}

THOMAS HART

WHO DIED NOVEM^{BER}

1689

Fig. 129. The Reverend Zachariah Symmes stone, 1707, Bradford, Massachusetts.

CONDITUM HIC CORPUS

VIRI VERE REVERENDI D

ZACHARIAE SYMMES, COLLE-

GII HARVARDINI QUONDAM

SOCII, EVANGELII MINISTRI,

PATRE AVOQUE, PRAECLA[RI]S EVA-

NGELII MINISTRIS, NAT[I]OM-

NIGENA ERUDITIONE ORNATI;

PIETATE VITAE QUE SANCTITATE

MAXIME CONSPICUI, ECCLESIAE

CHRISTI QUAE EST BRADFORDIAE

PER XL ANNOS: PASTORIS [VI]GI-

LANTISSIMI QUI COMM[UT]A-

VIT VITAM MORTALEM

CUM IMMORTALI. DIE XXII

MARTU ANNO DOMINI

MDCCVII AETATE SUAE . . .

[Buried here is the body of a man the Right Reverend Zacharia Symmes, of Harvard College a sometime Fellow, a minister of the gospel, whose father and grandfather were also distinguished ministers of the gospel, graced in every kind of learning: especially outstanding in the piety and holiness of his life; of the Church of Christ which is at Bradford for 40 years: a pastor of great vigilance who exchanged mortal life for immortality. On the 22 day of March in the year of our Lord 1707 his age was . . .]

Fig. 132. The Alice Hart stone, 1682, Ipswich, Massachusetts.

HERE LYES BURIED

ye BODY OF Mr^s ALICE

HART WIFE TO, M^r

THOMAS HART

WHO DIED: JUNE

ye 8 1682 AGED

ABOUT 70

YEARS

Fig. 133. The Sarya Wicom stone, 1705, Rowley, Massachusetts.

SARYA THE WIFE

OF DANIEL WICOM

DIED APRIL ỹ^e 9

1705 & IN ỹ^e

33rd YEAR OF HAR AGE

a tender mother

a prudent wife

at God's command

resind her Life.

Fig. 134. The Richard Goss stone, 1714/15, Ipswich, Massachusetts.

HERE LIES Y̆ BODY

OF MR RICHARD

GOSS WHO DIED

JANUARY Y̆ 24

1714-15 AGED

52 YEARS

For THIS DEPARTED SOUL

AND ALL Y̆ REST

THAT CHRIST HATH PUR-

CHASED

THAY SHALL BE BLEST

Fig. 135. The Deacon Nathaniel Knowlton stone, 1726, Ipswich, Massachusetts.

HERE LIES y̆ BODY OF

DEACON NATHANIEL

KNOWLTON WHO DIED

SEPTEMBER y̆ 24

1726 IN THE 69

YEAR OF HIS

AGE

Fig. 136. The Lieutenant Jonathan Pickard stone, 1735, Rowley, Massachusetts.

HERE LIES THE BODY

OF LEFT JONATHAN

PICKARD HO DIED

JANUARY $\overset{e}{y}$ 25

1735 IN THE

48 YEAR

OF HIS AGE.

Fig. 137. The Reverend Joseph Capen stone, 1725, Topsfield, Massachusetts.

HERE LYES BURIED

THE BODY OF the

REUEREND Mr JOSEPH

CAPEN A FAITHFULL MIN

ISTER OF CHRIST WHO

LIVED AN ORDAINED

PASTOR OF $\overset{e}{y}$ CHURCH

IN TOPSFIELD 42 YEAR^s

& DEPARTED THS LIFE Y

LAST DAY OF IUNE 1725

AGED 66 YEARS

DEAR . . . CAPEN thAt reuereD MAN

WhO DID the FAITH ^{of}CHRIST MAINTAIN

A LEARNED MAN IS GODLY TOO

NONE WILL DENIE THS WHO KNEW

Fig. 138. The Captain Joseph Little stone, 1740, Newburyport, Massachusetts.

HERE LYES BURIED Y^e

BODY OF CAPt JOSEPH

LIttLE WHO DEPARtED

THIS LIFE SEPtEMBER

y^e 6th 1740 - & IN

y^e 87th YEAR OF

HIS AGE

COME MORtAL MAN

& CASt AN EYE

COME READ tHY DOOM

PREPARE tO DIE

Fig. 139. The Elizabeth Wade stone, 1726, Ipswich, Massachusetts.

HERE LIES $\overset{e}{Y}$ BODY

OF MR^{S} ELIZABETH

WADE WHO DIED

JANUARY $\overset{e}{Y}$ 5

1726 AGED 76

YEARS

Fig. 140. The Captain Jacob Danforth stone, 1754, Billerica, Massachusetts.

Here Lies Buried

The Body of Capt

Jacob Danforth Who

Departed This

Life January y^{e}

2 A D 1754 Age

55 years 10 M &

16 D The Numbe^{r}

of our Months Are With God

Fig. 141. The Samuel Green stone, 1759, Lexington, Massachusetts.

Here Lies Buried

The Body of M^{r}

Samuel Green Who

Departed This Life

August y^{e} 10

A · D 1759

In y^e 63 year

of His Age

Fig. 142. The Esther Barrows stone, 1761, Mansfield Center, Connecticut.

In Memory of

Mr^s Efther Barrow^s

Con^{rt} to Mr Thomas

Barrows who died

March $\overset{e}{y}$ 17: 1761

in $\overset{e}{y}$ 64th year

of her Age.

Fig. 143. The Exercise Conant stone, 1722, Mansfield Center, Connecticut.

HERE LIETH

THE BODY

OF MISTAR

- EXERCISE -

CONANT - W$\overset{o}{H}$

DIED - APRELL

THE 28 - 1722

AGED - 85 - YEARS

Fig. 144. The Deacon Thomas Leffingwell stone, 1733, Norwichtown, Connecticut.

Here Lies Buried the Body of

Deacon Thomas Leffingwell the

Husband of Mrs Lydia Leffingwe^{ll}

& son to Mr Thomas Leffingwell

Deceafed & Mrs Mary Leffingwell

& . . . he had sarveed God &

His people, fell asleep ^{in} jesus

July 18 1733 in ye 60 year

of his Age. O Remembar

Death judgment & eternity

Fig. 145. The Abigail Huntington stone, 1734, Norwichtown, Connecticut.

Here lyes interred the

remains of Mrs Abigail

the wife of Mr Daniel

Huntington of Norwich

who died Dec 25 1734

In y^e 56 year of her age.

Fig. 146. The Deacon Christopher Huntington stone, 1735, Norwichtown, Connecticut.

HERE LYES INTERRD Y^e REMAIN^s

OF DEAC^N CHRISTOPHER HUNTIN^G

TON OF NORWICH BORN NOV$^{e\overline{\overline{M}}}$

BER Y^e =1=1660 & Y^e FIRST BORN

OF MALES IN Y^e TOWN HE SERVED

NEAR 40 YEARS IN Y^e OFFICE

OF A DEACON & DIED APRILL Y^e

24 = 1735=IN Y^e 75 Y^r OF HIS AGE

= MEMENTO = MORI== =

Fig. 147. The Hannah Huntington stone, 1746, Norwichtown, Connecticut.

IN MEMORY

of Mrs Hannah the

Virtuous and loving Confort of

Col. Hez Huntington Efq^r who

Departed this Life September

4th on AD 1746 and in the
46th year of her age

Ah Lavish death . . . this Narrow ſpace
In yonder Dome Made a Vaſt empty Place

Fig. 148. The Zeryiah Buckingham stone, c. 1746, Columbia, Connecticut.

IN MEMORY OF
the Well-beloved Gen^{t}-
woman Mrs Zeryiah Buckingham, wife to Capt:, Samuel
Buckingham. ſhe was a pattren
of Piety, Patience, & Virtue
and . . . ſhe had Lived
an Exempelary life many
years with the holy
Diſciple Lean herſelf upon
the Breaſt of her beloved, &
[Suddenly] fell aſleep in the
Cradle of Death, on the 17th
Day of September A:D
·   ·   ·

Fig. 151. The Deacon Nathaniel Bosworth stone, 1690, First Congregational Churchyard, Bristol, Rhode Island.

Here lyeth Interred
the Body of
Nathaniel Boswort^{h}
the first Deacon
of the Church of
Christ in Bristoll

who dyed August
ye 31st: 1690:in y^{e}:73st:
year of his Age.

Fig. 152. The Thomas Pelham slabstone, 1724, Governor Arnold Burying Ground, Newport, Rhode Island.

Here lieth Interred the body of
Thomas Pelham the Son of
Capt Edward Pelham and
Freelove his wife who deceas,
May the 14th:1724 in the 38:Year
of his age.

Fig. 153. The Sarah Harris stone, 1723, North Burial Ground, Providence, Rhode Island.

Here lyeth ye Body
of Sarah ye Daughter
of William Haris Esq;^{r}
and of Abigail his
Wife died Octo:^{r}
ye 4:th 1723 Aged
21:^{n} Years & 3 Months.

Fig. 154. The William Harris stone, 1725/26, North Burial Ground, Providence, Rhode Island.

Here lieth ye Body
of William Harris
Eſq. who died
January ye 4th
1725/6 in ye 53
Year of his age.

Fig. 155. The Job Harris stone, 1729, North Burial Ground, Providence, Rhode Island.

Here lies the body

of Job Harris who

died Decemb^{r} ye 17th

1729 in ye 5[9]thyear

of his age.

Fig. 157. The Captain Nathaniel Waldron stone, 1769, Old Common Burying-ground, Newport, Rhode Island.

IN MEMORY of

Capt.

NATHANIEL WALDRON

who departed this Life

January the 26th. A.D.

1769 in the 27th Year

of his Age.

Life how short!

Eternity how long!

Fig. 158. The Hannah Byles stone, 1771, Old Common Burying-ground, Newport, Rhode Island.

IN MEMORY of

Mr^{s}. HANNAH BYLES

Widow of M^{r}. JOSIAS

BYLES late of Boſton

deceased She died May

. . . 1771 in the 82^{d}.

.   .   .

Fig. 159. The Jonathan Wyatt stone, 1775, Old Common Burying-ground, Newport, Rhode Island.

> In Memory of
> MR.
> JONATHAN WYATT
> Son of MR.
> LEMUEL WYATT &
> SARAH his Wife, He
> died Sep. 28, 1775 in the
> 18th Year of his Age.
>
> J.S.

Fig. 160. The Elizabeth Sisson stone, 1774, Old Common Burying-ground, Newport, Rhode Island.

> This Humble Stone,
> is erected In Memory of,
> Mis ELIZABETH, daughter
> of M^{r}. JAMES SISSON,
> who departed this Life, the
> 22^{d}, Day of Auguſt A.D. 1774,
> in the 49th. Year of her age.
>
> J.Bull

Fig. 161. The Benjamin Wyatt stone, 1767, Old Common Burying-ground, Newport, Rhode Island.

> IN MEMORY of M^{r}.
> BENJAMIN WYATT,
> who died Decem^{br}.
> the 5th. A D 1767 in the
> 68th. year of his Age.

Notes

INTRODUCTION

1. For a brief but incisive account of iconoclasm during the sixteenth century in England, see Roy Strong, *The English Icon: Elizabethan & Jacobean Portraiture*, pp. 1–3.

2. Moses Coit Tyler, *A History of American Literature*, p. 228.

3. Carl Bridenbaugh, *The Colonial Craftsman*, p. 4; Roy Harvey Pearce, ed., *Colonial American Writing*, pp. v–vi.

4. Allan I. Ludwig, *Graven Images: New England Stonecarving and its Symbols, 1650–1815*, p. 43.

5. Ludwig, *Graven Images*, p. 4; Tyler, *A History of American Literature*, p. 228.

6. Ludwig says, "But in spite of what the zealots might have done in England, when they arrived in New England they rapidly changed their minds about imagery and began as early as 1668 to fill their burial grounds with emblems and symbols. This complex movement from iconophobia in England to iconography in New England is one of the most neglected transformations in our cultural history" (*Graven Images*, p. 44).

7. *An Addition to the Present Melancholy Circumstances of the Province Considered* (Boston: 1719), pp. 4–7.

8. *Ibid.*, p. 7.

9. See, for example, the diary of Joshua Hempstead, who was an eighteenth-century stonecarver in Connecticut; the account-books of the Stevens Family, stonecutters of Newport, Rhode Island; and the diary of Samuel Sewall, the Boston jurist.

10. Samuel Mather, *A Testimony from the Scripture against Idolatry & Superstition*, p. 6.

11. Ludwig selects an inappropriate passage from Willard's *Compleat Body of Divinity*, inveighing against the imaging of angels as folly but absolutely prohibiting the imaging of God (*Graven Images*, p. 33). Beyond that point (which is significant in its own distinctions), Willard goes on to elaborate about the Second Commandment in precisely Mather's terms: "THIS Command forbids the Worshipping of God by Images. . . . 1. THE Making of them is prohibited. Thou shalt not make. And under a graven Image and Similitude is comprehended, every manner of Representation of God, whether in Statues or Pictures. For this general prohibition doth not respect things meerly Civil" (*A Compleat Body of Divinity*, p. 621).

12. See Mason I. Lowance, Jr., Introduction to Samuel Mather, *The Figures or Types of the Old Testament*, pp. vi–vii.

13. For an account of the cultural anxieties of New England settlers during the latter part of the seventeenth century, see Perry Miller, *Errand into the Wilderness*, pp. 1–15.

14. Cotton Mather, *Just Commemorations*, p. 6.

15. For the iconographer the task of reading each and every image on New England gravestones would be overwhelming. Ludwig resolves this problem by claiming right- fully that "in all symbolism the value of many secondary motifs was not so much di- dactic, although to be sure it could be that too, as it was 'atmospheric.' The secondary symbols were meant to fill out the presence of symbolism rather than to define any specific dogma" (*Graven Images*, p. 14). Ludwig, of course, is interested primarily in the meaning of individual images, but he fails to acknowledge even in passing the meaning afforded by the formal patterns of imagery. By the same token, he maintains that "the scope of the imagery was limited" (*ibid.*, p. 65), while failing to recognize the rich variety of designs. The latter transcend the limitations of imagery and account in the main for the art of the gravestone.

16. *The Metamorphic Tradition in Modern Poetry*, pp. 1, 12.

17. Primary sources do not afford a comprehensive account of funeral practices in early New England, although Samuel Sewall offers at least surface details in his *Diary*, as he did for many contemporaneous events. In a complementary fashion, Cotton Mather's *Diary* provides some insight to the inner workings of the funeral. Historical renderings, some of which are inaccurate, and most of which treat simply the events of the ritual, are scattered throughout the nineteenth and twentieth centuries.

CHAPTER 1

1. John Winthrop, *The Winthrop Papers*, ed. Allyn B. Forbes, 5 vols. (Boston: The Massachusetts Historical Society, 1929–1947), 2:295.

2. Nathaniel Hawthorne, *The Scarlet Letter*, p. 38.

3. W. Lloyd Warner asserts that "the cemetery and its gravestones are the hard, enduring signs which anchor each man's projections of his innermost fantasies and private fears about the uncertainty of his own death—and the uncertainty of his ultimate future—on an external symbolic object made safe by tradition and the sanctions of re- ligion. . . . Rituals of consecration have transformed a small part of the common soil of the town into a sacred place and dedicated this land of the dead to God, to the sacred souls of the departed, and to the souls of the living whose bodies are destined for such an end. The rituals which establish graveyards tacitly imply formal rules and precepts which define the relations of the profane and sacred worlds of the living and the dead. The funeral—a formal rite of separation of the recently dead from the living—is, broadly speaking, an unending ritual, for although funerals are separate rites, they occur with such continuing frequency that they maintain a constant stream of ritual connection between the dead and the living" (*The Living and the Dead*, pp. 280–281).

4. In support of this view James Fulton Maclear claims that the neglect of the mystical element in New England Puritanism "has fostered the temptation to regard the Puritan mind as static rather than dynamic, as an entity installed in the New England landscape in 1630 rather than a development which within the first decade of settlement underwent ferment, revolution, decision, selection, and purgation" ("'The Heart of New England Rent': The Mystical Element in Early Puritan History," *Mississippi Valley His- torical Review* 42 [1956]: 622). Not only mysticism, as powerful a force as it was, but other attitudes and values, as we endeavor to show, animated Puritanism in dynamic ways.

5. Charles Feidelson, *Symbolism and American Literature*, p. 90.

6. For an extensive treatment of Ramus, see Walter J. Ong, *Ramus: Method and the Decay of Dialogue* (Cambridge: Harvard University Press, 1958). For a discussion of New

England Puritanism and Ramist logic, see Perry Miller, *The New England Mind: The Seventeenth Century* (Cambridge: Harvard University Press, 1954).

7. See Chapter III in Feidelson, *Symbolism and American Literature*, for a discussion of the analytic qualities of Ramist logic.

8. For a detailed study of this problem, see Clarence C. Goen, *Revivalism and Separatism in New England, 1740–1800* (New Haven: Yale University Press, 1962).

9. For an extensive discussion of these matters, see Edmund S. Morgan, *Visible Saints: The History of a Puritan Idea* (New York: New York University Press, 1963); and Robert G. Pope, *The Half-Way Covenant: Church Membership in Puritan New England* (Princeton: Princeton University Press, 1969).

10. Leonard Hoar, *The Sting of Death and Death Unstung*, p. 3.

11. Benjamin Colman, *The Hope of the Righteous*, p. 26.

12. *The Crown and Glory of a Christian, Consisting in a Sound Conversion and Well Ordered Conversion*, p. 21.

13. In his diary Wigglesworth recorded, "The Lord's Supper being nigh: I am afraid at the thought of it; and wel I may having a heart so vastly unsutable to be at any time near god, More fit to ly lowest in Hel that I might be farthest from him" (*The Diary of Michael Wigglesworth, 1653–1657*, p. 54).

14. Samuel Willard, *Covenant-Keeping The Way to Blessedness . . . .* , p. 49; Hoar, *The Sting of Death*, p. 22; Philip Pain, *Daily Meditations*, p. 16.

15. Colman, *The Hope of the Righteous*, pp. 17, 19–20.

16. Williston Walker, ed., *The Creeds and Platforms of Congregationalism*, p. 79.

17. *The Directory for the Public Worship of God*, p. 507. Horton Davies discusses this particular controversy: "The directions for the Burial of the Dead were also hotly disputed in the Committee and in the Assembly. The Independents, it might be imagined, had even more reason to regard burial as a civil concern than marriage. This time, however, they were joined by some of the Presbyterians. . . . The result of these protests was that only the briefest and simplest offices were permitted" (*The Worship of the English Puritans*, p. 139).

18. Thomas Lechford, *Plain Dealing; or, News from New England*, pp. 87–88.

19. *Directory*, p. 507; *The Diary of Cotton Mather*, 8:44.

20. *Directory*, p. 507; *Records of the Governor and Company of the Massachusetts Bay in New England, 1628–1686*, ed. Nathaniel B. Shurtleff, 5 vols. (Boston, 1853–1854), 3:162.

21. Nathaniel Morton, *New Englands Memoriall*, n. p.

22. *Ibid.*, n. p.; Mather, *Diary*, 8:96; *Diary of Samuel Sewall, 1674–1729*, 7:341–342.

23. *Diary of Samuel Sewall*, 7:341.

24. Mather's funeral sermon for Hannah Hull Sewall was entitled *The Valley of Baca . . .* (Boston, 1717). Written by John Danforth, the broadside elegy was entitled "Greatness and Goodness Elegized Madam Hannah Sewall" (*The Poetry of John Danforth*, pp. 162–164).

25. John Rowe, *Letters and Diary*, pp. 141–142.

26. *Proceedings of the Massachusetts Historical Society, 1920–1921*, Series 3, vols. 41–60 (Boston, 1922), 54:215–224.

27. Cotton Mather, *A Christian Funeral*, pp. 20, 22.

28. Mather, *Diary*, 8:96.

29. Sewall, *Diary*, 7:43–44.

CHAPTER 2

1. Johan Huizinga, *Homo Ludens*, p. 14.

2. In Chapter II of *Symbolism and American Literature* Charles Feidelson presents a theory of the symbolizing imagination which he then applies to the Puritans in Chapter III. For a full discussion of the symbol in theoretical terms, see Susanne Langer, *Philosophy in a New Key*; Ernst Cassirer, *An Essay on Man*; and Leslie White, *The Science of Culture*.

3. Harrison T. Meserole, ed., *Seventeenth-Century American Poetry*, pp. 384–385. The poem was written by John Wilson (*c.* 1588–1667). For a discussion of the relationship between the funeral sermon and the elegy, see Richard Henson, "Form and Content of the Puritan Funeral Elegy," *American Literature* 33 (1960–1961): 11–27.

4. *Diary*, 6:30–31.

5. Thomas Hooker, Preface to *A Survey of the Summe of Church-Discipline*, in Perry Miller and Thomas H. Johnson, eds., *The Puritans*, 2:673. For a general study of Puritan preaching, see Babette May Levy, *Preaching in the First Half of New England History* (Hartford: The American Society of Church History, 1945). For a brilliant interpretation of Puritan plain style in its complex dimensions, see Perry Miller, *Nature's Nation*, pp. 208–240. And for a history of the plain style in England, see John F. Wilson, *Pulpit in Parliament: Puritanism during the English Civil Wars, 1640–1648* (Princeton: Princeton University Press, 1968).

6. Michael Wigglesworth, *The Prayse of Eloquence*, in Miller and Johnson, eds., *The Puritans*, 2:674.

7. Ludwig refers throughout *Graven Images* to a "ministerial elite," but he ignores the evangelical nature of Puritanism. Though the ministers were indeed socially elite, emphasizing a hierarchical order for society, they keyed their sermons to the entire congregation by means of a "plain style." On the level of art, therefore, the ministers and their congregations were not necessarily at odds. Most significantly, it becomes difficult to contend, as Ludwig does, that gravestone art arose as a reaction against the theological abstractions of the ministers. There was not only a common discourse but a commonality of experience and shared values as well to dispel Ludwig's contention.

8. Wigglesworth, *The Prayse of Eloquence*, in Miller and Johnson, eds., *The Puritans*, 2:674.

9. Samuel Willard, *A Sermon . . . Occasioned by the Death of . . . John Leveret . . .*, pp. 1, 8.

10. Cotton Mather, *A Father Departing . . .* (Boston: 1723), p. 20.

11. Mather, *Diary*, 7:217.

12. "Thomas Dudley (ah! old, must dye)," in Kenneth Silverman, ed., *Colonial American Poetry*, pp. 132–133.

13. "Verses found in [Thomas Dudley's] pocket after his death," in Meserole, ed., *Seventeenth-Century American Poetry*, p. 365. In his history Nathaniel Morton reported: "The Verses following were found in his Pocket after his death, which may further illustrate his Character, and give a taste of his poetical fancy: wherein (it is said) he did excel" (*New Englands Memoriall*, p. 140).

14. Silverman notes: "No other form of poetry seemed so natural to them as the elegy. Far from disliking verse they awarded it an important public function. Death tests life. At death a man's lifelong daily struggle for salvation faces God's precalculated judgment. Then the soul knows whether it has won its way to glory or slid to eternal vomit of hell. Because death tested the conduct of a man's whole life, and because the passing of great men showed God's disposition toward the community, the elegy could stake as its province theological doctrine, social theory, and personal grief, while

elaborating the ideals of conduct Puritans valued and solidifying the community's scorn for heretics—could in short reach all domains the most public and most private of Puritan life" (Silverman, ed., *Colonial American Poetry*, p. 121).

15. In *The Poetry of John Danforth*, pp. 182–183.

16. "Greatness and Goodness Elegized," *ibid.*, pp. 162–164.

17. John Fiske, "Samuel Sharpe (Us! Ample-share)," in Silverman, ed., *Colonial American Poetry*, pp. 138–140.

18. In Ola Elizabeth Winslow, *American Broadside Verse*, p. 7.

19. See "Silence Dogood, No. 7," *The New-England Courant* (June 25, 1922), in Leonard W. Labaree, ed., *The Papers of Benjamin Franklin*, 15 vols. (New Haven: Yale University Press, 1959–1972), 1:23–26.

20. Henriette s'Jacob, *Idealism and Realism*, p. 3.

21. Ludwig, *Graven Images*, pp. 258–261. Ludwig's theory is supported by Roy Strong's contention that the neo-medievalism of Elizabethan court portraiture faded by moving to the provinces (see his *English Icon*, pp. 13–27). And from there, one might add, vestiges of the style were further dispersed to the colonies.

CHAPTER 3

1. Ludwig disputes Mrs. Harriette Forbes' theory that the Charlestown Carver actually worked out of Boston on the grounds that his stones would have then appeared south of the Charles River as well, when they do not (*Graven Images*, pp. 287–296). While Mrs. Forbes points out the fact that Joseph Lamson's work becomes difficult to distinguish from the Charlestown Carver's during the 1680's (*Gravestones of Early New England*, p. 41), we were first made aware of the possibility that the Charlestown Carver was more than one craftsman by Gerald Trauber. His specialized interest in lettering on New England gravestones allowed him to differentiate among some attributed stones. It is possible as well as probable, however, that the Charlestown Carver assigned the task of lettering to one of his apprentices.

The significance of the Charlestown Carver does not lie, as Ludwig suggests, in his boldness as an artisan who introduced religious art to an iconophobic culture (*Graven Images*, p. 296), because, as we have already indicated, the Puritans were not hostile to visual art as long as it was part of the civil realm. The Charlestown Carver deserves, rather, to be recognized as an artisan of substantial carving achievement.

2. Nathaniel Emmons defined a "plain preacher" as "one who has clear and distinct ideas in his own mind, and who conveys them to the minds of his hearers in plain language." He followed this standard definition by standard qualifications: "Sensible that *figurative* language is the voice of nature, and best adapted to explain and illustrate whatever is dark and obscure; he [Christ] made a free use of Images, which spread much light and perspicuity upon all the subjects he handled. He borrowed his Images, however, not from Music, Painting, Poetry, or any of the Arts which are confined to the learned Few; but from the most familiar appearances and productions of Nature, which lie open and common to every observer" (*Christ the Standard of Preaching*, pp. 6–7). Emmons' objections to the fine arts, then, were based on their esoteric quality, and hence their inutility for widespread communication. His anti-art attitudes do not go unqualified, and in nowise can they be considered as part of a heritage derived from a mythical Puritan hostility to art.

3. Ludwig, *Graven Images*, p. 295.

4. According to Ludwig, "By 1676 on the Thomas Call stone in Malden, Massachusetts (plate 164A), emblems such as the hourglass, the crossed bones, the shovel, the

coffin, the pick, begin to appear in a horizontal frieze set upon a thin lintel supported by three carved columns with stepped capitals. This stone may well be the first use of architectural ornament in New England" (*Graven Images*, p. 291).

5. Thomas Wilson, *A Complete Christian Dictionary*, p. 719. Wilson (1563–1662) was an Anglican rector at Canterbury and enjoyed good relations with those nonconforming members of his parish (see *The Dictionary of National Biography*, eds. Leslie Stephen and Sidney Lee, 22 vols. [London: Oxford University Press, 1959–1960], 21:607).

6. For an account of Lamson's development of carving skills, see Ludwig, *Graven Images*, pp. 300–313.

CHAPTER 4

1. Wilson, *A Complete Christian Dictionary*, pp. 96–97.

2. Benjamin Keach, *Tropologia: A Key to Open Scripture-Metaphors . . .* , p. 1 Keach (1640–1704) was a Baptist preacher in England.

3. Sewall, *Diary*, 3:347–348.

4. A casual search through *John Stevens: His Book 1705* reveals several references to cherubim. In an advertisement in the *Boston News-Letter* for July 30, 1772, Henry Christian Geyer made special mention of a cherub: "A monument has been cut in this Town by Mr. Henry Christian Geyer, Stone-cutter at the South End, to be sent to Connecticut: it is executed in the Composite Order with twisted Pillars, and other proper Ornaments, having a Cherub's Head on Wings, and the following label from his Mouth, Rev. XIV. 6, 7. The inscription follows" (in George Francis Dow, *The Arts and Crafts in New England, 1704–1775*, p. 285).

5. Wilson, *Christian Dictionary*, p. 97.

6. Cut on the Enoch Hopkins stone of 1778, on Copp's Hill, Boston, Massachusetts. The carving on this large (46 x 30 inches) slate stone is worn.

7. Keach, *Tropologia*, p. 104.

8. Ulrich Simon, *Heaven in the Christian Tradition* (New York: Harper & Brothers, 1958), p. 129.

9. Mrs. Forbes counted fourteen Dagon stones, three of which appear outside of Boston, in Dorchester, West Roxbury, and Portsmouth, New Hampshire (*Gravestones of Early New England*, p. 121).

10. See Gertrude Jobes, *Dictionary of Mythology, Folklore, and Symbols*, 2 vols. (New York: Scarecrow Press, 1961), 1:406; Louis Herbert Gray, ed., *The Mythology of All Races*, 13 vols. (Boston: Marshall Jones, 1916–1932), 5:80–83; Frank J. Montalbano, "Canaanite Dagon: Origin, Nature," *The Catholic Biblical Quarterly* 13 (1951): 381–397.

11. Robert H. West, *Milton and the Angels* (Athens: The University of Georgia Press, 1955), p. 10.

12. George F. Sensabaugh notes that Cotton Mather's reference to Milton in his *Magnalia Christi Americana* (London, 1702) was one of the earliest, although Roger Williams knew Milton (*Milton in Early America* [Princeton: Princeton University Press, 1964], pp. 38–39).

13. Quoted in George Wesley Whiting, *Milton's Literary Milieu* (New York: Russell & Russell, 1964), pp. 210–212.

14. William Bradford, *Bradford's History "Of Plimouth Plantation,"* p. 286. See Minor Wallace Major, "William Bradford Versus Thomas Morton," *Early American Literature* 5 (Fall 1950): 1–13, for a discussion of the affair.

15. Gunnar Berefelt observes that this particular posture of the flying angel was highly conventionalized, extending back to antiquity (*A Study on the Winged Angel:*

The Origin of a Motif, trans. Patrick Hort [Stockholm: Almqvist & Wiksell, 1968], pp. 8–10).

16. Mrs. Forbes identifies the carver of the Ruth Conant stone and others like it as the "Hook and Eye Man" because of the way he cut the faces of his cherubim (*Gravestones of Early New England,* pp. 101–102).

17. There is a possibility that Zerubbabel Collins did not carve the Jedidiah Aylesworth stone because of the attenuation of forms. Even so, the carver was certainly working closely in the Collins manner.

18. The painted chest offered as an example presents a compendium of motifs that were used on gravestones. In addition to all the floral variations, the profiles with vines extending from their mouths (painted on the two uppermost drawers) appear on the Captain James Lyman stone of Connecticut in 1769 and the Nicholas Larrance Stone of Charlestown in 1710. See Ludwig, *Graven Images,* plates 82 and 81, respectively. For an excellent analysis of motifs on colonial furniture, see John T. Kirk, "Sources and Development of Styles in Connecticut Furniture," *Connecticut Furniture: Seventeenth and Eighteenth Centuries* (Hartford: The Wadsworth Atheneum, 1967).

CHAPTER 5

1. Mather, *Diary,* 8:216–217.

2. Leonard Bliss, *The History of Rehoboth* (Boston: Otis, Broaders, 1836), p. 175; John Langdon Sibley and Clifford K. Shipton, *Harvard Graduates,* 16 vols. (Cambridge: Harvard University Press, 1933), 6:287.

3. This catechism is appended to *The History of the Holy Jesus, c.* 1750.

4. Sibley and Shipton, *Harvard Graduates,* 6:556.

5. Ludwig attributes the Rogers stone to either William Codner or one of his followers (*Graven Images.* p. 314).

6. Sibley and Shipton, *Harvard Graduates,* 6:556–560.

7. Ludwig identifies Codner as the carver of the Rawson stone (*Graven Images,* p. 316).

8. Mather, *Just Commemorations,* p. 37.

9. In addition to "Greatness & Goodness Elegized" (in *The Poetry of John Danforth,* pp. 162–164), the following poems bear the convention of a ship metaphor: John Fiske's "Anne Griffin"; Roger Wolcott's "Poetical Meditations" and "The Heart is Deep" (in Silverman, ed., *Colonial American Poetry,* pp. 140–142, 222–234); John Saffin's "An Elegie On . . . John Hull"; Captain John Smith's "The Sea Marke"; Richard Steere's "A Monumental Memorial of *Marine Mercy*"; and Benjamin Tompson's "Edmund Davie" (in Meserole, ed., *Seventeenth-Century American Poetry,* pp. 199–202, 378–379, 245–252, 223–224).

10. Franklin Bowditch Dexter, *Biographical Sketches of the Graduates of Yale College with Annals of the College History,* 6 vols. (New York: Henry Holt, 1885–1912), 1:375.

11. *Plymouth Church Records, 1620–1859,* 2 vols. (New York: New England Society, 1920–1923), 1:417.

12. For an excellent account of the Puritan family, see Edmund S. Morgan, *The Puritan Family* (New York: Harper & Row, 1966). It should be noted that, in addition to traits peculiar to a blend of Puritan values and New England environment, these people drew upon a strong Elizabethan tradition of portraiture. As Roy Strong has commented, "For the Elizabethans fame was connected with family and the portrait cult is another aspect of the genealogical mania which beset them. It is reflected in the hectic building of tombs and effigies in parish churches, in the use of ancestral heraldry (often in-

vented), in profusion in interior decoration and in the advent of published family histories. Pride of family with an eye to posterity inspired the commissioning of portraits." (*The English Icon*, p. 29).

13. Cotton Mather, *Right Thoughts in Sad Hours*, pp. 46–47. In a discussion of Puritan attitudes toward the death of children, Gerhard T. Alexis takes up the matter of Michael Wigglesworth's granting reprobate children "the easiest room" in Hell in his best-selling poem, *The Day of Doom*. He concludes that, while Calvinist doctrine distinguished even the youngest infants as elect or reprobate, Puritan theologians nonetheless attempted to ease the fate of condemned children ("Wigglesworth's 'Easiest Room'," *The New England Quarterly* XLII [December 1969]:573–583).

14. Mather, *Right Thoughts*, p. 48.

15. *Ibid.*, pp. 49, 54.

16. Edward Taylor, "Extract of a Letter," *ibid.*, p. 55. Thomas H. Johnson notes that Taylor's letter and poem (slightly different in the manuscript version) was originally to Samuel Sewall in response to the death of Sewall's child a few years before the extract was published in Mather's sermon. Sewall assumed the cost of printing this sermon and apparently gave the extract and poem to Mather to include in the publication ("A Seventeenth-Century Printing of Some Verses of Edward Taylor," *The New England Quarterly* XIV [March 1941]: 139–141).

17. Taylor, "Extract of a Letter," in Mather, *Right Thoughts*, pp. 55–56. "Upon Wedlock and Death of Children" can be found in its entirety in Taylor, *Poems*, pp. 468–470.

18. For an excellent essay on Taylor's poetry as meditative verse, see Louis L. Martz, Foreword to *The Poems of Edward Taylor*, pp. xiii–xxxvii. See also, Donald Junkins, "'Should Stars Wooe Lobster Claws?': A Study of Edward Taylor's Poetic Practice and Theory," *Early American Literature* III, No.2 (1968):88-117.

CHAPTER 6

1. A frame like that of a Chippendale mirror appears on the James Luce, Jr., stone of 1775 in Scotland, Connecticut, so as to border the face of a soul effigy and "reflect" life beyond the grave. Identification between the deceased and the viewer is further intensified by the conventional but, in this instance, highly appropriate saying: "Behold my Friend, as you pass by / as you are now so once was I: / as I am now so you must be, / Prepare for Death & Follow me."

2. Edward Taylor, *Poems*, pp. 468–470.

CHAPTER 7

1. For a full discussion of the history of typological interpretation, see Thomas M. Davis, "The Exegetical Traditions of Puritan Typology," *Early American Literature* 5, Pt. 1 (Spring 1970):11–50.

2. Feidelson, *Symbolism and American Literature*, p. 78.

3. Ludwig gives the source of the William Sinclear stone as the Cokayn broadside (*Graven Images*, p. 274).

4. Mrs. Forbes attributes these stones to William Codner (*Gravestones of Early New England*, p. 61).

5. Ludwig, *Graven Images*, pp. 88–100.

6. *Ibid.*, p. 274.

7. *Ibid.*, p. 89.

8. See Thomas Tileston, "Funeral Elegy" (1681), and Joseph Capen, "Funeral Elegy" (1681), in Thomas C. Simonds, *The History of South Boston* (Boston: David

Clapp, 1857), pp. 34–39. Acrostics were rarely used on gravestones, and anagrams apparently never, a curious fact considering their popularity in elegiac verse. The acrostic convention was used, however, in epitaphs on two stones in the Old Common Burying-Ground in Newport: the Sarah Mitchell stone of 1718 and the Jacob Dehane slabstone of 1751. Both these stones were cut in the John Stevens Shop.

9. Edward Taylor, 1 Meditation. Col. 2. 17, "Which are Shaddows of things to come and the body is Christs" (Taylor, *Poems*, pp. 83–84).

10. For a discussion of Taylor and typology, see Ursula Brumm, *American Thought and Religious Typology*, pp. 56–85.

11. Ludwig, *Graven Images*, pp. 124–133.

12. Wilson, *Christian Dictionary*, p. 8.

13. *Ibid.*, p. 440; Keach, *Tropologia*, pp. 43–44.

14. Wilson, *Christian Dictionary*, p. 30.

15. For a very similar woodcut of an ark, see *A New Hieroglyphical Bible* . . . (Boston, 1794), p. 10.

16. The obituary reads: "On Thursday evening last, departed this life, after a few days illness, in the 73d year of his age, CHARLES BARDIN, Esq; who justly merited through life the noblest of characters, that of an honest man. As a member of society, he was humane, benevolent, obliging, ever ready to assist and relieve his neighbour, as a husband, loving and affectionate, as a master, kind and indulgent; but as a tender parent, he shone with uncommon lustre, no man perhaps having manifested stronger marks of the truest affection, by attending with an anxious care to the educating and forming the manners of a numerous family of children, several of whose connexions and circumstances in life, in consequence thereof, afforded him a most pleasing return, and were a balsam to his declining years. He long sustained the office of a justice of peace, which he discharged with that readiness and uprightness which entitled him to a great share of business, procured him the esteem of the inhabitants of the town, and renders his death much lamented. His remains were interred yesterday" (p. 3).

17. Ludwig, *Graven Images*, p. 202.

18. Samuel Wilson, *A Scripture Manual*, p. 29.

19. Silverman, ed., *Colonial American Poetry*, p. 208.

20. Thomas Wilson, *Christian Dictionary*, p. 422.

21. Keach, *Tropologia*, pp. 417, 36–37.

CHAPTER 8

1. For a history of this stylistic change, see Ludwig, *Graven Images*, pp. 358–389.

2. For a brief account of the Byfield stones, see Lura Woodside Watkins, "The Byfield Stones—Our Earliest American Sculpture?" *Antiques* 84 (October 1963): 420–423.

3. *Bradford's History "Of Plimouth Plantation,"* p. 3.

4. A sense of death might have been all the stronger because Haverhill and the entire area experienced Indian wars throughout the latter part of the seventeenth century.

5. Dennis A. Fales, Jr., notes that "the design of the guilloche carving on the drawer [of the deedbox] resembles markedly the decoration in the borders of the gravestone of Thomas Dennis' first wife, Grace, who died in 1686" ("Essex County Furniture—Documented Treasures from Local Collections, 1660–1860," *Essex Institute Historical Collections* 101 [July 1965]: 165–244).

6. Joseph Capen, "Funeral Elegy," in Simonds, *The History of South Boston*, pp. 38–39.

7. Ludwig, *Graven Images*, pp. 358–371.

8. Keach, *Tropologia*, p. 78; Thomas Wilson, *Christian Dictionary*, pp. 571–572; Benjamin Woodbridge, "Upon the TOMB of the most Reverend Mr. John Cotton," in Silverman, ed., *Colonial American Poetry*, pp. 133–135; *The Crown and Glory of a Christian*, p. 33.

9. For an account of these theological ideas as they developed into Deism in the latter half of the eighteenth century, see Herbert M. Morais, *Deism in Eighteenth Century America* (New York: Russell & Russell, 1960).

10. Ludwig, *Graven Images*, pp. 380–382.

11. *Ibid.*, p. 416.

CHAPTER 9

1. *John Stevens: His Book, 1705* (Newport: privately printed), n. p. [p. 1].

2. *Ibid.* [p. 2].

3. John Cotton, *Christian Calling*, in Miller and Johnson, eds., *The Puritans*, 1: 319–327.

4. *John Stevens: His Book, 1705* [p. 93].

5. *Ibid.* [p. 71].

6. *Ibid.* [p. 74].

7. *Ibid.* [p. 10].

8. Mrs. Forbes attributes these stones to the Tingley stonecarving family of Attleborough, Massachusetts *(Gravestones of Early New England*, pp. 97–99). We attribute the Sarah Harris and the William Harris stones to John Stevens II, while the Job Harris stone may have been done by him or someone else in his style.

9. Thomas Wilson, *Christian Dictionary*, p. 653.

10. For information on Bull, see Henry Bull, 4th, "The Bull Family of Newport," *Bulletin of the Newport Historical Society* (October 1931): 1–36.

11. Ludwig, *Graven Images*, p. 331.

12. Silverman, ed., *Colonial American Poetry*, p. 129.

CONCLUSION

1. See John Singleton Copley, *Letters and Papers of John Singleton Copley and Henry Pelham, 1739–1776*, Collections of the Massachusetts Historical Society, vol. 71 (Boston, 1914).

2. For the February 1, 1770, issue of the *Boston News-Letter*, Geyer published this advertisement:

Henry Christian Geyer, Stone-Cutter, near Liberty-Tree, South-End, Boston, Hereby informs his Customers, and other Gentlemen and Ladies, that besides carrying on the Stone Cutting Business as usual, he carries on the Art and Manufactory of a fuser Simolacrorum, or the making of all sorts of images, viz.

1st. Kings & Queens; 2d. King George & Queen Charlotte; 3d. King & Queen of Denmark; 5th. King & Queen of Sweden; — Likewise a Number of Busts, among which are, Mathew Prior, Homer, Milton &c. — Also a number of Animals, such as Parrots, Cats, Dogs, Lions, Sheep, with a number of others, too many to enumerate: Said Geyer also cleans old deficient Animals, and makes them look as well as new, at a reasonable Rate. All the above mentioned Images, Animals, &c. are made of Plaister of Paris of this Country. (Dow, *The Arts and Crafts of New England*, p. 284).

Two years later, he published the advertisement for the Sandemann stone. Both ads suggest Geyer's increasing awareness of the artist's role, which, on the other hand, he was able to fulfill only through the production of *kitsch*.

3. Samuel Willard, for example, advised: *"When the Saints die beware of irregular Mourning:* though we are to lament their Death, yet we must beware that it be after the right manner. . . . It is we and not they that are indangered and endamaged by it: we may therefore weep for our selves, and there is good reason for it, but to mourn for them is superfluous. . . . Is it not a precious thing to be asleep in Jesus?" These are the stock Calvinist reasons that previously relegated the funeral to the civil realm, but even so, there is a "right manner" for mourning. In addition to prescribing proper forms, Willard further insulates the survivors against excessive grief by claiming that "it should more effect our hearts at the thought of this that they were *Saints*, then that they were our Father, or Mother, or Brethren, or nearest or dearest Friends, for this is that which makes their loss to be greater than any other Relation doth or can." By emphasizing the public role of the Saint, who deserved communal rites, Willard assuaged the immediacy of private grief (*The Death of a Saint*, in Miller and Johnson, eds., *The Puritans*, 1:371–372).

Selected Bibliography

An Addition to the Present Melancholy Circumstances of the Province Considered. Boston: 1719.

Bancroft, Thomas. *The Character of Anna, The Prophetess, Consider'd and Apply'd.* Boston: 1723.

Benes, Peter. "Nathaniel Fuller, Stonecutter of Plympton, Massachusetts." *Old-Time New England*, LX (Summer 1969): 13–30.

Bercovitch, Sacvan. "Typology in Puritan New England: The Williams-Cotton Controversy Reassessed." *American Quarterly*, 19 (Summer 1967): 166–191.

Bradford, William. *Bradford's History "Of Plimouth Plantation."* Boston: Wright & Potter Printing, 1898.

Bridenbaugh, Carl. *The Colonial Craftsman.* Chicago: The University of Chicago Press, 1964.

Brigham, Clarence S. *Paul Revere's Engravings.* 2nd, revised edition. New York: Atheneum, 1969.

Brumm, Ursula. *American Thought and Religious Typology.* New Brunswick: Rutgers University Press, 1970.

Bull, Henry, 4th. "The Bull Family of Newport," *Bulletin of the Newport Historical Society* (October 1931):1–36.

Burgess, Frederick. *English Churchyard Memorials.* London: Lutterworth Press, 1963.

The Burying Place of Governor Arnold. Newport: Privately Printed, 1960.

Cassirer, Ernst. *An Essay on Man.* Garden City: Doubleday, 1944.

Colman, Benjamin. *The Hope of the Righteous.* Boston: 1721.

Copley, John Singleton. *Letters and Papers of John Singleton Copley and Henry Pelham, 1739–1776.* Collections of the Massachusetts Historical Society. Vol. 71. Boston: 1914.

The Crown and Glory of a Christian, Consisting in a Sound Conversion and Well Ordered Conversion. 3rd edition. Boston: 1684.

Danforth, John. *The Poetry of John Danforth.* Edited by Thomas A. Ryan. Reprinted from the Proceedings of the American Antiquarian Society for April, 1968.

Davies, Horton. *The Worship of the English Puritans.* Westminster: Dacre Press, 1948.

Davis, Thomas M. "The Exegetical Traditions of Puritan Typology," *Early American Literature*, 5 (Spring 1970), Part 1:11–50.

Deetz, James, and Edwin S. Dethlefsen, "Death's Head, Cherub, Urn and Willow," *Natural History*, 76 (March 1967):28–37.

The Directory for the Public Worship of God. London: 1768.

Dow, George Francis. *The Arts and Crafts in New England, 1704–1775.* Topsfield, Mass.: The Wayside Press, 1927.

Draper, John W. *A Century of Broadside Elegies*. London: Ingpen and Grant, 1928.

Emmons, Nathaniel. *Christ the Standard of Preaching*. Providence: 1786.

Feidelson, Charles, Jr. *Symbolism and American Literature*. Chicago: The University of Chicago Press, 1953.

Forbes, Harriette Merrifield. *Gravestones of Early New England: And The Men Who Made Them, 1653–1800* (1927). Reprint. New York: Da Capo Press, 1967.

Goen, Clarence C. *Revivalism and Separatism in New England, 1740–1800*. New Haven: Yale University Press, 1962.

Harris, Neil. *The Artist in American Society: The Formative Years, 1790–1860*. New York: George Braziller, 1966.

Hawthorne, Nathaniel. *The Scarlet Letter*. New York: W. W. Norton, 1962.

Hempstead, Joshua. *The Diary*. Collections of the New London Historical Society. 4 Vols. New London: 1901.

Henson, Richard. "Form and Content of the Puritan Funeral Elegy," *American Literature*, 33 (1960-1961):11–27.

Hoar, Leonard. *The Sting of Death and Death Unstung*. Boston: 1680.

Huizinga, Johan. *Homo Ludens*. Boston: Beacon Press, 1955.

s'Jacob, Henriette. *Idealism and Realism*. Leiden: Brill, 1954.

Jantz, Harold S. *The First Century of New England Verse*. Reprinted from the Proceedings of the American Antiquarian Society for October, 1943.

John Stevens: His Book, 1705. Facsimile Reprint. Newport: Privately printed.

Junkins, Donald. "'Should Stars Wooe Lobster Claws?': A Study of Edward Taylor's Poetic Practice and Theory," *Early American Literature*, III, No. 2 (1968):88–117.

Keach, Benjamin. *Tropologia: A Key to Open Scripture-Metaphors* . . . London: 1681.

Kirk, John T. "Sources and Development of Styles in Connecticut Furniture." *Connecticut Furniture: Seventeenth and Eighteenth Centuries*. Hartford: The Wadsworth Atheneum, 1967.

Langer, Susanne. *Philosophy in a New Key*. New York: New American Library, 1956.

Lechford, Thomas. *Plain Dealing; or, News from New England*. Edited by J. Hammond Trumbull. Boston: Wiggin & Lunt, 1867.

Levy, Babette May. *Preaching in the First Half of New England History*. Hartford: The American Society of Church History, 1945.

Ludwig, Allan I. *Graven Images: New England Stonecarving and its Symbols, 1650–1815*. Middletown: Wesleyan University Press, 1966.

Maclear, James Fulton. "'The Heart of New England Rent': The Mystical Element in Early Puritan History," *Mississippi Valley Historical Review*, 42 (March 1956):621–652.

Mather, Cotton. *A Christian Funeral*. Boston: 1713.

————. *The Diary of Cotton Mather, 1709–1724*. Collections of the Massachusetts Historical Society. 7th Series. Vols. 7–8. Boston: 1911–1912.

————. *A Father Departing* . . . Boston: 1723.

————. *Just Commemorations*. Boston: 1715.

————. *Right Thoughts in Sad Hours*. London: 1689.

————. *The Valley of Baca* . . . Boston: 1717.

Mather, Samuel. *A Testimony from the Scripture against Idolatry & Superstition*. Cambridge: 1672.

————. *The Figures or Types of the Old Testament*. Edited by Mason I. Lowance, Jr. New York: Johnson Reprint, 1969.

Meserole, Harrison T., ed. *Seventeenth-Century American Poetry*. Garden City: Doubleday, 1968.

Miller, Perry G. E. *Errand into the Wilderness*. Cambridge: Harvard University Press, 1956.

_____. *Nature's Nation*. Cambridge: Harvard University Press, 1967.

_____. *The New England Mind: The Seventeenth Century*. Cambridge: Harvard University Press, 1954.

Miller, Perry G. E., and Thomas H. Johnson, eds. *The Puritans*. Revised Edition. New York: Harper & Row, 1963.

Morais, Herbert M. *Deism in Eighteenth Century America*. New York: Russell & Russell, 1960.

Morgan, Edmund S. *The Puritan Family*. New York: Harper & Row, 1966.

_____. *Visible Saints: The History of a Puritan Idea*. New York: New York University Press, 1963.

Morison, Samuel Eliot. *The Intellectual Life of Colonial New England*. 2nd edition. New York: New York University Press, 1956.

Morton, Nathaniel. *New Englands Memoriall*. Edited by Howard J. Hall. New York: Scholar's Facsimiles & Reprints, 1937.

Ong, Walter J. *Ramus: Method and the Decay of Dialogue*. Cambridge: Harvard University Press, 1958.

Pain, Philip. *Daily Meditations*. Cambridge: 1668.

Panofsky, Erwin. *Tomb Sculpture: Four Lectures on its Changing Aspects from Ancient Egypt to Bernini*. Edited by H. W. Janson. New York: Abrams, 1964.

Pearce, Roy Harvey. *The Continuity of American Poetry*. Princeton: Princeton University Press, 1961.

_____. ed. *Colonial American Writing*. New York: Holt, Rinehart and Winston, 1962.

Pope, Robert G. *The Half-Way Covenant: Church Membership in Puritan New England*. Princeton University Press, 1969.

Rowe, John. *Letters and Diary*. Edited by Anne Rowe Cunningham. Boston: Clarke, 1903.

Sewall, Samuel. *The Diary of Samuel Sewall, 1674–1729*. Collections of the Massachusetts Historical Society. 5th Series. Vols. 5–7. Boston: 1882.

Silverman, Kenneth, ed. *Colonial American Poetry*. New York: Hafner, 1968.

Taylor, Edward. *The Poems of Edward Taylor*. Edited by Donald E. Stanford. New Haven: Yale University Press, 1960.

Tyler, Moses Coit. *A History of American Literature*. New York: Putnam's Sons, 1878.

Walker, Williston, ed. *The Creeds and Platforms of Congregationalism*. Philadelphia: Pilgrim Press, 1960.

Warner, W. Lloyd. *The Living and the Dead: A Study of the Symbolic Life of Americans*. Yankee City Series, Vol. 5. New Haven: Yale University Press, 1959.

Watkins, Lura Woodside. "The Byfield Stones—Our Earliest American Sculpture?" *Antiques*, 84 (October 1963):420–423.

White, Leslie. *The Science of Culture*. New York: Grove Press, 1949.

Wigglesworth, Michael. *The Diary of Michael Wigglesworth, 1653–1657*. Edited by Edmund S. Morgan. New York: Harper & Row, 1965.

Willard, Samuel. *A Compleat Body of Divinity*. Boston: 1726.

_____. *Covenant-Keeping The Way to Blessedness* . . . Boston: 1682.

_____. *A Sermon* . . . *Occasioned by the Death of John Leveret*. . . Boston: 1679.

Wilson, John F. *Pulpit in Parliament: Puritanism During the English Civil Wars, 1640–1648*. Princeton: Princeton University Press, 1969.

Wilson, Samuel. *A Scripture Manual*. Newport: 1772.

Wilson, Thomas. *A Complete Christian Dictionary*. London: 1661.

Winslow, Ola Elizabeth. *American Broadside Verse*. New Haven: Yale University Press, 1930.

Index